wishing
for a happily
ever after

LISA HELEN GRAY

COPYRIGHTS RESERVED ©

Wish big, always.

Prologue

The sun is high in the sky. It beams down on my face, warming me from the inside out. A smile spreads across my face as I spin in a circle, my arms open wide as I enjoy the hot summer day.

I feel free, happy, blessed.

"Mummy! Mummy!" a little girl's voice calls, and for some reason, I know that voice is calling to me.

My head turns in the direction of the sweet sound, my heart soaring when a little girl with bright blue eyes and blonde curls comes running in my direction.

"Mummy, isn't this fun?" She holds her hands up in the air for me to catch her. I do, wanting her in my arms more than anything. The minute she's in my arms, everything feels complete, like there's nothing on this Earth that could feel better than this moment.

"You're getting dirt on Mummy."

I turn to the rich, smooth voice, the sun blocking the man from my vision.

"Mummy doesn't care, do you, Mummy? Tell Daddy he's being silly."

My gaze drifts back to the little girl, my eyes watering at the amount of love I feel for her.

The sky darkens and I'm now standing in a bare room, a single bed shoved in the corner looking lonely and out of place.

It should have a blanket, a toy or some teddies surrounding it. My heart hurts looking at it, like something isn't right.

I look for the little girl with blonde locks, needing her in my arms. I search, moving around the room until I hear snivelling coming from the closet.

"Hello?" I call, not recalling her name. But it's there, on the tip of my tongue.

Opening the door, I kneel down to the little girl, her swollen eyes sad. It breaks my heart in two seeing her so miserable and fragile.

"What's wrong, sweetie?"

"Don't you want me, Mummy?"

"Of course, I want you." I want a child more than anything. I want a family.

"Then why have you given up on me?"

"I haven't," I tell her, my voice filled with angst.

"But you have or you will. You need to hurry up if you want me, Mummy."

"I don't know what to do." Panic fills my veins.

"You do. You need to let yourself love again." This time the voice doesn't belong to the little girl but to someone else. When I turn around to face them, they're gone.

I shoot up from my bed, my breathing erratic as I try to forget the love I felt for the girl in my dreams.

If only falling in love and having a family was that easy.

Tears rush down my cheeks as I feel pathetic and lonely.

One day, *one day*, I will have it. I have to believe that; otherwise, what else do I have to live for?

Chapter One

"*P*agan, your eleven thirty appointment just called to cancel," my assistant and best friend, Alison, says, dropping a stack of papers on my desk with a thud.

I sigh, running my fingers through my tangled blonde hair. Trust me to be in such a rush this morning that I forgot to brush it. Hell, I'm surprised I remembered to brush my teeth.

When I started my business four years ago, I was excited, overjoyed that I was given the opportunity to start my own company. Yeah, I worried about getting the clientele I needed to keep it running, but I shouldn't have. The first year I had to turn work away because we were that booked up, and the second year I decided to open another office, hiring other event planners.

Four years on and I have three more offices, more staff and a fully booked schedule. The only thing I don't have is a life.

No joke.

I don't go out anymore unless it's to do with work. All my social events? Work. Dinner dates? Work. Everything in my life is work, work,

work. I even live above my office. That's how much my work has leaked into my life.

The last time I went on a date was over four years ago, and let's just say I'd rather forget about that experience. He turned out to be my brother's wife's ex-boyfriend, who was a raving lunatic. He kidnapped her, beat her, and well, it's a long story but thankfully he's dead now. That's all that matters. But still, he used me to get to her, and I'll never forgive myself for putting her in danger.

At the beginning, that was the reason I put off dating, but after time, my work was enough to make me happy. It's not enough anymore.

I want the love I see in each of my wedding clients. I want the love my brother has with his wife, Lola, and what my parents have after fifty years of marriage. I want to be able to leave work and go home to my husband, where we can just be *us*. I want children. Hell, at the moment, I just want a life that consists of something other than work. I never thought I'd ever even think those words.

I love my job, love the order of it, the routine. I like seeing something start at nothing and build its way up to something spectacular. And that feeling I get when the client sees the end result makes it all worth it. But lately, I don't feel the same excitement I once did. I know I'm missing something—and that something is a life.

"Thank you, Alison. Are you packed?" I ask her, looking up through tired eyes.

We leave in a few days to go to London, where we'll be for three weeks organising a wedding for one of our new prestigious clients. Her son is getting married, and she wants only the best for him.

He's a partner at one of the best law firms in London, but based on the size of this wedding, you'd think he was the prince.

They've also only given us six weeks to plan the wedding, and three of those will be spent in London with them.

"Yeah. I'll be around tomorrow to pack yours." She smiles, picking up some folders.

"How did you know?" I groan. She knows me too well, because I haven't packed a damn thing. In fact, the only thing I've done in preparation for our trip is to make sure that everything is booked for the big day.

4

"You need me to remind you to eat, and I'm pretty sure if I didn't text you at night, you'd still be awake until the morning." She chuckles, shaking her head.

"True. You are a godsend. Tell me, when was the last time I gave you a raise?" I tease.

"Last week, which I told you I didn't need." She scoffs, rolling her eyes.

"Well, you need another," I laugh.

"What are you going to do for the two hours you have free?"

"Um, work?" I ask, knowing it's not really a question but a statement. I have so much to do before we leave.

I'm leaving my other event organiser, Catherine, in charge while I'm away. However, I don't trust anyone other than myself to get everything done. People pay me more because I'm good at what I do; one bad event and my whole life's work could go down the drain.

"No. You're going to go out into the reception area, where Brooke and Lola are waiting with Cece to take you out for lunch. Now go," she orders, handing me my coat.

I give her a soft look, taking the coat from her. "Come with us. We could both use the break."

"Oh no, I don't want to intrude."

"Don't be stupid. Brooke and Lola love you. Now come on. I could use a drink before we have to deal with Mr. Harrington." I shudder and she does the same, looking at me in horror.

"Yep, we definitely need a drink to deal with him."

Mr. Harrington works at the local vet and is always in here, hiring us to help organise a fundraiser to help the stray animals brought in to him. But he's slimy. Instead of making eye contact when he's talking to you, he stares at your chest. It's worse for Alison because she has a bigger chest than me and has to deal with him for longer periods of time.

We walk out into the reception area and I smile when I see my niece with her head inside a book.

Just like her mother and father.

She looks up when she sees me, her chubby face breaking into a wide smile, and I can't help but return it. At four years old, my niece is a genius, but more than that, she freaking rocks. I love her to bits and can't imagine my life without the little madam.

"Auntie Pagan, look what Mummy bought me," she shouts, twirling around in a princess dress.

"You look beautiful." I smile humorously down at me niece.

"I know!" She grins, twirling again before launching herself at me. I bend down, picking her up and resting her on my hip.

Sheesh, the kid is putting on weight. Soon I won't be able to pick her up. That thought kind of sucks.

"Hey, Pagan. We're going out for lunch and were wondering if you and Alison wanted to join us?" Lola, my sister-in-law, asks, smiling beautifully. Every time I see her smile, something inside me shifts. She's come a long way from the girl who turned up here five years ago, alone, broken and lost. She's gone through hell, but with her strength and with help from my darling brother, she's made it through to the other side. She also gives me hope that one day I'll find someone who loves me like my brother loves her.

"Yeah. If anyone could drag me away from my work, it would be my favourite niece and my two faves." I grin, bumping Cece in my arms, making her giggle.

"I'm your only niece," Cece pouts.

"Not for long," I tell her, winking. Lola is six months pregnant—not that it shows. She can cover her bump with a few baggy tops and no one would even know. She's stunning, no matter what she wears, but pregnant, the woman glows.

"I want a brother," Cece tells me. "I want to be the only princess Daddy has."

I giggle along with Brooke and Lola. Cece's a daddy's girl through and through. In fact, she has all the men in our family wrapped around her little finger. My dad can't say no to her, and the same goes for my twin brother, who makes it his life mission to give her everything she asks for.

Alison walks back into the room with her coat and bag, and I turn her way. "You ready?"

"Yep. I hope they're ready for us. I have a feeling this afternoon is going to be a long one."

"Let's go, then. Where to, Your Majesty?" I say dramatically to Cece.

She giggles and points to the door. "To the car!"

~

A few hours later, I'm leaning back in my chair, my belly stuffed with yummy food. It actually feels good not to eat on the run, or another dreaded pot noodle. The company isn't so bad either. And I called Catherine to handle Mr Harrington, so that's a bigger bonus. Not having to deal with him has made my day.

"So Lola said you're leaving in a few days to go to London. You excited?" Brooke asks, looking as full as I feel.

"To stay with what is most likely a snobby family for three weeks and have a bridezilla bossing me around? Um, no." I shudder, my face pinching together.

"Only because you like being the one to do the bossing around," Lola giggles, covering her mouth.

I give her a mock glare before groaning because it's true. I do prefer to be the one doing the bossing around. It's just in my nature. "It's not that. I normally just send Catherine to do our out-of-town events or have one of the other offices closer do it, but for some reason this family has requested me specifically and are paying triple the rate I would normally charge. I'm just worried the triple amount won't be worth it if I have to deal with a bunch of snobby rich people, especially when they won't let us book into a hotel. They've requested I be there at their house to help run things."

Lola knows all too well that I don't play nice with rich people. We used to run a charity event for one of the local companies, but one of their associates attacked Lola at one of them, leaving her in a bad state. We dropped all ties with them and started throwing them ourselves after that. Ever since then, I don't do too well around entitled people. I see them all as the same, and I know I shouldn't. Not everyone is stuck up their own arses. But I've only met one rich person who doesn't think their shit doesn't stink, and she's sitting right in front of me.

"I don't think they're like that, Pagan," Alison answers, her black bob bouncing around her chin. "And I'm excited. I can't wait to see what it's all going to look like. I mean, they have doves, ice sculptures, and don't get me started on the actual venue."

I think about it for a second. "Probably. I mean, the mother, Pamela, was really nice on the phone, but from past experiences, that could just be a ruse to get me to take the job. And I haven't seen the venue yet. I'm hoping the measurements they gave me are all correct. They seem to be on a larger scale than we're used to."

"I've spoken to her, and the nan, Ada. The nan seemed pretty crazy but legit," Alison tells me, but I don't say anything, not wanting to jinx myself.

I remember the last prestigious wedding I did and it wasn't fun. The bride was a monster. If I believed in the supernatural, I would actually believe she was a demon. By the fifth day, I quit, walking out and never looking back. I didn't even care that they didn't leave a glowing recommendation. She wasn't worth the pay cheque, and definitely not the headache. But I can't let that happen again, not if I want to keep my business running as smoothly as it is.

"Yeah, but still, London," Brooke says dreamily. "You get to visit Big Ben, the London Eye, Harry Potter studios, the Natural History Museum—"

"There are children present," Lola teases, referring to Brooke's hazy expression.

She shakes her head, grinning. "Sorry. I've never been and have always wanted to go. There's so much to do there. All those museums, all those tourist attractions—"

"You're doing it again," Lola sings, interrupting. We all giggle this time.

"Sorry." Brooke blushes before turning to me. "You get my drift. You're going to have a blast."

"You did hear the part where I'll be working, didn't you?" I ask, my lips twitching.

She waves me off, scoffing. "You can probably get that shindig organised in three days tops. You'll have a blast."

"And you might get to meet Prince Harry and get him to propose," Lola says, grinning.

Always the dreamer.

8

Now it's my turn to scoff. "I should be so lucky. I'd probably have more luck talking one of those statues outside Buckingham Palace into proposing to me."

"Don't be stupid. The prince would be lucky as hell for you to agree to marry him," Alison butts in, giving me a stern expression.

"You say that like it's a real possibility I may run into the prince and get him to fall in love with me," I say dryly.

"Meh, weirder things have happened."

I laugh, shaking her off. "Well, you'll stand a better chance, since you'll have more time off than I will."

"Hey, I'll be working right alongside you."

"Aw, why can't my staff be as good as yours?" Brooke smiles.

I turn to look at her and frown. "You've *still* not fired her?" I ask, referring to the young girl Brooke hired three months ago fresh out of college. She has no idea what to do when it comes to kids, and I'm pretty sure she spends most of her time on the phone instead of actually working. Both times I've seen her, Brooke's been running around and the girl just looked around in a daze, like she's forgotten why she's there.

"No," she sighs. "Every time I build up the courage and talk to her, she starts crying, telling me something bad's happened in her life. Her nan died last weekend."

Lola's expression hardens. "I swear her nan died the first time you tried to fire her."

"Maybe both her nans died?" Brooke says, actually looking hopeful. Not about two people dying but about her employee telling her the truth.

"Nope. Remember, she called earlier and said she was going to be late because she was looking after her sick nan," Lola grunts.

I frown, not liking my friend being taken advantage of. "Do you want me to come over and fire her? Surely you have a list of written warnings and other stuff piled up by now."

"Really?" Brooke asks, her eyes lighting up. "Firing someone's never bothered me before, but for some reason, with this girl I just can't. She reminds me so much of myself at her age, so lost and confused—just without the lying part."

I look to Alison and we both share a grin. Firing staff is a specialty of mine. I've done it so many times, but girls like this one really rile me up. If you're going to work, no matter if it's at McDonald's or as a surgeon, you work damn hard to earn that money. After all, everyone needs to make a living.

"I'd love to. Let's go do it now. You can go next door with Lola and Cece while we clear her out."

"Are you sure?"

"She's positive." Alison beams at them, then at me.

"Why do you both look positively happy about firing someone?" Lola asks warily.

"Because it's a stress reliever," I answer, waving her off.

"Shall we go now?" Alison asks me. Lola and Brooke eye each other, probably wondering what they've gotten themselves into.

"Yep," I answer cheerfully, my day definitely looking up.

Chapter Two

I'm glad I brought Alison along with me for this trip. At first it was to make sure I didn't walk out on another job, but now I'm just glad she's here to keep me sane.

What should've been a five-hour drive has turned into eight due to traffic, a pile-up on the motorway, and the much-needed rest stops. My legs feel like jelly and my arse is completely dead. I'm choosing to ignore the rumbling in my stomach and the pressure in my bladder because we're pulling up to what have to be the largest iron gates known to man. I'm pretty sure Buckingham Palace doesn't have this kind of security. I wouldn't be surprised if soldiers jumped out of the trees and proceeded to search us.

"Holy fucking shit-balls," I gasp, taking in my surroundings.

"I told you." Alison grins. "You should see the pictures I found online. They did an article for *Now Times* magazine and it featured the house. This is nothing."

I gape at her, wondering what the hell we're walking into. She presses the buzzer next to the gate and a voice sounds over the intercom.

"Hello, may I help you?"

"Hi, we're from Salvatore Events. Mrs Donovan is expecting us," she tells him politely.

"Come on through. If you drive to the end of the path, someone will be waiting outside the main entrance and will help you with your luggage and park your car."

"Thank you."

When the gates open, my jaw drops further. The lights leading along either side of the gravelled road turn on and I'm in awe. Trees line each side with Christmas lights swirling from each one. My breath hitches when we near the end.

"Holy shit. It's a fucking castle."

Alison giggles. "It's not a castle, it's a mansion. Stop gaping. You've seen houses just like this."

"No, Alison. This is not a fucking house, this is something else. I feel like I should be wearing a ballgown. Oh my God, they're going to kick us out thinking we're riff-raff."

She laughs at my expense, steering the car around a large water fountain—yes, a freaking water fountain!

"If they have staff, why didn't they just get them to organise the wedding and events leading up to it?" I mutter, my nerves fluttering inside my chest. I never get nervous—ever! But this... this is intimidating.

"Stop panicking. You're going to be fine, and they'll love everything. Now come on, they're coming over," she whispers, opening her door.

Panicked, I pull her back in, ignoring her shocked gaze. "We need to go. We can't be here," I screech.

Seemingly flabbergasted, she turns to me. "Why the hell not?"

"Look at the place! I'll break something. I'll fuck this up. What if they think we're common as muck and kick us out? How does that look for my reputation?"

She laughs in my face. *The nerve.* "Pagan, you're doing that overreacting thing again. You need to calm down. It's just a house."

"Just a house?" I scoff, looking at the beautiful mansion once again. "Just drive. We'll think of some excuse for why we couldn't come."

"They know we're here," she reminds me dryly before stepping out of the car.

"Alison," I hiss.

I sit for a moment, still in shock, before following her out of the car. It's not like she gave me a choice. I'm totally going to fuck this up for my business. This is a palace. If Prince Harry greets me at that door, I wouldn't be surprised. I'll pass out, for sure.

Instead we're met by three men impeccably dressed, their expressions blank.

Well okay then.

"You must be Ms Salvatore. I'm Shane, head of security here at Donovan's Manor. Mr and Mrs Donovan will be out shortly. In the meantime, Jeff here will help Lee with your bags, and I'll park the car around the back."

I push past my nerves, straightening my spine, because I can do this. I can.

I hope.

"Thank you, Shane. I'm Pagan Salvatore, and this is my personal assistant and good friend, Alison Mills."

"Pleasure to meet you both," he says, bowing slightly. I turn, giving Alison a wide-eyed look. She just grins, her excitement showing, and I shake my head.

"Pagan, it is so lovely to meet you." I turn around to the sweet voice and find the most stunningly dressed woman I've ever met. She's in an elegant cream suit with a white blouse, accessorised with white pearls around her neck. Her dark hair seems to be in some sort of updo that I would never be able to perfect. Next to her is a handsome older man, his silver-fox hair and soft features reminding me a little of George Clooney.

"Hello, it's nice to meet you too...."

"Oh how rude of me. I'm Pamela Donovan, but you can call me Pam. This is my husband, Adam Donovan. We're so happy you could make it. How was your journey?"

"Long," I sigh, smiling. "As you know, I'm Pagan, and this is my personal assistant and good friend, Alison Mills."

"Oh how terrible for you both. Come on in. I bet you're hungry from the long drive. And it's a pleasure to meet you face-to-face, Miss Mills."

"Please, call me Alison. And we ate not too long ago. We needed a rest from the dreadful traffic."

Adam grunts. "We heard about the traffic on the news, my dear. Why don't we show you two girls to your sleeping quarters? You can rest for the night, and we can talk about everything else tomorrow," he says, gesturing for us to head inside.

We follow and I have to try my hardest not to keep gaping at my surroundings. The ceilings are high enough for me to start wondering how the hell I'm supposed to add twinkling lights at the wedding reception. The floors are marbled, and there are stone pillars on either side of the door as we enter. However, it's the various antiques and furnishings that have me wary.

I'm totally going to fucking break something.

Don't get me wrong, I'm not a klutz. I just have a serious case of bad luck. I could walk through Poundland and not break a thing, but walk me through a store with the lowest item in its hundreds and I'm fucked. Seriously. Last time, my luck cost me four grand.

But this place is something else. I'm almost too scared to touch anything. Knowing my luck, I'd leave sticky fingerprints all over the place.

A grand wooden staircase breaks off into two directions. Looking up, I can see they lead to different sections of the house.

"Your house is beautiful," I tell Pam.

Smiling kindly, she says, "It is, dear. It's far too big for just the two of us, but we promised Adam's parents we would keep it in our family, just like it has been for generations."

"I don't know... I'm feeling claustrophobic," Alison teases.

My eyes widen and I turn to look at her, wishing the ground would swallow me up. I'm surprised when both Pam and Adam start laughing, Adam taking Alison's arm.

"You, young lady, are a breath of fresh air. Most people never know what to say."

"I can see why. This place is kind of intimidating," she chuckles, walking ahead of Pam and me as we turn to the right at the fork in the stairs. I notice it splits again, my eyes widening further as I wonder just how big this house is.

Pam must see where I'm looking because she explains, her voice polite. "To the right is where our old staff quarters used to be. Emily, our housemaid and cook, uses one for her knitting and sewing, which she sells at a church car boot on the weekends. She lives with Jeff in the guest house at back of the property. They've been married twenty-five years. Shane and his men did stay in that side, but with the rotation and different men working, we built the building on the side of the house for them to use. To the left is where my son stays when he's here. He likes being close to the stairs that lead to the gym," she tells me as we reach the end of a corridor. I notice the stairs and look down them, seeing them spiral at the end. "This wing of the house mostly goes unused, but we thought you and Alison would like your privacy and had the rooms set up."

"It's a beautiful home. I don't know how you don't get lost," I laugh, amused.

She chuckles. "The plan on this side of the house is pretty simple. It's the other side where people tend to lose their way."

"I can imagine. Are you sure you don't want us to book into a hotel? I hate to intrude when you have guests arriving in a few short days."

"Nonsense, dear. It'll be a joy to have young ones in our home again. We enjoy the company, and we have the room. Most people live nearby or will be sleeping in the other quarters. Please don't worry." Pam stops as we reach the door at the end of the hall where Alison and Adam wait just outside, listening to our conversation.

"She's absolutely right, dear. We're alone a lot now that the kids are all grown up and have their own homes. It's nice to have the house full again," Adam says, agreeing with his wife.

"If you're sure?" I ask, knowing how generous this is of them. Normally I'd say no to a client, opting to stay at the nearest hotel or bed and breakfast, but with the Donovans, I've found they don't like taking no for an answer.

"We are. Now, the stairs to your left, the ones we just passed, lead down into the gym area. We have a pool, fully equipped gym, sauna, and steam room. You're welcome to use any of the facilities here at the manor. We'll give you a proper tour tomorrow, but for tonight, you have everything you need.

"There's a phone in your rooms. If you press extension one, it will go straight to Emily. Ask for anything you need and she'll bring it right to your room. Each room has an en suite bathroom that's stocked with fresh towels and toiletries. Breakfast is served at eight thirty, and I'll have someone waiting to greet you at the bottom of the grand staircase to show you the way. This will be your room, Pagan, and Alison's will be next door," Pam finishes as Adam opens the door for me.

I look inside the spacious room and feel like I've died and gone to heaven. In the middle of the room, pushed against a dark wooden wall with carved patterns, is a four-poster king-size bed. Big, puffy gold pillows and blanket make the bed welcoming and inviting. And with the drive I just suffered through, I can't wait to collapse on it.

That's as far as I look before seeing my suitcase and bags at the end of the bed.

Well crap, that was pretty quick.

"Thank you so much. This room is fantastic," I beam, happy when Pam's shoulders seem to relax as she smiles widely back at me.

"I'm glad. We'll let you get settled and see you in the morning. We'll see Alison to her room. Goodnight, Pagan, and thank you again for coming and agreeing to work with us."

I want to say I had no choice, that they just kept upping their price and I didn't want them to think I wanted them to go higher, so I said yes. But looking at the glorious couple in front of me, I'm glad I took the job. They're nothing like I imagined them to be and seem to be really good, down-to-earth people.

"Goodnight. I'll see you in the morning." I watch as they lead Alison down the hall a little, standing between two doors. I don't see which one she walks into before I shut the door for some much-needed sleep. Fourteen hours, preferably.

The room is much bigger than I thought, painted a warm red, matching the dark mahogany furniture in the room.

On the left is a bathroom, gleaming white with marble flooring similar to the flooring downstairs, but what has my eyes widening is the glass fireplace that separates the bedroom and the bathroom, letting you see right through. It's burning bright, adding to the warm glow in the room. It only makes the bathroom look that much more tempting, but a yawn escapes me, reminding me that I've been awake since four this morning, making sure I left everything organised for Catherine. I plan to take full advantage of it in the morning though.

Picking up my overnight case, I grab my toiletries and pyjamas before heading to the bathroom to get ready for bed.

Once I'm changed and ready, I walk back into the room, heading over to the large window that looks out over the front of the entire estate.

A box seat is set against the window, a throw blanket and a few pillows strategically placed on the cushion. Looking at it, I'm glad I brought my Kindle along with me for when I get some downtime. *If* I get some.

My hands are on the curtains, ready to draw them shut, when the lights leading down to the house flash on, gaining my attention. The water fountain at the front switches on next, beautiful from this view with the water lit up a sparkling blue. The place is magical, truly breathtaking, and by far one of the nicest houses I've ever seen or been to.

When the sound of tyres crunching gravel reaches my ears, I look up to see a Range Rover Sport SVR coming down the lane. The car is slick, the lights from the road shining off its gleaming white body. I sigh, wishing I could afford a baby like that as I step away from the window, not wanting to be caught ogling the beautiful car.

Drawing the curtains, I move back over to the bed, wondering how on earth I'm going to get out of such a high bed in the morning without breaking my neck. Still, I'm tired, and those sheets really do look welcoming. All I can do is pray I don't fall out of it in the middle of the night and knock over one of the expensive-looking lamps on either side of the bed.

Yawning, I crawl into bed and close my eyes, hoping the Donovans will be the same tomorrow as they were tonight.

Chapter Three

The next morning I wake up rested after a full night's sleep. I can't remember the last time I slept through the night, let alone gone to bed before 2:00 a.m. I'm completely refreshed, and I'm totally on board for getting used to this. I think the fact that the bed is the best one I've ever slept in helped a lot too. I wonder if they'll let me keep it.

A girl can wish.

Stretching, I look up at the ceiling, noting the large gold chandelier that escaped my notice last night. It's extravagant, something that belongs in a dining room or a grand ballroom, not a bedroom.

Sitting up, I grab my phone to check if Catherine has called or messaged me, but when I see the time, I panic.

Shit!

It's just before eight in the morning, and I have to be ready by half past to meet with the Donovans for breakfast.

Shooting from the bed, I get tangled in the sheets and land on the floor, my legs stuck in the sheets.

"Fuck," I curse, kicking them off and rushing into the bathroom.

Moving quickly, I brush my teeth before jumping in the shower.

The feel of hot water running down my body makes me wish I could stay under longer and enjoy it. I'm also kicking myself for not taking one last night when I could've appreciated it more.

Jumping out, I wrap a towel around my hair and one around my body, loving the soft, fluffy fabric against my bare skin. It's luxurious, and I start a list in my head of things I'm hoping the Donovans won't miss when I take them home with me.

It doesn't take me long to go through my morning routine, only throwing on a bit of foundation and a little mascara for my make-up, knowing I don't have time to do anything else. But when I go to grab my hairdryer, I can't find it.

"Where are you?" I mutter, throwing everything out of my suitcase, making a mess of the room. "Ugh." Not having time, I leave my room, knowing Alison will have packed one, or possibly have mine. I take the door to my right, barging in.

"Holy balls," I gasp, frozen in place.

Standing as naked as the day he was born is the sexiest man I've ever seen in my entire life, and I've seen *a lot* of beautiful people in my line of work.

"Hello, *you*," he drawls.

Piercing blue eyes with specks of silver stare back at me, his smouldering gaze burning into me. My stomach flutters. I know I should probably look away. I try, I really do, but I can't stop staring at him.

My gaze follows the line of his strong jaw, liking the rough-shaven look he has going on. My lips part when I see his full plump ones, kissable, biteable.

I lower my gaze to his large muscled chest and wide shoulders. He has a thin layer of hair on his chest, making his dark tan seem dirty. I want to run my fingers through it to see if it's as soft as it looks.

Then my eyes travel lower and I gasp, horrified when his dick—his *very* large dick—twitches.

He chuckles, most likely at my expression, and I close my eyes, mortified. "Oh my God, I'm so sorry," I squeak before rushing to the door. My head smacks against something hard and I hear the door slam shut. Pain radiates through my head to the back of my skull, and I lift my hand to the small lump forming on my forehead.

Not wanting to be here a moment longer and embarrass myself further, I reach out with my free hand for the door handle and swing it open with more force than necessary.

Thud.

"Fuck!"

I turn around, stunned when I see the gorgeous stranger holding his head, his face scrunched in pain.

"Oh no! I'm so sorry... again," I cry, rushing to his aid.

I trip over my own feet, falling forwards. I reach out to stop my fall, but it's too late and I end up on my hands and knees.

"Jesus! Are you okay?" I hear him rumble, his voice close.

Not able to look at him right now, wanting to catch my breath and try to find some dignity, I lift my hand to wave it off, but I come into contact with something smooth and *very* hard.

"Well, while you're down there," he teases.

Asshole.

I snap my hand back and quickly get up off the floor. "I'm sorry," I tell him once more, glaring in his direction before heading towards the door, keeping my eyes open this time.

As I step out into the hall, Alison opens the door in front of me, holding none other than my hairdryer. Her eyes are round as saucers as she stares behind me, no doubt at the good-looking arsehole. Hopefully he used his head and picked up a freaking towel.

I stomp over to her, snatching the hairdryer. Then with one last glare in her direction, I stomp back to my room, not saying a word. I'd probably just make the entire situation a whole lot worse by opening my mouth, and I don't need any further embarrassment.

"Hi, I'm Alison."

Just as I get to my door, I hear his rumbling, rough voice and feel his eyes on me, the tingling at the back of my neck a warning that I'm totally fucked.

"Drake."

Yep, I'm royally fucking screwed.

∽

I meet Alison outside her room, hoping the stranger in the next one isn't there as we carry on down the hallway.

I try not to look at his door, I really do, but my eyes flicker in that direction more than once.

My face is still hot, and no doubt red from embarrassment. I pride myself on appearance and presentation, so when I fuck up the way I did earlier, I want to kick myself.

How I get myself into those situations is beyond me, but when they happen, they really suck.

"What was that earlier?" Alison whispers when we reach the main staircase. An older gentleman wearing a navy-blue suit is waiting at the bottom of the stairs. He greets us with a smile, his eyes bright and practically beaming with happiness.

"It was nothing," I whisper back, then turn to the man with a smile.

"Hello, we didn't get to formally meet last night. I'm Jeff, the house butler of sorts and gardener. I'm to escort you to Mr and Mrs Donovan in the garden room."

"Hello, Jeff. I'm Pagan and this is Alison," I reply polity, then turn to Alison and mouth, "Garden room."

She shrugs and together we follow Jeff into another hallway before turning left into a large room.

"Oh my," I whisper in amazement. The whole room is made up of glass, with roses and wild flowers surrounding the room. It's extraordinary.

"We're glad you like it. This is my favourite room in the house," Pam says as she walks up to greet us. Instead of taking my hand like I expected her to, she pulls me in for a hug before doing the same to Alison. "I hope you both rested well?"

"Best night's sleep in ages," I gush before I can stop myself.

She laughs. "I'm glad."

"She's right. I slept like a princess." Alison smiles.

"Come join us. We thought we could have breakfast in here today since it's such a lovely day. Come, sit."

"Hello, ladies," Adam greets as he walks into the room dressed impeccably. He strolls up to his wife, pulling her in for a kiss, and I smile, watching how loved up they are. They remind me of my parents. "Sit, sit."

We sit down and I look around, my eyes never once focusing on one thing. Everything looks incredible. I'm about to compliment Pam on the room when the door behind us opens.

"Son, we heard you arrived late last night. I hope everything is well?"

"Hi, Dad. Everything is perfect, especially after my wake-up call this morning."

The deep rumbling voice belongs to the sexy stranger I met this morning. My eyes bug out, my cheeks heating.

Oh my God, he's their son!

I'm gonna die.

Someone kill me, please.

I don't turn around, scared my face will give everything away. *What's up with all this 'wake-up call' bullshit? Is he trying to get me fired?*

"Wake-up call? Was everything okay?" Pam asks, a worried frown on her face.

"Everything was fine, Mum. I'm just teasing. And who are these fine women?" he asks, taking the seat next to me. I try to shift away but there's nowhere to go.

Why is he acting like he hasn't met either of us? Hell, he introduced himself to Alison in the hall.

Not that I gave him a chance to introduce himself to me or anything, what with my hand on his dick and all.

"This is Pagan Salvatore, and here is Alison Mills. They're from Salvatore Events. They're here to organise Jesse and Amelia's wedding."

"Is that so," he says.

I feel his eyes burning into the side of me, but I don't turn to confirm it, keeping my expression blank as I stare ahead. Alison's 'what the fuck' look catches my attention from across the table. I just glare, inwardly pouting. *Can't she leave me to wallow in my own misery?*

"Yes. Isn't it wonderful that they could come for the entire three weeks?"

"Yes, it is. I'm Drake, by the way," he says, his arm brushing against mine as he leans over to shake Alison's hand. She grins widely, shaking his hand with much enthusiasm.

I'm so gonna fire her arse.

When he turns, my face heats further, hating all his focus on me. "It's nice to meet you." The amusement in his voice is thick as he holds his hand out.

I take his hand with a firm grip, and bolts of electricity shoot up my arm. I pull away quickly, my mouth agape at the sensations running through my body.

"You too." I swallow hard, looking away.

"We had our chef cook up a full English breakfast. We weren't sure what you'd like, so we asked for a bit of everything," Pam says just as an older lady walks in pushing a tray of food. My mouth waters as if it knows it's going to be fed.

"How many sausages would you like, miss?" the lady asks, standing next to me.

I open my mouth, but Drake answers for me. "She'll have the biggest sausages you have, Emily. Something tells me she loves her sausages."

My glare is fierce when I turn around to face him, wondering if they'll fire me if I happen to slip and punch him in his arrogant, handsome face.

"She really loves her sausages, but she hasn't had any in ages," Alison speaks up, and my glare turns her way at the innuendo. Her lips twitch, looking everywhere but at me.

"Thank you." My attention turns back to Emily as she places other yummy treats on my plate. I'm so hungry and focused on my food, I don't hear my phone beeping until a slight nudge to my right has me jumping.

"Your phone," Drake whispers against my ear, and a shiver runs down my neck.

"Yes, um, excuse me," I tell the table, hoping they can't see my blush.

Seeing my office number for here in London, I answer, "Hello, this is Pagan."

"Hi, Pagan, it's Jessica. We have a problem."

My sigh is loud and I turn to face the table, giving them an assuring smile. I hold my finger up, letting them know I'll be a minute before turning my back to them. "What's going on? Is everything okay?"

"No. The British Army fundraiser was being held at the Metropolitan, but they've had a kitchen fire that spread, so all events held there have been cancelled. I've called around everywhere that hires a hall big enough to hold three hundred guests and have nowhere. We're coming up blank."

"Oh no," I whisper, my face paling. The British Army fundraiser is one of our biggest. We raise money for not only the families of our fallen, but for soldiers who need long-term medical treatment or any renovations that need to be done to their homes. "I... leave it with me. I'll get back to you within a few hours."

"Okay, Pagan. I'm sorry to throw this at you. We called Catherine and she said you were out of the office and actually in London. With the office being new, we're stuck on what the protocol is."

"No, I totally understand and it's fine. I'll sort it. We only have a few things to check up on here, so we're pretty much free."

"Okay. Thank you again. I'll talk to you later."

"Bye." I hang up and sigh, wondering what on earth I did this morning to wake up to such a shitty day. And it's hardly even begun.

"Everything okay?" Alison asks when I sit back down, my appetite now gone.

"No. The hall booked for the fundraiser for the British Army has fallen through. They had a fire that spread, and Jessica's called around for last-minute halls and can't find anything. We need to do a wider search."

"Have it here," Pam blurts out before Alison can answer.

I turn, shocked at her offer. That's over three hundred guests in her home that she doesn't even know.

"We couldn't—"

"You can. When is it?"

"It's tomorrow night," I answer suspiciously.

"Well, that's settled. I'm guessing you have caterers and whatnot already booked, so it's literally just the hall. We have a bar in the main ballroom, but it isn't stocked at the moment. However, we know a company that will be able to supply us at short notice."

I mull it over, but as much as I think about it, it doesn't seem right. These are my clients.

"I'd just nod and agree. Otherwise she'll just call whoever you were on the phone to and make arrangements through them," Drake says. I gaze over at him, his eyes so beautiful I stop breathing for a second.

"But—"

"So it's settled," Pam gushes before turning to her husband. "I knew hiring them was going to be life-changing. Oh, it feels good to have a house full."

"I'll let housekeeping know. If you need anything else, please don't hesitate to ask," Adam says.

My mouth is agape, looking back and forth between the two, wondering when the hell I agreed to hold the party here.

"Pagan, breathe. It's all going to be okay," Pam assures me.

I nod, hoping like hell she's right. "Thank you."

"It's my pleasure. Will it be okay for us and some of the wedding party who are arriving tomorrow to attend? I'd like to donate if I can," Pam asks.

"Pam's grandfather was in the army," Adam explains.

"Of course. This is your house, after all. The more the merrier. I know Jessica will be thrilled to hear you're hosting. She's new and opened the office here in London six months ago, so she's still getting used to everything."

"Whenever you need a place to hold an event, you're more than welcome here," Adam says.

"This place would be great." Alison smiles widely. She would get excited; she's the one who goes and scouts for new places to hold events, negotiating prices with the owners. She's amazing at her job.

"Have the day off today. Go see what London has to offer. We have to go pick my mother up from the airport, but there's always someone here to let you in or out."

"You didn't tell me Grams was going to be here. I thought she couldn't make the wedding because she was on a singles cruise?" Drake says nervously from beside me, but Pam ignores him, waiting for my reply.

"Okay. We were hoping to go over the plans for the family dinner on Sunday," I tell her.

"Oh dear, it's Tuesday. We have plenty of time to go over all that. You and Alison can go out and sightsee for a bit, go out on the town."

My lips twitch at her usage of 'out on the town'. It seems so foreign coming from someone so impeccably well-mannered and dressed.

"We do have the best tourist attractions," Drake muses. "Maybe I could show you around?"

I wish he'd stop flirting. It makes me nervous.

"Um, no. Thank you, but we'll be fine."

"Are you sure, dear? My Drake knows his way around," Pam says.

"I bet he does," I mumble under my breath.

"What was that?" he asks, a smirk lighting up his face.

"I'm sure you do." My eyes stay locked on his, my back straighter.

"Well then, that's settled. You two go enjoy your day, and Pam and I will inform the staff about tomorrow. If you can get Jessica to call my personal line, we'll help coordinate," Adam tells me.

"Thank you so much for helping us out with this. It's very kind of you."

"It's our pleasure. Plus, we'll owe you once you meet my mother." Pam giggles and Adam laughs, throwing his arm around her.

Why does everyone seem to be on edge about her mum? Even Alison mentioned the nan being nuts.

I look to Alison for help, knowing she's spoken to them a lot over the past few weeks, but she just shrugs, looking as baffled as I feel.

"May God bless our souls," Drake whispers before getting up and leaving the table.

Now I'm wondering just who the hell her mother is.

Chapter Four

My feet are killing me, and I'm pretty sure that, even after using factor 50, I've caught the sun. My skin is stinging and as the sun sets, my body is starting to shiver from the light breeze.

"Never again am I going sightseeing with you." I curse as we step out of the car, glaring over the roof at my friend.

"Hey, you had the best experience of your life," Alison mutters as she hands the keys over to the guy we met last night.

"I'm pretty sure you were out to kill me, Alison. In the worst possible way."

"Oh come on, that sushi place was something you had on your bucket list," she argues, but she seems pretty distracted.

"Yeah, whilst I'm in Japan, not in London. I don't even like sushi." I'm so grateful I decided to skip and just watch Alison stuff her face.

"I feel sick," she grumbles.

"I did tell you not to eat it, but you didn't listen. I've heard stories about sushi," I scold, shuddering as we step inside.

"You had it on your bucket list, Pagan."

"Yeah, because having boring stuff that I've already done sounds

27

lame. I also had 'eat snails in France' on that list. Doesn't mean I'm gonna do it."

"I think I'm gonna be sick." She holds her hand over her mouth, looking rather green for someone who's been out in the sun all day.

"Are you okay?" Pam asks as she walks into the main foyer, accompanied by a sweet old lady. I'm guessing this must be Ada, Pam's mother.

She doesn't seem so scary.

"She looks like she's about to spew," the old lady comments, grinning. It takes me by surprise because the smile looks downright terrifying.

"Let's get you to bed," I tell Alison before turning to Pam. "She had bad sushi."

Alison makes a gagging noise and quicker than I thought anyone could move, let alone a small old lady, Ada grabs a bronze vase from the table. She tips the flowers and water out all over the floor and rushes over to Alison, holding it in front her face. Within seconds of holding the vase, Alison is throwing up.

I gag, looking away from Alison and breathing through my mouth so I don't have to smell it.

"Wow, you had the rice sushi? That sucks to throw back up," Ada mutters. Alison groans in agreement, throwing up more.

Who is this woman?

"Mother," Pam scolds.

"Oh shush, Pammy. I got this. Come on, dear, let's get you upstairs. I've got something to make you feel *all* better."

"Do not go giving her that godawful drink, Mother."

"What drink?" I ask, looking between Pam and Ada.

"It's not even a drink. It's a bunch of expensive alcohol mixed together. Grams drinks it like it's pop, but to the rest of us, it makes us vomit," Drake says, walking out of the kitchen.

"It's better she gets it all out of her system." Ada defends. "Now why don't you and Pagan here go watch a movie in the theatre?"

"Theatre?" I ask, then remember the cinema room down the hall from the kitchen on the tour this morning.

"Please," Alison groans between puking and gagging.

"Come along. Just don't go getting any on me. Now that expensive

28

rug outside your room—go for it. Ugly thing." Ada shudders, helping Alison up the stairs.

"Mother," Pam shouts, shaking her head.

"Is she going to be okay?" I ask, my eyes following Alison and Ada.

"It's probably food poisoning, which might take a few days to get over," Drake says, looking down at me.

Wow, I didn't realise how tall he is.

"I meant Ada with Alison. Will she be okay to look after her?"

"Oh." He chuckles, turning to his mum for an answer.

"I'll go hide her stash of alcohol," she mutters before rushing off.

"So would you like to go watch a film?" Drake asks, turning back to face me.

Shifting on my feet, I look away. "I should go check on Alison."

"She'll be fine with Grams. Plus Grams will only send you away. Come on, I'm sure we've got some movie you like."

I don't get a chance to refuse as he takes my hand and drags me up the tall staircase.

"I thought the cinema room was downstairs?" I ask, breathless as we turn right on the staircase.

This side of the house seems more like a maze than a home. There are so many corridors, stairs and doors.

"It is. I'm taking you to my old room. It's been turned into a games room now. I got fed up of going up and down to get to the gym when I couldn't sleep."

"Oh." We hit another flight of stairs, these thinner and longer. He places his hand on my back, letting me go first. Cautiously I do, noting the paintings on the walls instead of family pictures.

My mum and dad's house is filled with family photos. Hell, the reception lodge is filled with photos of us with guests who are regulars. But one thing I've noticed in this huge home is that they don't have many family portraits hanging, unless you count the mammoth-sized photo above the grand fireplace in the main room.

Drake sees where I'm looking and speaks up. "Mum has a fascination with famous artists. The house is filled with various works and antiques, as you can see, but her love of art will forever adorn these walls."

"They're beautiful. I can't help but compare it to my parents' home is all. Theirs is full of family photos hanging on the walls. We have a few paintings, but more for decorative reasons."

"Ah, I see," he mumbles.

I hit the top of the stairs and my eyes widen. Shit, both of my brothers would have a field day up here. Not only do they have a state-of-the-art television hanging on one of the main walls, but there are gaming chairs, a sofa, a pool table, a ping-pong table and, if I'm right, an arcade-style Pac-Man machine against the farthest wall.

"Holy crap, this room is amazing.... Wait, is that a balcony?"

Drake chuckles. "If a roof counts as a balcony, then yes. Do you want a tour?"

"Does a priest pray?" I ask, giddy as I rush to the glass doors.

Before he's fully pushed the doors open, I look out onto the back of their house, my eyes widening further. Holy crap, I thought my parents owned a lot of land, but these guys... they don't mess around.

Large greenery as far as the eye can see in the dim moonlight spreads out before me, settling into a forest with trees so high it almost looks magical.

"What do you think?" he asks. The amusement in his voice would normally ruffle me, but I don't care with a view like this. I can even forget I touched his dick accidentally this morning because nothing could pull me out of this fantasy.

"It's breathtaking. What I don't understand is why the hell you gave up this room for the one downstairs. I'm not saying it's shabby or anything, but this one... it's everything," I breathe, gazing up at the stars.

"That it is, but when you've walked the length it is from here to the gym a few times, you'll understand. Plus it was much harder to sneak girls up here," he says, chuckling.

"I bet." I giggle, looking over the side of the house.

Holy crap, that's a long way down.

"Come on, let's put a movie on. Do you have any preferences?"

"As long as it's not horror, I'm fine."

"No to watching *The Blaire Witch Project*, then?"

I shudder. "God no."

"Duly noted." He laughs and walks over to a door I hadn't seen before.

WISHING FOR A HAPPILY EVER AFTER

I follow, curious as to where he's going, when I see the rows and rows of DVDs stacked high in a room the size of my bedroom back home.

"You got enough films?" I ask sarcastically.

"Meh," he mutters absently, looking along the rows of movies.

"I'll just get comfy, then." I take a seat on the largest, deepest sofa I've ever seen. The minute I plant my arse, I get sucked in and sigh, lost in heaven, wondering if this too would go unnoticed when I leave.

I seriously need to get a start on that list.

~

I'm tipsy.

Yes, tipsy, and I've only had three beers.

I giggle again when Roman tells Mia to hide the baby oil in *Fast and Furious 7*, but the minute Hobbs tells Roman to hide his big forehead, I fall to my side, laughing my arse off.

No matter how many times I've watched it, it never fails to make me laugh.

"I love this film," I tell Drake, hiccupping. I wipe the tears of laughter from under my eyes as I sit back up.

"I can see," he murmurs. I turn to find him doing the whole staring thing again, and I give him a small smile. His lips twitch as his expression warms.

He reaches out, tucking a strand of hair behind my ear. A nervous flutter swirls in my stomach and I freeze, wondering what he's going to do next. But he just turns back to the television, ignoring the emotions he's stirred inside me.

We've spoken a lot during the two films we've watched, and I've found out a lot about him. He's currently between jobs since he left his practice, wanting something more. He's a doctor, working between two hospitals as a step in.

We've talked about my family, his family, and managed to keep the subject light and fun. He also told me all about the manor's history, which I found fascinating. Apparently the house has been in his family for generations, being passed down to the firstborn ever since his great-great-great-great-grandfather built it.

Knowing something has been passed down to each generation, keeping the family alive, is kind of special. I can see my dad doing that for us.

My granddad owned Cabin Lakes before he passed away and left it to my dad. He plans on passing it down to Dean when the time comes. It's only a start for us, but I kind of like knowing that in years to come, our great-great-great-whatever will own Cabin Lakes, know where it started, and will add their own touch to it. I'm actually thinking about talking my dad into starting a journal or a family one of sorts so it can be passed down.

A yawn escapes me. I try to hold my hand up to cover it, but I'm too late.

Drake hears and turns to me with a smirk on his face. "It's only nine, you lightweight."

Pouting, another yawn starts but this time I have chance to cover my mouth. "I was also pranced around London by my best friend, who I might add acted like she had never left Winchester before. Therefore she dragged me to every shop she laid eyes on, eating everything from liquorice, candy floss, burgers and, heaven help me, sushi. I'm dead on my feet, and I also think I've got a little sunstroke. Oh, and I'm a teeny bit tipsy."

His eyes widen and I can't help but giggle at his expression. I didn't mean to bite his head off.

"Can I have my head back now? I'm kind of fond of it."

I giggle, shaking my head at his meaning. "Whatever. I'll leave you to it. Thank you for keeping me company tonight. I've had fun."

"My pleasure."

His eyes warm and I look away, trying to hide how much he affects me. I get up from the sofa, stretching my back when I do and trying not to sway. I hear a groan and look to Drake to find his heated gaze on me. And that's when I realise my dress has ridden up and he got a good view of my arse.

I blush, ducking my head as I hear him chuckle darkly. "Well, you've seen mine. It's only fair I get to see yours."

"Asshole," I mutter before moving towards the stairs.

"You'll come to love me, Pagan," he says, and the heat behind his words causes a shiver to race down my spine.

I don't turn around, leaving him with a quick "Goodnight" before rushing down the stairs.

In my haste, I don't really watch where I'm going, so when I come to another turn five minutes later, I sigh in frustration, knowing there weren't this many turns when we went to the games room.

"Seriously, they should have maps on the walls in this place," I grumble, walking down another corridor, one that looks far too familiar.

Just as I turn the next corner, I slam into a hard body, my hands going to their waist. "I'm so sorry." I look up into Drake's eyes and huff out a breath when I see his amused and cocky expression.

Asshole.

"Did you come looking for me?" He grins.

Not wanting to admit I got lost, I straighten and take a step back. "Yes. I thought it would be decent for you to walk me back to my room like a true gentleman."

"We're not on a date," he points out, grinning wider now. "And have you really been waiting down here for me for ten minutes just so I could walk you back?"

That's when I notice the stairs to the game room on the left of me and I growl, frustrated.

At least I was heading in the right direction.

I think.

"Yes, I just didn't think you'd be this long," I say rather snottily.

"You got lost, didn't you?" he chuckles.

I sigh, defeated. "Yes," I snap. "If you could point me in the right direction, or even walk me to the stairs, I'll be able to find my way."

He laughs. "Come on, princess. If you ever get lost again, follow the paintings of landscapes to the stairs. And if you need to check that you're going in the right direction, just lift the painting a little and on the bottom left-hand corner there will be a tiny arrow pointing the way."

"Are you serious?" I ask, peeved and kind of impressed. Not that I'm willing to admit that to him.

"Yes," he laughs. "As a kid, I'd get lost all the fucking time, and our favourite games to play were 'hide and seek' or 'murder in the dark'. It wasn't fun not knowing where you were. Scared the shit out of me."

"But you've lived here your whole life," I point out, confused.

"Yeah, but I swear the walls move in this place." He shudders. Warily, I look around, hoping he's not insinuating that the place is haunted.

"So you drew underneath expensive artwork just so you could find your way around?"

"Yep."

"Wouldn't it have been easier to get a map put up down every hall?"

He laughs. "You've seen the place. You really think my mother would have a map of the building hanging up? Plus if we're ever robbed, which is highly doubtful, the robbers wouldn't know where to go and would end up getting caught."

"Wait," I say, as we reach my door. "On the wedding itinerary, it says 'hide and seek' or 'murder in the dark' is due in three days. I thought it was just a joke."

"Nope. We loved it as kids. Even as teens we would get our friends around to play. Best fucking game ever, especially when you're drunk."

"So, what's the difference between the two?"

"Well, both are the same, except we play 'murder in the dark' in, well, the dark. 'Hide and seek' is for any time of day, lights on or off."

"Oh my God, it says murder in the dark. Which means we're gonna have drunken adolescents running around in this huge house... in the dark."

"Um, yeah," he says, looking confused.

"I have to play that game as wedding planner. Oh my God! I'm gonna get murdered first, and then I'll be the one on, and I won't be able to find anyone in this godforsaken house. You'll all end up falling asleep or passing out waiting for me. I'll ruin your fun. Or worse, you could all die from starvation while waiting for me to find you. The staff will find your corpses a week or two from now."

"One, it takes a lot longer for a body to die of starvation and a lot longer to turn into a corpse. Plus we know our way around now. Sort of. But in any case, I'll make sure you don't get caught first and, as groom, my brother Jesse will be on first, so I'll show you the good hiding places," he chuckles.

What the hell have I gotten myself into?

"Okay, whatever. It'll be fine," I tell him, taking a deep breath. "Thanks for walking me to my door."

"My pleasure. And I'll see you for breakfast. My brother and everyone else won't be arriving until the night, so we won't see them until the party."

"Okay. See you in the morning." Once again I stare at his handsome profile as he walks to his door. I watch him go, ogling his fine arse.

"Oh, and Pagan?" he calls once he reaches his door. "If you need to drop by again in the morning, feel free." He winks, then saunters off.

I stare in astonishment at his closed door, my mouth opening and closing like a fish as I try to come to terms with what he said.

Was he flirting with me?

No, surely not. Not someone as handsome as he is.

"Oh God, I'm in so much trouble," I mumble before I let myself into my room.

Chapter Five

*A*fter another peaceful night's sleep, I was glad I set my alarm an hour earlier than normal so I could enjoy more time in the shower.

It was better than I imagined.

Loads better.

I just wish I could transport their bathroom to my place. It would make showering and getting up earlier so pleasurable to deal with.

After dressing in another floral, cream summer dress, my hair down but clipped back from my face, I leave my room.

I never got to check on Alison last night, so before heading to breakfast I stop by her room, knocking lightly on the door just in case she's still asleep.

A hoarse croak comes from behind the door. "Come in."

Walking in, I immediately wince at the sight of Alison lying in bed, a pale green. She also looks relieved to see me.

"Hey," I greet softly, moving over to her bed. The second I reach her, she clasps my hand in a strong grip, using strength I didn't think she was capable of in her current state. I wince, pulling my hand away and shaking out the pins and needles as I take in her anxious expression. "What's wrong?"

"Don't you dare leave me with that woman ever again," she announces heatedly.

"Good morning to you to, sunshine," I reply sarcastically. "Are you talking about Ada? She seems like a sweet old lady."

She scoffs, looking offended. "You cannot be serious, Pagan. That woman... that woman... God, I can't even explain *what* she is, but she is *not* sweet."

"Alison, don't be ridiculous." I roll my eyes at her dramatics.

"She tried to kill me!"

"What?" I shriek, my eyes widening in horror.

"Yes! She gave me this green poison to drink, forcing it down my throat... literally," she declares.

I relax and a small chuckle escapes. "Alison, she was just trying to look after you. She wasn't trying to kill you, she was just being kind."

"There were things in that drink that moved, I swear." She shudders.

I laugh loudly, amused by her exaggeration. A disgruntled look crosses her face.

"Sorry, but—" I choke out, laughing too much to continue.

"Stop laughing! It's not funny. I had it coming out of both ends, and she wouldn't give me any privacy. None. What. So. Ever! It was mortifying."

I fall to my back on the bed, laughing harder than before. My side hurts and when she kicks my hip, I laugh harder, a snort escaping.

"Pagan," she whines, sounding weak.

"I'm sorry, I'm sorry. I'll try not to leave you with her again." My lips twitch as I avoid looking at her.

She growls, narrowing her eyes on me. "I hate you."

I roll my eyes. "You love me. But in all seriousness, how are you feeling today?"

"I haven't vomited or gone to the toilet for a few hours, so I guess I could say I'm doing a little better."

"Teach you to eat—"

"Stop! Don't even say it because I'll throw up all over you and your pretty little dress," she says, turning a shade greener.

"Okay, okay. So you won't be joining us for breakfast this morning?"

She gives me an annoyed, dry look, one I can't help but find amusing instead of threatening. "Hell to the no. I'm going to stay in this bed. Pam said last night that she'll have one of the TVs brought up for me. Will you be okay with work? I tried calling Jess to come in earlier but she didn't pick up, so if you need me—"

I cut her off, holding my hand up. "No, no. I've got this. You rest and concentrate on getting better. Your health is more important. I hate leaving you when you're ill, but I really need to get going. I've got some things to go over with Pam before I meet with Jess. If you need me or need anything, text me. I'll be picking up dresses tomorrow morning instead of today, so I'll be around if you need me. Are you sure you'll be okay on your own?"

"As long as you keep that woman away from me, yes."

I shake my head, laughing as I get up to leave the room. I can't even make that promise because something tells me there's no stopping Ada when she puts her mind to something.

"Pagan! Pagan, answer me, dammit," Alison calls out as I walk down the hall.

She's totally going to quit on me.

~

I'm invited back to the garden room for breakfast again when I reach the bottom of the stairs. When I walk in, Pam smiles up at me warmly from her seat at the table.

"Good morning, Pagan. How is Alison feeling this morning?"

I slide my gaze to Ada as I take one of the empty seats. Turning to face Pam, I'm about to answer when Ada makes a disgruntled noise, interrupting.

"I told you already, she's fine. I made sure of it. Now, Pagan, tell us more about you. Are you single? What do you think of London? What are your parents like?"

Blown away by the rapid-fire questions, I give Pam a kind smile, not wanting to ignore her. "Alison is fine and resting in her room." Ada is giving her a smug look when I turn her way. "I am single, London is beautiful from what I've seen, and my parents are great people."

She smiles broadly, like I just gave her the answers she wanted. I actually feel like I'm being duped when she clasps her hands on the table.

Why does she look like she's about to take over the world?

"My grandson is single," she murmurs, more to herself than to the room.

"That I am, Grams," Drake's deep, rumbling voice announces.

Looking to my left, my mouth goes dry at the sight of him walking into the room wearing only a pair of basketball shorts and a towel wrapped around his neck.

Holy mother of God!

Sweat glistens on his hard, ripped chest, and I lick my suddenly dry lips. What would it be like to run my tongue down his hard body, right down to where the sweat trickles into the elastic band of his shorts?

I bet he tastes as good as he looks.

My thighs clench together when the image of him above me, his hard chest pressing against mine, flashes in my head.

He sits next to me, snapping me out of my daydream. Having him so close is doing things to my body, so I distract myself by lifting the Donovan file and notebook from my bag and turning to Pam, clearing my throat.

She's looking from me to Drake with rapt interest, a small smile playing on her lips.

"Pam, I've called the Hilton to confirm your rooms and booking. Your driver will be here tomorrow at eleven to take you, Mr Donovan, and Ada. He'll be there until you leave Friday morning. I'm also advised to inform you that you can call on him anytime you're there for his car services.

"I've also gone ahead and booked a table at a five-star restaurant with a wide range of foods, so everyone should be happy with the choice. Tickets for the play are ready to be picked up at the front desk at the Hilton. Just give them your name and they'll hand them over," I tell her as I read through my notes, checking everything off as I go. Not that I need my notes; it just gives me something to concentrate on instead of my eyes straying back to Drake, which they've been dying to do for the last five minutes.

Pam looks at me, relief in her eyes. "Thank you. I completely forgot about the hotel and tickets. It's been a busy few weeks."

I smile, tilting my head to the side. "It's my job, Pam. It's why you hired me, to keep everything running smoothly and to make sure you are where you need to be."

"Still, thank you, dear. You really are a godsend."

Her approval makes me blush a little, and I clear my throat once again before looking at the next topic on the agenda. "Okay... next is the fundraiser. Since you've let us use your hall, the house is going to be really busy today. My colleague Jessica, who should be here shortly with the catering staff, will be running everything. The rest will flow in and out throughout the day.

"We already had two bouncers and six security guards hired for tonight, but because it was originally at a hotel, we didn't feel the need for any extra security. With the items of value around your home—"

She waves me off. "Shane was informed yesterday morning about the change of schedule and has hired a valet parking service and my normal security staff. We use them for other events like this one. They'll make sure everyone is kept in the ballroom and the gardens. We've have the stairs roped off, along with the left side of the manor. But to be safe, if you could get your team to check in with Shane when they arrive, he'll instruct everyone on where to be so there's no confusion."

That's actually brilliant. It takes another load off Jessica and me.

"Thank you, that will be a huge help."

"It's our pleasure. And I've already had the kitchen prepped and the ballroom cleaned and ready for you. Is there anything else you'd like to discuss about tonight?"

Looking down at my notes, I see I've gone through most of it. "Not today, but I would like to sit down with you and Amelia when you're back from your trip."

She nods before turning to Ada, giving her a knowing look. "Did you pack?"

Ada huffs, glaring at her daughter. "No. I still don't understand why I can't stay here with the kids. You know I hate all that uppity crap. And a play? I'm gonna be bored out of my brain."

"Mother, we've talked about this. The kids want the house to themselves for the night," Adam tells her, treading carefully.

"Yeah, and I bet they have more fun than me. And they'll have alcohol."

Drake chuckles under his breath, and goosebumps run up my arms. For a moment, I forgot he was even there.

Shirtless.

Sweaty.

Hard...

Yeah, I totally need to get laid, or find a new hobby.

"Grams, the police were called the last time we were alone with you," Drake says, causing his dad to chuckle and Pam to glare at both of them.

"Revenge is best served sweet," Ada says, shrugging as she twirls her knife.

Sweet?

Huh!

I don't tell her the saying is 'Revenge is best served cold.' I don't want to get on her bad side, especially with the way she's eying that butter knife.

"You put a laxative in his drink," Adam reminds her.

"And his pudding," Drake adds.

"After you somehow made sure none of the toilets were working," Pam says, sounding a little sceptical.

What on earth?

She's just a tiny old lady.

I'm actually starting to think I should've taken Alison's pleas for Ada to stay away a little more seriously now.

This is just plain crazy.

"He cheated on me, then had the balls to bring her to *my* favourite restaurant, where he took *me*," Ada snaps, spinning the knife a little too hard.

Why is Cher Lloyd's "I Want You Back" ringing in my head?

"Mother, you sent them a voucher to get them there," Pam tells her, sounding vexed.

"And forced Jesse and me to take you there under false pretences," Drake says, sounding more amused than anything.

"And you hit a waiter with your bag," Adam adds, his lips twitching.

Okay, next job I'm totally doing background checks—on the whole family. Are they not worried about that knife she's freaking spinning at all?

"Like I told the copper, it was an accident. I was aiming for *him*," she tuts, rolling her eyes.

"It's a moot point since you're still coming with us. I don't want you getting the kids into trouble this close to the wedding."

"Whatever," Ada mutters before sulking off. She looks like a kid who just had her tablet confiscated.

When she's gone, I'm able to relax. The knife is still there, which has to be a good sign. Though I still can't help but wonder how someone her age, someone who looks adorably sweet, can be so... so... I don't even know what to call it, but it's *something*.

"You do realise she's gonna be here for every other gathering for the wedding?" Drake points out, shovelling eggs into his mouth.

Lord, even his mouth closing around a fork is sexy.

"She'll be on her best behaviour," Adam says, avoiding eye contact with anyone.

"Yes," Pam agrees, taking a sip of her drink.

And, I note, also avoiding our gazes.

"They're lying, aren't they?" I whisper to Drake.

He grins, all straight white teeth on show, with a little dimple in his cheek. I find myself sighing at his perfection.

"Yep," he says, popping the 'p'.

I close my eyes, seriously hoping I don't have to deal with anything she does. I can only handle so much. And I don't want to get arrested. I wouldn't look good in a prison uniform.

My phone beeping has me looking away from Drake's amused eyes and down to the screen. I groan when I read the message.

ALISON: If you don't come and save me right now, I'm quitting. I should be getting paid danger money. And why the fudge does she want a copy of the wedding itinerary?

Oh no!

"I have to go!" I rush out, glaring at Drake when I see his shoulders shaking in laughter.

Without looking back, I race out of the room, leaving Drake to explain to his parents about my sudden departure.

As I run up the stairs, I pray like hell that I won't need to find a new assistant by the end of the three weeks.

Chapter Six

*B*eing an event planner means being on the go constantly. You have to know the where, when and who. But when you haven't been on the project for more than a day, it sucks. It's guaranteed that there will be more than one mistake, and trust me, today has been a day of mistakes.

First, the caterers mixed up their menus, cooking for a venue they have for tomorrow. Then we had a mishap with the live band, but thankfully it wasn't anything that couldn't be fixed. Then the hotel wouldn't let Jessica's assistant pick up the raffle prizes and auction donations, even after giving them permission over the phone, so I had to hold the fort while she went to sort that out.

By the time I left Jessica less than an hour ago to greet the guests arriving, it was too late for me to do my normal 'get glammed up' routine. And now my mood is dwindling. To feel great, I have to look great, but I just don't. I don't even have time to moisturize since I was already expected to be downstairs half an hour ago.

I barely have my silver strapped heels on when there's a knock on the door.

"Come in," I call out, finishing up my buckle.

"Hey, Jessica—" Drake starts, stepping in, but then he stops. I look up to see what has him so distracted and find his eyes on me, his expression heated.

His intense appraisal has me blushing and running a hand down my dress self-consciously. I'm not ugly, but the way I've thrown my outfit together doesn't warrant a look like that.

My hair's in a messy bun, leaving a few strands framing my face. I didn't have time for full make-up, so I gave my cheeks a good pinch and applied pink lip gloss.

My silver silk gown falls to my ankles. It was something Alison had packed in case something happened to one of my other dresses. Boy I'm glad she did.

Drake shakes his head, his gaze travelling up my body, clearing his throat when he meets my eyes. "You look beautiful," he tells me hoarsely.

Blushing, I tuck my hands behind my back. "Thank you." I clear my throat, looking anywhere but at him. "Um, you mentioned Jess?"

"Oh yeah, she wanted me to come check on you and let you know the auction will be starting soon."

Yep, totally freaking late.

I nod, taking his arm when he offers. "Have the wedding guests arrived?"

"Yeah, and Jesse and Amelia brought the best man and maid of honour with them. My sister Gabby won't be here till tomorrow morning."

His tone when he mentions the best man and maid of honour has me giving him a sideways glance as we make our way down the hall. "Isn't the maid of honour Amelia's cousin?"

"Yeah, and she's a freaking bitch, just like Amelia's mum. How Amelia came from her or even survived it still surprises me. She's everything her mum isn't. Angela's mum, Amelia's aunt, is a peach though. Lovely woman."

"That bad?" I ask, gulping.

One thing I can't deal with is bitches. I'm a cheerful, bubbly person, so when someone around me wants to sour that, it riles me up and I end up doing and saying shit I shouldn't.

45

"She's the spawn of the Devil himself. Amelia's mum is the Devil's sidekick."

Hmm.... "And you don't like your brother's best friend?"

He grunts. "No. He's an entitled prick, or acts like one. He's a snake, but my brother is too nice to say anything. He helped Jesse out in law school and they've been inseparable ever since. But the guy is a dick, a total womanizer. He tends to treat every female like gold until he gets what he wants. Like I said, a snake. Just be careful around both of them. Something about him has always bothered me," he warns me as we reach the bottom of the stairs.

I'm about to ask why but Jessica steps in front of us, her headpiece on and a clipboard in hand. "Hey, you made it," she beams.

"Hey. Where do you want me?" I smile.

"I don't. You've got the night off to enjoy yourself. Mr and Mrs Donovan agreed with me."

"But the auction—"

She waves me off. "We have it covered. I just wanted to make sure you were in attendance. I know you were looking at bidding on the spa weekend."

"Are you sure?" I ask, since nothing really went to plan today. I bite my bottom lip, ready to get to work, but Drake places his hand on my back and I bite back my words. His hand is warm through the thin material, and tingles shoot up my back.

"She's sure. Now let's get you a glass of champagne," he says.

Jessica grins, her eyes sparkling as she eyes the both of us like she knows something we don't. I guess with how close Drake is, and with him touching me so intimately, we must seem like we're a couple to her.

She winks at me, waves and turns to leave. I roll my eyes, letting Drake steer me towards the ballroom.

"That was rude to assume," I remark, smiling at people as I pass.

"Just relax and have some fun."

Everyone is dressed to the nines. My eyes rake over everyone, admiring the beauty surrounding me. And I don't just mean the people, but the room too.

It's absolutely breathtaking.

I left the floor staff to sort out the room around noon, so I'm seeing this for the first time. How they managed to pull this off in one day is incredible.

Jessica didn't order decorations for the event since it was being held at a hotel. Somehow, with the large chandelier, twinkle lights surrounding the doors and bar, and with the architecture of the room, it doesn't need any fancy decorations. Although, picturing what this room will look like for the wedding has me giddy with excitement.

Glancing around, my eyes land on the stage where a live jazz band is playing and I smile. Jessica really went all out when she acquired everything for tonight. What amazes me more is that she got it donated or at a discounted price.

Guests seem to be enjoying themselves, socialising, some dancing, and all chatting and having a good time.

Waiters and waitresses are walking around handing out champagne and appetisers. The second one is near, I snag a glass off the tray, Drake doing the same.

"Wow, I didn't realise this many people would be here," he says in awe, glancing around the room with the same expression I just had.

"It's one of our biggest fundraisers. There are a lot of wealthy people here, and family of fallen or injured soldiers," I explain. "Once word spreads, tickets usually sell out within a week or two. Our other biggest fundraisers are for children in need and women's aid." His expression burns into me so I turn his way. "What?"

"You really love this, don't you? Organising events." He stares down at me.

I smile, gazing right back into his eyes when I answer. "I do. It's the best feeling in the world, but when we do fundraisers, it means something much more to me. Knowing a community of people—rich or not—who probably never speak, know each other, or get along can come together to support something so meaningful and worthwhile... I don't know. It's spectacular. It shows that as people, as a country, we can come together peacefully. And knowing we could help someone, at least *one* person, with the money we raise is a gift no money can buy." I trail off, thinking about all the women we've helped with our women's aid fundraisers.

He probably thinks I'm a certifiable nutjob.

Great!

He shocks me when he places his hands on my waist, pulling me against him. I gasp, meeting his eyes in shock as tingles rush through my body. My heart slams into my chest as I try to control my emotions.

His eyes dilate and a look I can't decipher flashes through them. His expression is warm and, if I'm reading him correctly, loving.

"You really are special, Pagan Salvatore," he whispers, lowering his head towards me.

My heart beats against my chest.

Holy crap! He's going to kiss me.

And I think I'm going to let him.

And maybe kiss him back.

"Pagan, Drake, there you are. My, don't you look dashing, dear," Pam calls out from nearby.

We jump apart, turning to his mum who pulls me in for a quick hug, pecking both cheeks.

"Hi, Pam. So do you," I tell her, gesturing to the red sequined dress she's wearing. Pam can certainly pull off most outfits even women *my* age can't.

"Thank you." She smiles. "I'd like you to meet my son, Jesse, and Amelia. You'll also get to meet Aaron and Angela." Her expression scrunches in disgust when she mentions Angela's name, making my lips twitch.

When Pam gestures for us to follow her, I give Drake a wide-eyed look but find him too busy staring down at my lips, seeming lost in thought.

Not wanting to think about what may or may not have just happened between us, I clear my throat, pointing in Pam's direction. "We should follow her."

Snapping out of it, he places his hand on my lower back, nodding mutely.

"Are they really that bad?" I ask, wanting to get rid of the awkwardness between us. Or maybe it's just me who feels it and I'm making it awkward.

He gives me a smile and a wink, seeming more like his normal self.

"Nah. Aaron is a pansy, and Angela is just a witch who likes to throw tantrums."

I nod, straightening my back when we come to a group Pam's talking to. I notice Adam and Ada straight away. Two people have their backs to us, but Jesse and Amelia, who I've seen pictures of from Pam, I recognise right away. But even without having seen pictures, the way they're acting together would've confirmed it. I can tell they are totally, irrevocably in love with each other.

They're practically glued at the hip, but it's the way they look at each other that cements my notion of them being in love. They look blissfully happy, and seeing something so beautiful makes me smile. The way they are together, I already know I'm going to enjoy working for them.

Still, I can't help but be a little envious of what they have. Reminds me so much of what my brother has, and my mum and dad. I desperately want what they have more than ever, but love like theirs can't be forced, or found. It's magnetic, pulling together two people who belong with one another.

"There you two are." Pam beams, turning to face us. "Pagan, I'd like to introduce you to my son, Jesse, and my future daughter-in-law, Amelia."

I smile wide and take a step forward, ready to give handshakes, but the two people who had their backs to me turn around and the smile falls from my face. I pale, taking a shaky step back.

Aaron.

Fucking Aaron.

Aaron, my high school boyfriend till we were eighteen. Then I found out he cheated on me. Right before he dumped me, saying he got some girl pregnant and was leaving to be with her.

That's all I got after five years of being with him. No 'I'm sorry', no explanations and no goodbye.

The break-up destroyed me, leaving me broken-hearted. I think it took just over a year for me to move on, to finally get over it. But when I did, it was to my sister-in-law's ex, who was abusive to her. He used me just to get to her, and being used twice made dating less and less appealing for me.

I pick some real winners.

That said, this is the first time I've seen him since.

"Pagan? Pagan Salvatore? Oh my gosh, hi." He smiles widely, stepping forwards to hug me.

I don't think so, buddy.

Taking one huge step back, I end up bumping into Drake. Not apologising, I keep my eyes on Aaron, narrowing them. "Aaron," I hiss.

He hasn't changed much since I last saw him. He still has a baby face, one struggling to grow facial hair. His face is what drew people to him, especially the older women in town. They thought he was the town's golden boy.

He dresses a lot smarter now, clad in a three-piece suit instead of the ratty jeans and T-shirts he used to wear to piss his parents off.

"Well, will you look at that," Ada mutters, sounding rather amused. I ignore her, continuing to glare at him.

"You know each other?" Drake asks, an edge to his tone.

I open my mouth, but whether it's to excuse myself or to tell *him* to fuck off, I don't know. Nor do I get a chance to find out because the jerk pastes on a fake smile right in front of my eyes and answers before I can.

"Yeah, we were close friends at school."

I scoff, taking a step closer to Drake, drawing from his strength and needing his support as I ignore everyone's eyes on us.

"Is that right? Marvellous!" Pam is either oblivious to the tension or trying to avoid it.

Having had enough, I turn to Pam with a fake smile. "No we weren't. We started dating in high school until we were eighteen. Then one day, he went to go home to change for our date—"

"Pagan, don't," Aaron hisses, his expression changing to the one I'm used to.

"Oh no, Pagan, continue," Ada says giddily, clearly enjoying the show.

Ignoring her too, I glare his way, scoffing at the audacity. "What? Don't tell them how I waited three hours for you to pick me up, only to have you send me a message to tell me you got some girl pregnant and were leaving to be with her. Don't tell them how I went straight to your house to find you already gone? Or don't tell them how you didn't even say sorry or give me a goodbye!" I yell, all the anger I felt towards him bubbling up to the surface.

"You tell him, girl," Ada hoots.

When my surroundings come back to me, I find everyone staring at me. Well, everyone except Ada. She's busy glaring holes into Aaron's head.

I close my eyes as embarrassment washes over me and take a second to gather myself before turning to Pam. "I'm so sorry, Pam. That was rude of me." I feel my throat close up. Glancing at Amelia and Jesse, I give them a small smile. "And it was lovely to finally get to meet you both in person. I can't wait to catch up with you. Now if you'll excuse me, I have to... I have to go." As soon as I'm finished, I turn towards the bar, ignoring Pam's outstretched hand to comfort me. Once I know they won't hear me, I mumble, "To get really, really shit-faced."

"Pagan, wait," Aaron calls, but I continue walking away.

"Leave her the fuck alone," Drake snaps, hopefully stopping him from following me.

Walking up to the bar, I wave the bartender over, fighting the angry tears from falling. I never thought I'd have to see him again, let alone speak to him.

"Shot of tequila and a double vodka, lime and lemonade, please," I tell the bartender.

"Hey," Drake says softly, standing beside me against the bar.

"Hey," I whisper, turning to face him. "I'm so sorry for that back there. It was unprofessional of me, and I'll completely understand if your mum wants me to leave."

He turns my whole body to face him, giving me a soft expression. "She's actually in the middle of Grams handing Aaron his balls. I don't think she minds. She seemed pretty pissed on your behalf."

I glance in that direction just in time to see Ada throw a drink in Aaron's face. Before he can recover, she kicks him in the balls.

Ouch!

Holy crap she can move quick.

"Is it wrong that I don't even feel sorry for him or his nuts?" Drake blurts out, his face scrunched in pain like it was him who was just kicked.

Men!

I laugh and turn back to the bar, throwing back my shot. My throat burns, but it feels good as I chase it down with a sip of my drink.

"He never did have big balls. My guess, he's playing it up to make it look like she hit the mark."

He laughs, throwing his head back. I smile at the sight, feeling a little better already as my own laugh threatens to slip free.

"Do you want me to get Mum to book him into a hotel so he's not in your face?"

Shit, I didn't even think about him staying here. I'd been too shocked about seeing him to think of anything else. But I know I can't fuck this job up. I just pray they make sure he's on the other side of the mansion.

"No," I sigh. "I'll stay out of his way. And if he even thinks of pissing me off, I'll be setting Ada on him."

He chuckles but sobers quickly. "Are you okay? What he did was pretty fucked up. That must've been hard."

I think about it for a second before shrugging. "I'm mostly angry. I never got to be the teenage girl who got to take her anger out on him or make him jealous of what he lost. We were together for five years and he didn't even say goodbye or apologise to me. I didn't get any closure, and I spent a lot of time wondering what the hell I did that was so wrong he would cheat on me. It had taken me a long time to realise I never did anything. He was a jerk and we were young, practically kids."

"Young or not, it was a really shitty thing to do. But there's a pro to him being here."

He grins mischievously and my eyes scrunch together, wondering what he's up to.

"And what's that?" I ask dryly.

"Well, you have three weeks to take out as much anger as you want on him. Don't hold back either. And don't worry about him, I'll make sure he stays out of your way."

My heart melts, grateful for him being here, for being here for *me.* "Thank you."

It's his turn to look confused. "For what?"

"For being kind, for stopping him coming after me." I shrug.

"It's my—"

"Hey, darl, as soon as you're up for some sweet revenge on the cheating scumbag, come find me. I have some ideas," Ada says, startling me from behind.

When I turn, she disappears just as quickly as she materialised, and my gaze shoots back to Drake. We stare at each other wide-eyed before bursting into laughter.

Yep, definitely going to be an interesting three weeks, that's for sure.

Chapter Seven

*I*t seems I didn't need to get shit-faced to forget all about fuckface. I just needed to get merrily drunk and find a fabulous dance partner.

I've successfully avoided Aaron at all costs. Whenever he's tried to approach, Drake or a member of his family has intervened. They weren't even sly about it either. I think they wanted him to know what they were doing to warn him off, but like a dumbass, he never got the memo.

I'm drunk, dancing to Jackie Wilsons "She's So Fine" with a retired soldier called George. Jessica introduced me to him and his wife, Betty, earlier on in the night.

He's a hoot, and I'm having the time of my life dancing with him.

And my new friend tequila is partly to thank for that.

"You'll get me into trouble with the missus," George laughs as he twirls me around again.

Laughing and shaking my booty, I look over in the direction of where I last saw Betty. She's dancing with Drake, also having the time of her life.

"I think your wife is enjoying the company," I tease.

His gaze flickers back over to his wife, a warm look replacing the happy, teasing expression he was wearing.

"Looks like I'm up. I want to get a dance in before some other yahoo moves in and steals my chance to woo my wife."

I smile and let him walk off, about to turn around to see if Drake wants to dance when a firm hand takes mine. I smile wide, ready to tease Drake about his dancing skills, but end up coming face-to-face with Aaron.

Pulling my hand out of his grip, I glare at him. "Go away, Aaron. I have nothing to say to you," I hiss quietly.

There's no way I'm going to make another scene, and if he has a decent bone in his body, he won't either.

"Dance with me," he slurs.

Still can't hold his liquor, I see.

Pansy.

He pulls me against him before I can move away, using strength I didn't know he was capable of, especially in his condition. He starts swaying us side-to-side, full-on 'boat rocking at sea in the middle of a storm' swaying.

"Let me go!" I hiss, pushing at his chest, but he doesn't budge.

"No! Dance with me. I'm sorry, Pagan. I made a mistake. I should never have left."

I manage to somehow get loose, so I take the opportunity to step back, ready to leave. "Just leave me alone. Goodbye, Aaron."

He takes my hand in a tight grip, spinning me around. With so much alcohol in my system, I topple over, falling into him.

He groans in pleasure, disgusting me. But when his hands land on my arse, pressing himself against me, I shriek, "Get off!"

"You need to get over what happened. We were kids, Pagan. It didn't mean anything back then. But fuck, if I knew you'd turn out this hot.... Come on, Pagan, we were good together."

No, we really weren't, jackass.

I gape, shocked at what I'm hearing. There's no way I could have heard him right. No, I must be hallucinating, or the alcohol is affecting me way more than I realised.

Since I've frozen in shock, too stunned to even move, he must see it as me giving him the green light because he keeps groping me. By the time I overcome the madness I just heard him spout, he's humping my leg.

And he's hard.

I pull back, slapping him as hard as I can. The red handprint forming on his cheek doesn't give me an ounce of satisfaction, especially when my hand feels like it's on fire.

Now stringing him up by the balls... that would be a start.

"You have got to be kidding me!" My voice rises, echoing around the room as the song changes. He grins, coming in for a kiss.

Everything moves in slow motion, like a really bad horror movie coming true.

First I see his approach, then his intent. The next thing I know, my hand is raised, ready to give his other cheek the same treatment.

Only he's pulled back in a blink of an eye and I end up slapping Drake instead.

I cover my mouth in shock as I wait for what he'll do. He just blinks at me, rubbing his red cheek.

"Seriously?" he asks dryly.

Rushing up to him, I wince. "I'm so sorry. He was about to kiss me, and I got angry and just snapped. I didn't even see you."

Ada cackles from beside me and I jump. "You got 'im a gooden."

"Not now, Grams," he mutters before turning on Aaron, who's struggling to stand up. "And you! Go to bed and sleep it off. When you wake up tomorrow, you can apologise to Pagan for your behaviour. You're lucky I don't kick your arse."

Wow! He looks serious too.

And hot.

"We're gonna have sex, just you wait and see," Aaron slurs, swaying.

I think I just threw up in my mouth.

Looking at him now, I can't believe I ever thought I loved him. I shake my head, disgusted. "Yeah, over my dead body, buddy."

"We were good together."

"So much so that you cheated on me."

"Yeah, you cheatin' scumbag," Ada pipes in.

I nod, totally agreeing. "He is a cheating scumbag. Now if you don't mind, I'm going to find my new friend tequila."

"Ah, good ol' tequila. She's been my BFF for a while." Ada winks, linking her arm through mine as she pulls me away from Drake, who's trying to remove Aaron from the room.

"Shame she sucks arse in the morning," I grumble.

She cackles, throwing her head back. "I may just like you even more."

We make our way over to the bar, and with a huge grin at the bartender, I order another shot of tequila.

"I'm sorry but the bar's closed, ladies."

The man's crazy. No way is the bar closed. I forbid it. Doesn't he realise how much I need a drink? "But how? Why? We need a drink."

"Yeah, we do. Why don't you just pour us one? We won't tell the owners," Ada says, leaning over the bar a little.

I grin, wondering why I even thought she was a little whacko. "It *is* her daughter's house," I mutter.

He frowns, looking down the bar. Yes! He's going to get us a drink. I want to whoop, but then he winces before turning back to us. "I'm sorry, but I'll lose my job if I serve you. We're only contracted to serve till twelve. If we serve after that, we'll be fined."

"Who's gonna know?" I ask him, my voice rising.

"Who's gonna know what?" Drake asks, stepping up behind me.

My smile widens as I turn swiftly to face him. "Drake. You're here."

"I've been here all night." He grins.

"You know what I mean. Can you do me a huge favour?"

"And what's that?"

"We need a drink, and this arse won't serve us," Ada interrupts. She's staring daggers at the bartender, who's moved down the bar, cleaning glasses. However, he's watching her from the corner of his eye warily.

Clever man.

"Please?" I bat my eyelashes, swaying slightly on my feet.

He chuckles deeply, shaking his head. "I think you've had enough. Why don't you go up to bed?"

I pout, thinking it over when Ada interrupts. "The night is young. I've got a stash of sherry in my room."

"Grams, Mum's warned you about hiding the alcohol, and don't you have to be up early?" he asks, giving her a pointed look.

"Pish, I don't get hangovers. I'm too old. I'll be up before your mother and father."

"Maybe so, but Pagan needs her rest," he argues.

A yawn escapes me just as I'm about to decline. I snort, giggling. "Okay, okay! I think bed is in order."

"I thought you were different," Ada mutters before storming off.

"She hates me," I whisper, shocked that I'm kind of hurt. I feel like we were just having a true bonding moment. She seems like a really good ally to have.

"She doesn't. She's just off to find the next willing victim. Now, are you okay to get to your room on your own, or do you need me to draw you a map?"

I scoff, waving him off. "I'll be fine, thank you. I'm only a little bit drunk… thanks to Aaron sobering me up."

Chuckling, he steadies me. "I'm sure."

"Well goodnight and farewell," I sing.

"Goodnight, Pagan," he rumbles before moving off in the direction Ada went.

"I don't need a map," I mutter to myself before turning in what I hope is the right direction to my bedroom.

"Ha! I showed him," I whoop quietly when I reach my door.

It's open when I go to push it open and I frown. Looking around, I make sure I'm at the right room. The stairs to the gym are just down the hall a little, so I know I am.

Stepping inside, I immediately sober, anger filling my veins. Passed out in my bed, wearing only his boxers, is Aaron.

"Get out!" I yell, walking over to him.

I immediately regret coming near him when the stench of vomit has me gagging.

Pinching my nose, I move closer, slapping him. It seems to be tonight's theme. When he doesn't wake or even stir, I growl in frustration. "Wake up, you arsehole. You're in *my* bed."

Great, now I sound like the little bear confronting Goldilocks.

Looking around the room, my eyes land on the bathroom and an idea occurs. I grab the jug resting on the dressing table and move to the sink, filling it with cold water.

If this doesn't wake the fucker up, nothing will.

But when I walk back into room and stand above him, Drake's earlier words come back to me. *'You've got three weeks to take out as much anger as you want on him.'*

I want revenge. I deserve it, goddammit.

And I know just what to do.

Walking over to my work case, I grab my pencil case and move back over to the bed. An evil grin forms across my face as I stare down at him.

Up first is his eyebrows, so grabbing the brown Sharpie, I start to colour in some real thick eyebrows, making sure to get them as perfect as possible with shaky hands.

I giggle when I'm finished, grabbing the red Sharpie next and colouring in his lips, making them look bigger.

He doesn't even stir, the only movement his chest rising and falling from his deep snores.

God, I got lucky when he left me. I'd have smothered him in his sleep by now.

Not wanting to stop there, I grab a dark blue, colouring in his eyelids, which is harder to do when I'm trying to keep a steady hand.

Really shouldn't be doing this drunk, Pagan.

I'm hoping I don't accidentally on purpose poke his eye out. Not that I'd care.

When I'm finished, he looks like a drag queen gone wrong. The thought has me laughing.

Finishing, I grab the pink, drawing small circles on his cheeks and colouring them in.

Now to wake the arsehole up. He can walk back to his room and hopefully bump into every living soul looking like this on his way back.

Grabbing the jug, I trickle the water on his chest, wanting him to see my face when I pour the whole jug in it.

And... nothing!

Not even a twitch.

Growing frustrated, I pour it on his boxers, growing annoyed by the second when he doesn't wake up. No way am I going to sleep in the same room as him, and I'm sure as hell not going to find my way through this maze of a house just to ask for another bed.

Leaving him in bed to wake up thinking he pissed himself, I storm out of the room. I'm ready to knock on Alison's door, then pause with my fist raised in the air. With the way she felt earlier, before the party started, I don't want to interrupt her. I'd left her waiting for food before rushing into my room to get ready. She looked tired and worn out.

I notice the stairs to the gym and make my way towards them. Looking down, I see a faint glow of a light reflecting off the walls. The stairs spiral as I make my way down them and when I come to the bottom, I gasp.

In the middle of the room is a swimming pool, a hot tub at the top with stairs on the other end leading into the deep pool.

My gosh, it's beautiful.

Another yawn and I'm looking around—for what, I don't know. When I see a line of reclining deck chairs, I smile to myself. It seems someone is listening to my pleas after all. I really didn't fancy sleeping somewhere someone could find me, and the only sofa I've seen is in the main foyer, where guests were still passing through as I reached the stairs to come up. That would've been awkward.

I'm just about to get comfortable when a dressing gown hanging on the wall near another door has me walking that way, grateful the Donovans think of everything. It's a soft towel material and I smile as I walk back over to the recliner.

I'm totally taking this home with me.

With a yawn, I lie down, getting comfortable. Before I know it, my eyes close and I'm drifting off to sleep.

Chapter Eight

*C*onsidering I went to sleep on a plastic sunbed, I feel pretty flipping comfortable. Too comfortable, in fact.

My head is on something soft, my left leg cocked over something even softer, and a cold breeze is blowing over my bare legs and arse—

Holy crap!

My eyes open as I twist around and shoot up in bed, looking around the room in a panic.

Why the hell am I in Drake's bedroom, and how did I get here?

How drunk was I last night?

This is definitely one of those moments where I wish like hell I had listened to my inner conscience instead of my brain and *not* gotten drunk. I'm positively certain I went to sleep in the pool room after finding Aaron in my bed. However, I once woke up believing I'd met Elvis Presley, so certain in fact that I bet my dad and brother a hundred pounds that I did. Turns out I only met a life-size cardboard cutout of him.

But no matter how hard I try, I don't remember coming to Drake's room.

Better yet, I don't remember getting dressed in a blue T-shirt.

Out of all the shit I've done after I've had a drink, forgetting how I got into bed with a sort-of stranger is not one of them.

A door opens, startling me. I'm ready to attack Drake with a million questions, but when I look up, it's Ada walking through the door.

I lift the sheet to my chest, looking around the room with a new kind of panic. "Ada, hi. I, um... I can explain," I start to tell her, gesturing to the room.

She waves me off, grinning from ear to ear. "We're all grown-ups, but I already saw that douche canoe coming out of your room this morning. It's why I'm here."

"*Here?* I don't even know *how* I got here," I squeak.

How did she know I was here?

Just as she's about to reply, Drake comes out of the bathroom wearing only a towel around his waist.

Good God, he really needs to cover that body of his up. I'm already struggling to think, and he's not helping matters.

"Grams, what are you doing in here?" he asks, pulling the towel tighter. He shifts, looking uncomfortable, but not as much as I am right now.

"Hey! What am *I* doing here?" I ask.

"I came to give this to Pagan," Ada answers him.

"Give her what?"

"Hello, let's talk about me for a second. How did I get here?"

He's about to reply when Ada interrupts, dropping a shoebox into my lap. "As much as I'd love to stick around and enjoy the awkward conversation you're about to have, I need to get going. Pam is just about ready to put some baby reins on me or electrocute my arse into gear. Now, there aren't any condoms in there, but I do have a stash in my room if you need any. I love kids, but I'm not ready to be a great-grandma."

My eyes bug out as my mouth hangs open in shock. I'm still stunned when the door clicks shut behind her.

What the hell just happened?

"Um," Drake starts. My head turns in his direction, and for a split second, he looks a little uncomfortable. But then he grins, his eyes raking down my body. My face heats and I look away, fiddling with the sheets. "Last night was amazing."

I squeak, my face burning for an entire other reason. "What? We... I... what?"

He laughs, throwing his head back. He has a good laugh, deep and sexy. "Relax, I'm kidding. I went down to the gym after dealing with Grams and saw you sleeping. I carried you back to your room but you had a guest. I'm guessing he was an unwanted guest?"

I give him a dry look, not amused. "Not funny. And what do you think?"

"By the look of his face, I'd say unwanted," he laughs. Then I remember what I did to Aaron's face last night and giggle lightly. He's going to suffer for days trying to get that off his face. They're the best Sharpies I've ever had.

I just hope Amelia and Jesse aren't mad. It's not like he'll look like that at the wedding.

"He wouldn't wake up." I shrug, then notice the T-shirt I'm wearing and look back up at Drake, who is still half-naked. "How did I get into your T-shirt? I don't even remember coming up here." I'm also well aware I'm only wearing a thong underneath. I'm pretty sure I had a bra on before I fell asleep too.

I'm pretty mortified over waking up with my arse hanging out. There's no hoping that he hadn't seen the goods, though I'd flaunted them without knowing.

He grins, sitting on the edge of the bed. "You were out like a light, snoring away."

"I do not snore," I snap.

"Trust me, you do. And drool," he teases. Being mature, I stick my tongue out, smiling lightly. "And don't worry, I managed to change you without seeing anything. Although, I'm pretty sure you copped a feel or two while I was getting you undressed. And who the hell made your shoes, NASA? It took me twenty minutes to get them off."

"Oh God," I groan, leaning back against the pillows and covering my face. I ignore the comment about the shoes because I wouldn't win the argument. They are a pain in the arse. "Please tell me you're joking."

He chuckles. "No, you really have a thing for my abs."

That makes me blush harder, and I start to giggle. "I'm so sorry. And thank you. I'd dread to think how I'd be feeling right now if I had slept downstairs."

"It's not a problem. Although, you owe me now."

I can see he's serious. He turns to the far side of the room and I follow his gaze, smiling when I see a throw blanket and pillow on the small leather couch.

"I'm sorry. Thank you for giving up your bed. I'm pretty sure I would've fitted better on that than you though."

"It's fine. I've slept in worst places at work between shifts. Now can you please open that box? I'm desperately dying to know what my Grams is up to."

The box rattles when I shake it and I give Drake a wary look. "She wouldn't put a snake or spiders in a box, would she?"

He laughs, shaking his head. "I don't think so, but with Grams, you never know."

My eyes widen as I move the box off my lap and closer to Drake. "I swear, if something crawls or jumps out of that box, I'm gone. You'll see smoke coming from behind me."

Laughing, he knocks the lid off the box and then frowns, looking inside. "Oh God."

"What?" I ask, then peer inside, laughing when I do.

It's a box of tricks. Not magic tricks, but pranks. The first thing that catches my eye is the box of laxatives, and I remember the conversation the Donovans had at breakfast the morning before.

It's the duct tape that has me confused and a little worried. Picking up the note left on the side, I read it out loud.

"Laxatives are old-school but they do the trick. Make sure you swap his toilet roll with the duct tape though—wouldn't be funny otherwise. Now I only had a few hours to get some research done, but luckily for you, I already had some stuff on the slimeball. It comes in handy, so don't judge me. Anyway, he's a clean freak, hates feeling dirty, so I've left some itching powder and stink bombs in the box. You're probably wondering what the toy snake is for. Well, I heard through the grapevine that he's petrified of them and mice. I didn't have a toy mouse on me, but wait till I get back. I do have some better tricks up my sleeve. Now I know what you're going to say—why would I help you? I'm doing this because we girls need to stick together... and okay, things here were getting really boring. Until I return, Ada."

I pause, reading over the letter once again.

"Ah, the duct tape makes sense now. I was worried for a second," Drake chuckles.

I shoot him a look, wondering how any of this makes sense. "Is she trying to get me fired?"

He laughs. Yes, *laughs*. "No, but she means well. Plus, after what he did last night, he does deserve payback. I haven't had this much fun in ages."

"Glad to amuse you," I mutter dryly, picking up the packet of stink bombs before dropping them back into the box. "I can't do this. I'm supposed to be working. I'm a respectable businesswoman. No one would hire me if they heard I acted like a three-year-old."

"No one will know. If you don't do it, Grams is only going to do it herself, and who knows what else she has planned."

I look over the letter again and shake my head. "I still can't believe she thought the first thing I'd think of is to ask her why she's helping me."

"What *was* your first thought?" he chuckles.

"Why none of you have had her sectioned," I joke.

Laughing, he gets up from the bed, walking over to his drawers. Then it dawns on me that I'm still in his room, in his T-shirt and in his bed.

"I'm going to go get changed," I rush out, thankful to see the T-shirt falls to above my knees when I climb out. Picking up the box and letter, I head for the door, turning to Drake when I reach it. "Thank you again for last night."

He smiles. "Pleasure was all mine. I'll see you for breakfast."

My body locks up, not wanting to leave him, which gives me pause.

What the hell am I doing? I'm working. I'm not here to sleep with my client. Not that he's my client, but he's a relative of the client and well... I don't know, it's just not ethical.

"You forget something?" he rumbles.

Shaking my head, I give him a fake smile and turn to leave, smacking my head into the door. "Fuck, I really hate this door."

"Oh my God, are you okay?"

"Yeah, yeah," I tell him, rubbing my head.

Before he can come over, I rush out of his room and straight into Alison's. She's looking a lot better this morning with more colour in her cheeks.

"Hey, you okay?" I ask when I notice her stormy expression.

"No, I'm not okay. Do you not look at your phone?"

I frown, then remember. "I'm sorry. I left it in my room."

"Wait, what are you wearing? And where have you been all night if you weren't in your room?" she asks, sitting up straighter.

I shrug, sitting on the edge of the bed. "Long story, so first, why don't you tell me what has your beautiful face all frowny."

"Flattery will get you everything you want," she chuckles before the smile dies on her face. "Last night some drunken idiot got into bed with me, practically naked, telling me how we belonged together."

"What?" I ask, shocked. "What did you do?"

"I didn't have to do anything. I woke up screaming, which made me gag, and I puked all over him. After that he stumbled out of the room without looking back."

"By any chance did he have a baby face and dark hair?" I ask, realising where this is going.

"Um, yeah. How did you know?"

"His name is Aaron Beckett."

Her eyes widen, her mouth gaping open. "Your ex Aaron?"

I nod. "The one and only."

"Holy shit. What is he doing here?"

Her expression says it all. She's just as shocked as I am. Not that she would've clicked that they were the same person, even if she knew his name. Because come on, what are the chances your ex-boyfriend happens to be a part of the wedding party you're planning?

"Turns out he's the best man and still a complete jackass. I don't know what I ever saw in him."

She closes her mouth before opening it again. "I'm totally speechless. I don't even know where to start with the questions. Has he said anything? Did he recognise you? What am I saying, of course he did. What are we going to do? Do you want me to take over?"

"Wow, slow down. I'll be fine. He got drunk, then started harassing me last night. He even got into my bed and passed out. I left him with Sharpie all over his face and went to sleep downstairs in the pool room. Drake found me and carried me back to his room. Ada also left me a box of pranks to get back at him for what he did to me." I let out a huge breath and wait for her reaction. A lot of emotions are crossing over her face as she blinks at me.

Shaking herself out of it, she squeals, "You slept in Drake Donovan's bed?"

Rolling my eyes, I hold my hands up, quieting her before checking to make sure no one's opened her door. "Keep it down. And yes—"

"Oh my God, this is great. He is *fine*." She giggles, her face lit up with excitement.

"He slept on the sofa in his room. Nothing happened. I didn't even know he carried me up until I woke up this morning."

"I'm having an information overload moment. I can't even process any of this until I've had some coffee and more sleep."

"You still not feeling any better?"

"Did you hear the part where I threw up on your ex?" she deadpans.

I laugh. "Oh yeah, sorry. Are you sure you don't want to head back home? I'm sure I could hire someone to take you."

"No, I'm feeling so much better. A little weak still, but I think some sleep will help with that. I'll be back in full swing by tomorrow, I promise."

"Are you sure? Jessica offered to come in and help if you're still not any better."

"Are you kidding? I wouldn't miss this wedding for anything. Is that the box Ada left you?" she asks, snatching it out of my hand.

"Help yourself," I mutter. "I need to go shower and get ready. Do you want me to bring you up something to eat?"

She doesn't look away from the box as she laughs at its contents. "No, I'm fine. Emily's already been in to ask what I needed."

"Okay, well I'll see you in a little while."

"Yeah, yeah," she says distractedly, still looking through the box.

"I'll just see myself out, then." I get up from the bed and walk over to the door, opening it a little. She still doesn't move a muscle. "I might jump off the roof," I say, trying to get her attention. She grunts but still doesn't look up as she finds the letter. "Better yet, I might go have sweaty, dirty sex with Drake right on the breakfast table."

"Now *that* is what I call a good breakfast," Drake rumbles from behind me. I scream, turning around to find him standing in the open doorway, a big grin on his face.

"Don't sneak up on people like that!" I yell, my face red with embarrassment.

"Will you go have sweaty, dirty sex on the breakfast table already. I have plans to make," Alison interrupts.

So she was *listening. Little traitor.*

I turn my glare her way, finding her grinning at me with a twinkle in her eye. She's seriously loving this.

"I like this plan," Drake adds.

"Me too," Alison laughs.

"Grrr." I stomp my foot. "I can't believe you two."

"It was your idea, darling."

I can't even look at Drake when I turn back to Alison. "I hate you." With that, I stomp down the hall, wondering if this is gonna be how I spend every morning—making an arse out of myself.

Chapter Nine

My nerves are skyrocketing as I make my way down the main stairs to meet everyone for breakfast. I've never had a problem talking to people, but after last night and then again this morning, meeting Jesse and Amelia scares the crap out of me. I'm worried of what they'll think and if they'll still want me to plan the wedding. Not that they have much of a choice since the wedding is in less than three weeks, but still, they could ask me to leave. The thought of leaving so soon, even before I get to see the finished touches, saddens me. I don't know why, of course, considering I'm leaving anyway at the end of the three weeks. I guess the Donovans get under your skin.

Or one in particular.

In the short amount of time I've spent with the Donovans, I've actually grown fond of them. They're nothing like I imagined. I like them, even if Ada is batshit crazy,

"Hi, Pagan. They're in the dining room. It seems everyone had a lie-in this morning," Jeff tells me as I meet him at the bottom of the stairs.

I smile at the old man, taking his arm when he offers. "I think it's the booze that did it."

He laughs, squeezing my arm gently. "It probably was. My Emily had to put Miss Ada to bed after she found her asleep outside by the pool."

"Oh no!" I chuckle. Can't help it.

Poor Emily.

"Jesse, Amelia and their sister, Gabriella, are already in there. Angela's gone out for breakfast, and Drake just stepped outside to answer a call. I've not seen Mr Beckett this morning."

My smile turns tight when we arrive outside the dining room. "I'm sure he'll make his presence known."

"Yes, I'm sure. Be wary of that one," he says, gazing down the hall. "Go on in. Emily will be in shortly with breakfast."

"Thank you." Leaning up, I kiss his cheek, giggling when a blush rises on his face. "See you in a bit, Jeff."

He clears his throat. "You too. Now eat."

When I enter the room, everyone turns to me with bright smiles.

"Hi, Pagan. This is my sister, Gabriella. She got in this morning." Jesse is all smiles as he introduces me to his sister.

"Hi, Gabriella. It's lovely to meet you," I tell her.

My, the Donovans must have good genes. All three of their kids are beautiful.

Gabriella has flawless milk-coloured skin, dark silk brown hair and bright blue eyes like her brother's. Except hers don't hold anything on his. His are sharp, piercing, like they can see right through to your soul.

"I'm so glad you could make it. When Grams said she hired you, I didn't believe her. A few of my friends and I attended a women's aid charity gala in Wales last year. It was incredible," she gushes as she walks up to greet me, kissing me on each cheek.

I beam, proud of that gala. "I'm so glad you enjoyed it. We do one every year."

Jeff pops his head through the door, clearing his throat. "Emily will be serving breakfast. Would you like me to wake Mr. Beckett?"

"He's awake," I blurt out without thinking. Not wanting to implicate myself, I add, "Ada spoke with me this morning and mentioned she passed him."

"All right. I'll let Emily know."

I nod and turn back to the room. Gabriella puts her arm around me, steering me towards the large oak table. "You have to tell me everything about your job. It's so fascinating. You must meet loads of gorgeous men whilst working," she says excitedly.

If only she knew her brother is the only one.

Stunned at the thought, I trip over my feet. My hands land on the table, knocking over a plate, fork and whatever else was there.

"I'm so sorry," I say, bending down to pick up the smashed plate.

"Hey, it's fine. I'll get a broom from Emily. Don't touch it," Gabriella says before rushing from the room.

I ignore her, picking up the broken pieces and placing them in a pile.

"You really don't need to do that," Jesse says.

"It's fine, nearly done," I explain. I'm just picking up the last big piece when I notice a fork under the table. On hands and knees, I crawl under it a little, grabbing the fork.

"Well, you really were literal this morning. But with so many eyes?" Drake's voice sounds from above me.

Shooting up, I bang my head on the table. "Ouch."

"Shit! This is becoming a pattern." He comes into view as I get to my knees, a smug grin on his face.

"Ugh, why are you always there when I do something incredibly embarrassing?"

"Better question, why do you keep falling all over yourself in front of me?"

I glare at him. "Your ego is impressive," I tell him sarcastically. Jesse and Amelia laugh and my face heats.

I'm really never going to get a glowing review after this job.

"I know, right?"

I continue to glare and get up from the floor, dusting off my leggings and top.

"I've got the broom," Gabriella yells as she comes barging back in. "Hey, I told you not to touch it. Did you cut yourself?"

Smiling, I shake my head. "No, I'm fine. Here, let me do it since I made the mess."

"No, you sit down. Emily's coming now."

Seeing she's not going to let me clean my own mess, I take a seat, growling when Drake drop into the one next to me.

He leans over, making sure no one else can hear him when he whispers in my ear, "Admit it, you're totally thinking of having sweaty, dirty sex on the table right now, aren't you?"

Turning, I narrow my eyes at him. But now that he's put the thought in my head, I'm actually thinking about it.

Grr, I hate him.

"Actually I'm thinking of how I'm going to make it through breakfast without stabbing you with my fork." I smile sweetly.

"Feisty. I like them feisty." He winks, turning to the door when Emily walks in with a rolling tray of food. "Emily, that smells amazing."

She giggles. "Thank you, Drake. Enjoy."

A message alert goes off and a small smile touches my lips when everyone rushes to grab their phones.

Jesse frowns down at his as he looks over the screen.

"Everything okay, honey?"

"Um, yeah. Aaron can't make it to breakfast. He said he's had an allergic reaction to something and his face is swollen."

I choke on air and Drake starts laughing, patting my back. "You okay?"

"Yeah," I croak out.

"Is he okay?" Amelia asks, looking concerned.

"Yeah. Emily, can you take some food up for him? He's hungover, and I don't want him to be ill all day because of an empty stomach."

"Of course. I hope he's okay. I'll have to see if I have any cream for him," Emily assures him before leaving the room.

"Looks like it's just us," Gabriella beams, seeming happy that Aaron won't be joining us.

When Amelia and Jesse asked me to meet them in their father's office after breakfast, I thought for sure they were going to fire me. After what happened last night, then sleeping in their brother's bed and drawing on the best man's face, I was pretty certain. What I didn't expect was to be handed a non-disclosure form.

"I don't understand," I say, reading through it. It seems pretty simple, and in my line of work, I've had to sign a few of these. I just don't understand why I would have to with Amelia and Jesse. Yes, they're wealthy, but from what I know, they lead simple lives. Amelia runs a successful clothing line and Jesse is a lawyer. Both great jobs, but none that would really require this.

"We'll explain once you've signed. We couldn't say anything over the phone since we didn't want our engagement getting out so soon."

I nod, signing the paper once I've finished reading the last page. "It's fine. I'm just surprised is all."

Handing it over, I give them a reassuring smile, hoping they don't confuse my surprise with disapproval.

"Amelia's last name isn't Hudson. It's Fisher," Jesse tells me.

I raise my eyebrows, wondering if that's supposed to mean something to me. "I'm sorry, I'm still not following."

He chuckles and Amelia smiles. "It's okay. Many people don't know, but the ones who do make my life hell. I'm Amelia Fisher, Eric Fisher's daughter."

Eric Fisher. Eric Fisher. Eric Fisher.

Oh.

Eric Fisher.

"The prime minister, Eric Fisher?" I ask, swallowing hard.

"Yes."

Holy crap!

Eric Fisher has been hounded in the press after he was accused of abusing his power as prime minister. He was accused of living in sheer hedonism and pure greed, but from what the press released on TV, he lives a day-to-day life like any other person.

"I see you've heard?"

"Um, yes. I'm sorry for what's happening in the papers," I tell her. They are brutal. If it weren't for the testimony from a spokesperson and pictures of his home that were revealed, I'd have believed the newspapers.

"Thank you. It's been hard for him, constantly defending his name and title. He does everything he can for our country, but there's always someone wanting to get higher in their job," she seethes, a lost look in her eyes.

"Hey, it's fine. Your dad's been wrongfully accused. People will know that," Jesse says, hugging his fiancé lovingly.

A pang of jealousy hits me. I try to mask it, but a part of me desperately wants what they have. I'd love someone to comfort me or hold me when some idiot has royally pissed me off at work. But most of all, I want someone to look at me the way Jesse is looking at Amelia.

"I know, I know. I'm sorry. I just get upset over it," she explains, wiping under her eyes.

"It's fine. I understand now why you've wanted to keep this on the down-low." I smile softly.

"They've been following us around since it all came out. We're worried that when the news hits we're getting married, they'll use that as another way to get at my father. He's a wealthy man, was before he was even elected, but they won't mention that. They'll be too focused on the money spent on our wedding."

My heart aches for her. Her wedding day isn't supposed to have a black cloud hanging over it.

"I promise I'll do everything in my power to make sure your day is special. But something tells me there's more to why you brought me in here."

"There is," Jesse says, smiling now. "We have a few trusted magazines who have been supportive of Eric and are close with my parents. We want to make an announcement to those magazines in a few days. We were hoping you'd arrange for that to be done."

"That's fine. If you give me names and numbers or email addresses, I'll put it on my schedule. But how have they not found out already?"

It's Amelia's turn to smile now. "We actually got engaged six months ago, but it happened the same time my dad was accused, so we've only told family."

"That's why you haven't sent invitations out," I say almost to myself. I always thought it was weird since most people need time to arrange sitters or get time off work.

"Yes. Close family know the date already, but we didn't want to risk it getting out if we told friends. It's another reason why I got stuck with my cousin as maid of honour. My best friend, Hallie, knows, but we've been friends since we were little."

"I've listed names and addresses in here for invitations. We've looked over everything you sent Mum and we love all of it. And again, thank you for organising our wedding on such short notice. We couldn't have done it without you," Jesse says.

"It's what I do." I smile, taking the list from him. "Would you like me to get my colleague to sign a non-disclosure form, or would you like to take care of it?"

"We'll let you sort that out. We trust you. Now if you'll excuse me, I have to go get some things for tonight," Jesse tells me, grinning.

After he leaves, I turn to Amelia. "Is there anything you need me to do before I grab your dress for the engagement party?"

"Can I come with you? I'd like to try it on one more time to make sure it fits."

"Of course you can. I have to go to the baker for a taste testing of your cake. I think he's just worried with the size, thinking it'll go to waste if it's not liked."

She laughs. "Roberto's, right?"

"Yeah."

"My mum had hers made there for her third wedding. She didn't bother taste testing because she was worried about putting weight on. He refused to make it until it was tasted. I got the pleasure and it was superb. I'd be happy to go," she tells me, and I giggle at her dreamy expression.

"Let's get going, then."

"We should ask Gabriella. We can make this a girls' day and go for lunch," she offers.

"Sounds like a plan. Let me grab my things and I'll meet you outside. I'll drive."

Chapter Ten

*L*ying on the bed next to Alison, I let out a loud groan, making her giggle. "It's not funny. I thought it would be fun to have the girls join me, but we kept distracting each other. Don't get me wrong, I love shopping as much as the next girl, but my God, today I think I felt an ounce of what Lola feels when me and Mum drag her shopping. My feet are so sore."

"Did you even get what you needed done?"

Another groan. "No." She laughs and I nudge her in the belly with my elbow. "Anyway, how was your day?"

"Well, Jeff took me outside for some fresh air earlier, and on the way out we bumped into a woman called Angela. She was being a bitch to Emily. Who is she?"

"Ah," I murmur, wondering how I explain her. "She's Amelia's cousin and maid of honour."

Her eyes bug out in horror. "Really? But... how? Why? She's horrible."

"Yes, I'm afraid so. From what Amelia told me today, her mum isn't the nicest of people and can be controlling. So, when she found out about their engagement, she guilt-tripped her into letting Angela be maid of honour."

"There's going to be two of them?" She swallows, looking anxious.

Laughing, I nod. "Don't worry, apparently Angela's mum is a sweetheart and makes sure to put the two in their place. I met Amelia's best friend, Hallie, on the way in. She arrived when we got back. She seems lovely, so hopefully we'll only be really dealing with her. I don't think Angela is the type who does something for others, let alone maid of honour duties."

"Well thank Christ for that. Who else is arriving tonight? I feel bad that you have to deal with all this on your own. I bet you're behind schedule."

"I've only missed a few things, so don't worry over it. But I do need you to email the caterers and the florist to make sure everything is still as planned. And as for the guests arriving tonight," I begin, taking out my tablet, "we have Jon and Toby, the groomsmen, arriving shortly. And Veronica and Harmony, who are Gabriella's guests, arriving any second."

"So full house, huh?"

"Yep. Which reminds me, I should be going down for dinner," I tell her, getting up from the bed. "Get some sleep because tomorrow, we need to get our arses into gear."

"Promise. I'm feeling much better, just tired."

"I know. I'm just teasing. You can take as much time as you possibly want. Right, I'll see you in the morning."

"Have fun," she sings, switching on the TV.

I laugh, shutting the door behind me, bumping into Drake when I do. He has a mischievous grin on his face when he sees me.

"Just who I was looking for."

"Why are you looking at me all creepy-like?"

"Am I?"

I giggle, shaking my head. "I'm teasing, but you do look a little shifty. What do you have planned?"

"Well, I'm glad you asked. I had to spend the day with Aaron and my brother—"

"Please don't tell me he's fallen in love with you."

"Who wouldn't?" He grins. "But no, he did nothing but talk to Jesse about how you'll go crawling back to him. Telling him how you belonged together—"

"Well aren't you Chatty Cathy today."

"Will you stop interrupting me for one minute?" he asks, giving me a stern look.

I try to fight my grin, I really do. "Go on."

"Anyway, not only did he keep going on about you, but he talked non-stop about himself. He's driven me freaking nuts all day, especially over his face—which has been funny as shit, by the way. And then to top that shit off, he scratched my car."

I gasp, horrified. "Oh my God. Your Range Rover?" He nods, his face relaxing when he sees I get him. "What did you do?"

How dare he! Why would anyone want to do anything to that car? Hell, even dropping a bread crumb on the interior is a crime.

"It's what *we're* gonna do." He grins.

Scrunching my face up in confusion, I give him a questioning look. "We?"

"Yeah. You've still got Grams' box, haven't you?"

"Yes," I answer cautiously.

"Great. Go get the stink bombs. And let's be rebels, grab the itching powder too."

I giggle at his boy-like expression. "And what are you going to do? Cover him in them at the dinner table?"

"Do I look stupid? I am Grams' grandson, after all. I'm going to cover his flipping bed in it."

I think about it for a minute. *Why the hell not. It's not like he'll know it's me.* "If we get caught, I'm blaming you."

He holds his hands up, grinning. "I swear I'll take full responsibility. Come on. He's downstairs at the minute chatting up one of my sister's friends."

I roll my eyes and quickly open the door to Alison's room. "Sorry, just grabbing something," I tell her when she looks up. She eyes me curiously before turning to Drake at the door.

"Hey, how you feeling?" he asks, casually leaning against the frame.

"I'm better, thank you. Um, Pagan, what are you up to?" she asks quickly when I grab the two packets from the box.

"Nothing."

"Doesn't look like nothing."

"We better be going or we'll be late for dinner," I rush out, smiling widely at Alison. "Speak later."

Before she can say anything or warn me of the consequences, I shut the door shut and grab Drake's hand. We laugh as we run down the hallway, but I come to a stop at the end, not knowing where I'm going.

"Where to?"

"Come on," he laughs, pulling me now.

A rush of excitement floods through me knowing we could get caught at any second. "Is it wrong that I'm seriously ecstatic right now? I feel like I'm twelve years old."

He laughs, slowing to a steady pace. "Nah. I'm a doctor and even I can admit this is the most fun I've had in ages. I've always secretly wished Grams would do something to him for years. I'm just glad it's me who will get the pleasure."

"Well, I've always wanted to do this," I giggle.

"This is it. You ready?"

"Hell yeah."

My heart is pounding as he opens the door. The room is laid out similar to mine, except Aaron doesn't have a window bench or a fireplace attached to the bathroom. It's the same colours and décor, but the bathrooms on this side of the house are shared, separating two rooms.

"You got the bombs?" Drake asks, pulling the bedspread away.

With sweaty palms, I hand over the pack. "Let's do the itching powder first. I don't know how long I'll be able to stay in here with that thing going off."

He chuckles. "You do the honour, then. Make sure you get the pillow."

"Which side does he sleep on?"

He looks at me like I've lost my mind. "You dated him, not me."

I roll my eyes at him. "Yeah, when we both slept in single beds at our parents' houses. Let's just cover both of them to be sure. If we need to get more, ring Ada."

He steps away from me, a smirk on his handsome face. "You look kind of scary right now. Remind me never to piss you off," he laughs. "And don't let my Grams rub off on you."

"I think she already has," I tell him, smiling. My fingers slip once again as I try to tear the packet open. "I'm sure these things are for children, so why can't I open it?"

"Stop pouting. Here, let me try."

Moving the packet away, I pull harder. "No, no, I—" The packet rips open, a little of the powder blowing into Drake's face. "Oh my Gosh, I'm so sorry."

He wipes frantically at his face, sneezing as he does. "It's fine. It's fine. I don't even feel anything."

I don't have the heart to tell him it takes a few minutes to start working. "Good, good. Let's do this before he comes up." Walking over to the bed, I sprinkle a little on some of the pillows. Then from the corner of my eye, I notice his suitcase, and an idea forms.

"What are you doing?" he asks, still wiping his face.

I grin, opening his case. "Well, we have just under half a packet, so why not use it on his prize gem."

"You wouldn't," he says, sounding horrified.

Turning around, I find him rubbing his jaw. "Stop messing. Go wash your face before dinner. And yes, I totally would." Pulling out a pair of boxers, I cringe but somehow manage to cover the front in itching powder. Grinning evilly, I get up, chuckling when I find Drake scratching furiously at his jaw.

"My God, this stuff is fucking lethal. Why won't it stop?"

Laughing, I walk over, slapping his hands away. "Come on, I'm sure I have something that will stop the itching."

"I'll google it, thanks. I don't want to make it worse."

Giving him a 'whatever' look, I walk into the hall. "Quick, then. We still have dinner to get through and we're running behind schedule."

"God, you're bossy."

"I know." I grin.

"Shit, I left my phone in my room," he says, patting his pockets.

"Hold on." Grabbing mine out of my back pocket and clicking on google, I make quick work of finding what I need and burst out laughing.

"It says here it's the first scratch that makes it worse. The more you scratch, the itchier it'll be."

"Wish I had known that before," he tells me dryly.

"It's not my fault the packet split. And what would you have done differently?"

"Worn a bloody space suit." His voice is high-pitched and I laugh loudly. "Oh you think this is funny, do you?"

With the tone of his voice and the look in his eye, I step away a little, getting ready to run. "Yes, it is pretty funny."

He grins, showing all his teeth, and the dimples in his cheek pop out. "You're so gonna get it."

Squealing, I race down the hall, my laughter echoing. "No, don't you dare."

"You asked for it," he says, coming up behind me. He grabs me and I giggle, wiggling to get down.

"No, don't," I beg.

But he does.

He rubs his jaw over my cheek, and no matter how hard I laugh, beg, or squeal, he doesn't give up.

"Put me down."

He does and turns me round with a wide smile, his eyes twinkling. "Now we're even."

"Oh we *so* aren't." I gaze up at him, my smile as wide as his, and get lost in him. He tucks a strand of hair behind my ear and my breath hitches. "We should, um... we should go wash our faces and put some vinegar on, just in case."

He clears his throat. "Vinegar?"

I look away, my face heating. "Yeah. Before you attacked me with your powdered face, I saw someone used vinegar."

"Seems reasonable. People use it for stinging nettles."

"Let's go, then." I smile, trying to hide the emotion I'm feeling right now. My heart is beating ten times as fast as it was back when we walked into Aaron's room. My palms are sweating, and for the first time in a while, a male has me tongue-tied, stuck on what I should do. Because I'm pretty sure he was going to kiss me.

Or I was going to kiss him.

That or it would've been mutual.

~

Tonight was meant to be fun and games, but the minute we entered the dining room, I wanted to walk straight back out.

Angela was moaning at Emily about her dietary plan and that the food didn't meet her requirements.

Then Aaron kept trying to strike up conversation with me, which I ignored. No one questioned my rudeness, or called me out on it, thankfully.

But it was the minute the wedding was brought up during dinner that I wanted to pull my hair out. Hallie asked Angela how her speech was going, and Angela didn't take it too well. She seemed very confrontational over everything. Needless to say I think I'll work with Hallie to write one up for Angela to read that day. I'll just keep it short and sweet and make sure Hallie gets hers perfect.

At last, dinner is over and everyone is ready to play 'murder in the dark'. Well, almost everyone. I'm still wondering if they'll let me hang out in my room since a surprise guest of Amelia's arrived during dinner.

"Are you playing, Angela?" Jesse asks, trying to include her. All dinner he's been trying to keep her satisfied, steering everyone away from topics that get her mad. How he puts up with her, I don't know. I'm guessing his love for Amelia is stronger than his annoyance for his future cousin-in-law.

"Gosh no. I'm not a child," she replies snottily.

"She never played as a kid," Amelia mumbles under her breath.

I fight my grin. "Are you sure, Angela? The lights will be off in the house. I'm sure it will be more entertaining than being in your room."

She turns her nose up at me, giving me a distasteful look. "I've got better things to do than run around the house in the dark. Now if you don't mind, I'll be away for the night. My aunt Sharon is taking me out."

"Mum's picking you up?" Amelia asks, hurt clear in her voice and expression.

Angela smirks. "Yes. Didn't she tell you? We're going out for drinks with her new husband and family."

"No, she didn't."

"Oh well, not to worry. You get to play your *game*. Toodles."

She walks out of the room, her hips swinging side to side. Everyone's gone silent, but then Hallie speaks up. "Anyone else happy she won't be here to poop on our fun?"

I would've been happier if she'd taken Aaron with her, but I don't voice that.

"Come on, let's get started. I've been dying to play this for a week." Jesse stands, his face lighting up.

Outside in the garden, I grab the small box that was delivered earlier today and open it. "You'll each wear ten ribbons around your neck, each of you having a different colour. Once you're caught, you have to hand a ribbon over to Jesse, who will be on first. Once he has six different coloured ribbons, he can come back outside and choose a ribbon for who will be on next. That way, the people still hiding inside won't know who is on and who to hide from. Here is the meeting point for those without ribbons, but once a new person is chosen to be on, you're all back in the game until you run out of ribbons. The front left-hand side of the mansion is off limits, and so is outside of the property. Does anyone have any questions?" I ask, looking up to see another light flicker off. It's a bit of a good job Shane knows his way around the mansion or we might be searching for him.

"Don't forgot everyone who's caught has to do a shot when they reach outside." Jesse grins. You'd never think he was a lawyer, too boyish and innocent looking.

"The first person to lose all their ribbons has to drink a pint of... I don't even know what it is, but it's look vile," I tell them, scrunching my nose up at the offending drink on the table.

"It's one of Grams' concoctions," Drake chuckles.

Well that explains it all.

I'll be drinking that vile drink within the hour, I just know it. I can practically taste it already.

"Don't worry, I'll protect ya," Aaron says, seeing my expression.

I give him a dirty look, wondering what planet he's on. "I'd rather drink the drink."

Drake laughs next to me, covering it with a cough. "Right, let's go. First to go in are the girls. We boys will follow in a couple of minutes."

I give him a wide-eyed look, wondering if he's lost his mind. I was hoping to follow him so I didn't get lost myself.

Maybe I could get away with sneaking to my room.

"I'll find you," Drake whispers, making me shiver.

Smiling, I nod, then go to follow the girls into the house. "Wait, you need to do a shot first," Jesse tells us, handing each of us a glass.

I down the shot, wincing at the burn in my throat, then move to follow behind the others who are giggling. Once I walk into the house, the girls are gone and a shiver runs down my spine. The thick heavy curtains do a perfect job at blocking out the moonlight from outside, so finding my way into the main hallway is harder than it should be.

"For fuck's sake," I curse when I walk into a door. Reaching out in front of me, I feel my way down a short hallway, coming to what I hope is the main staircase. I'd been planning on hiding out in Drake's old bedroom on the balcony, but when I hear a door open and close behind me, followed by Aaron's muttered curse, my feet carry me down the hall towards the pool.

The room is dark, but once my eyes adjust, I walk towards the door to the steam room, hoping no one will think to go in there. There's no way I'll be able to handle drinking that drink. It was green, for heaven's sake.

Please don't let anyone find me.

Chapter Eleven

J'm not sure how long I've been hiding in here, but it's become too stifling in the small room. I feel like I've been in here hours. Someone must have used it earlier in the day, because the condensation is making me sweat and I feel like I can't breathe.

Why did I decide to hide in here?

Because you're a dumbass, that's why.

Deciding enough is enough, I get up from the corner of the room and open the door as quietly as I can. The room is silent, the only noise to be heard a light buzzing sound from one of the machines. Stepping out, I head towards the back stairs, hoping no one will hate me if I head up to my room for the night. But out of nowhere, a dark figure jumps out in front me, scaring the bejesus out of me.

Screaming, I step back, tripping over something behind me. Strong arms wrap around me, holding me to them. Drake's chuckling reaches my ears and I bite back a curse.

"Oh my God, Drake, you scared the fucking crap out of me. What were you thinking?"

"Be quiet," he whispers, still chuckling under his breath.

I slap his chest, breathing hard. "Well that wouldn't be an issue if you hadn't scared me."

"Sorry, I couldn't help myself. I came in and noticed you opening the door. I knew it was you straight away. How long have you been in there?"

"Too long," I mumble. "Have you been caught yet?"

"Six times, you?"

"None."

"Really?" he asks, surprise in his voice.

"Why is that so hard to believe? Everyone probably forgot I was even here."

He chuckles again and I become aware of him still holding on to me, my body pressing against his. "Nope. Everyone is determined to find you. I didn't believe them when they said you still hadn't been caught. Apart from you, I'm the one with the most bands left."

"Really?" I ask, surprised and kinda relieved that it won't be me drinking that nasty concoction.

"Yeah. Aaron is on now. He's got one ribbon left."

"Great," I mutter, not exactly thrilled with the news.

"Fuck, what was that?" he asks. My heart starts beating wildly as I look behind me, hearing a door close by before someone screams, then laughs. "Fuck, we need to hide."

Panicked, we both look around before moving. Problem is we both move into each other. Arms flailing, I try to grab a hold of Drake, who tries to reach out and steady me, but instead we both end up falling... into the pool.

"Holy crap!" I cough, spitting out water when I reach the surface.

"Shh," he whispers, pulling me to the side as quietly as he can. The pool's edge cools my back as he presses me against the side, his hand covering my mouth. He pushes closer and my breathing escalates, worsening when I hear the door open.

He's so close.

Footsteps sound across the floor and I press harder against the wall, wanting to remain unseen. Drake does the same, dipping down into the water until his face is close to mine, his warm breath fanning my cheek.

Yep, seriously close.

"Where are you?" I hear Aaron mutter just as another door opens and closes. I'm assuming he just checked the steam room because movement sounds right above where we are. My whole body is tight, the rush of being caught seriously intense.

He must give up because the door to the pool room opens and closes with a thud. I breathe out a sigh of relief, my whole body sagging against Drake.

"That was close," I whisper. My breathing speeds up for another reason when I feel Drake's hard body pressed against mine.

And I mean *hard*.

Every inch of him pressing against my stomach.

"Yeah," he croaks hoarsely, staring at me intensely.

I don't know who moves first, me or him, but all of a sudden, his hands move to my arse at the same time I'm wrapping my legs around his waist and we're kissing.

No, not kissing.

This is more.

It's everything.

I sway, moving into him as my nipples harden, pressing against him. My eyes roll to the back of my head, moaning when he presses his groin against my core. I feel like I'm losing my mind, especially when he grips my arse possessively, rubbing me against him harder.

I deepen the kiss, gripping his hair tightly, needing him closer.

Perfect.

He's perfect.

Fuck, this kiss is perfect.

"Pagan," he moans. Hearing my name come from his lips turns my insides to liquid.

My lips tingle from the kiss, but nothing could pull me away. I've waited twenty-eight years to be kissed like this, and it's better than I ever imagined it could be.

His hands roam up the front of my body, cupping my breasts, squeezing gently and making me wild with lust.

"I... ohmigod," I moan.

He pulls away from the kiss, making me groan from the loss, but the second his lips land on my neck, trailing down to my collarbone, I'm lost again. His kiss is like his touch, hungry and desperate, and I can't get enough as I grind myself against him.

I want him.

Now.

He stares into my eyes and I feel like he can read every thought I'm having.

"Pagan," he groans, brushing his thumb against my erect nipple.

When did he get under my top? How did I not notice?

Reality slams into me like a loaded truck and I push him away, my face flushed with embarrassment.

"Pagan?"

The uncertainty in his voice hurts, nearly breaking my resolve. "We can't do this," I gasp, my entire body in flames. I'm so turned on I'm surprised I can even think straight.

"What? Why? Did I hurt you? Push you?" he asks, moving closer.

I push him away again. "No, you didn't. I... we... I work for your family. We can't," I tell him, not having any other reason than the fact that he scares me. He scares me shitless because I've never, not once in all my life, felt the way he just made me feel. The mansion could've been on fire and I wouldn't have cared or even noticed.

He'll break your heart, my inner voice teases me, and I bite back a curse.

"Pagan, listen," he starts, but I ignore him, swimming to the stairs and walking up them.

"I'm sorry, Drake," I whisper, taking my ribbons off and grabbing the dressing gown from the chair before rushing towards the staircase leading to our rooms.

"Pagan, wait," he calls out. I hear him getting out of the water, but I'm already halfway up the stairs.

When I reach Alison's room, I barge in, not bothering to knock. She jumps away from watching the television.

"Hey... Pagan, what are you doing? Are you okay? And why the hell are you wet?"

Catching my breath, I just stare at my best friend before bursting into tears. "Oh, Alison, I just made a big mistake. The best one I'll ever make."

"Hey, what happened?" she coaxes gently, patting the bed.

I'm about to move when I hear knocking from down the hall. I freeze, looking at the closed door behind me.

"Pagan, open the door, please. We need to talk," I hear Drake call and my eyes water, ashamed of the way I left things.

"Uh, what happened?"

"I... I just need a minute. Let me go get out of these wet clothes," I tell her. Instead of waiting for her to reply, I rush into her bathroom, quickly stripping out of my clothes. When I realise I have nothing to change back into, I curse.

There's a knock at the door and I still, hoping it's not Drake. I still can't believe I kissed him, or he kissed me.

"Pagan, I have some pyjamas here for you," Alison calls out quietly.

I breathe out, kicking myself for being so stupid. Opening the door, I take the pyjamas from her, giving her a small smile. "Thank you."

"It's all right. Now hurry up."

I change quickly, towel drying my hair once I'm done before leaving the room.

"He's left. I heard him go into his room."

I stare for a split second before rushing over, jumping into bed with her under the blanket. "I kissed him."

"And by your reaction I take it he didn't kiss you back?" she replies, though she doesn't sound convinced.

"Oh he kissed me back."

Boy did he kiss me back.

"I'm at a loss. Why are you in here and not bumping uglies with the hot guy? Totally better than Prince Harry if you ask me," she teases.

"Because we work for his family. Because he lives five hours away from us. Because I don't have a great track record when it comes to men. Take your pick, Alison. There's a long list. The way he kissed me...." I look at her, feeling lost. "It was like being on a fast roller coaster that never ended. He's already gotten under my skin. But this, tonight, the kiss... I've totally fucked up."

"Babe," she sighs, moving to her side to face me. "You can't stay single forever. As much as I hate what Aaron did to you, he's right about one thing. You were kids. That wasn't your fault, not at all. And as for

Rick...." She shakes her head, her eyes dropping sadly. "That wasn't your fault either, babe. He was good at manipulating people, charming them. That doesn't say anything about you or your choice in men. You can't let their decisions dictate the rest of your life. Drake seems like a well-respected man, and according to Ada, he's a gentleman. Always has been."

Her words register, they do, but it doesn't stop the doubt from worming its way through me. "It's not just because of them. It's me. He lives here, in London, and we work for his parents."

She rolls her eyes. "You just kissed the bloke. He didn't propose."

I smack her arm lightly. "I know that, but I already feel like there's something between us. There's this connection, and my God, when he touches me...." I smile, remembering the kiss. "He's amazing. I just don't want it to go further and get my heart broken. We still have over two weeks here. A lot can happen. I get excited at the thought of seeing him and his family already. They're amazing. I know I'm being dramatic, but with my track record, I'll make a mess of everything."

"I think that's what scares you the most. It was just a kiss, babe. He's not asking anything of you, and you're not asking anything from him. You enjoy his company, and he clearly enjoys yours," she says, waggling her eyebrows.

"Shut up," I laugh.

"Pagan, you've slept with one person in your life. Having a little fun won't hurt. Don't overthink things, please. You deserve to be happy, but the more you stress over it, the worse you'll feel."

I groan, covering my eyes with my arm. "You're right. God, I made a fool out of myself. I just ran off, not even explaining. He most likely thinks I'm a weirdo now. But you have to admit, kissing him was wrong, especially when I'm working for his parents. And this is their house."

She giggles. "Look, as your assistant, I'm not gonna lie and say it was the best decision to kiss the client's son. But as your friend, I will tell you to go for it. No one's going to get hurt, and if I'm reading them right, I think his parents won't mind. They seem like really down-to-earth people."

Sighing, I uncover my eyes and look at her. "You're right. I know you are. Argh, I'm such a drama queen. I'll just find him tomorrow and apologise for running off like I did."

"Good. Now, how was the kiss?"

Laughing, I look up to the ceiling, my smile wide and expression dreamy. "Out of this world. It was like nothing I've ever experienced."

Chapter Twelve

The next morning after showering and changing, I head down the hall to Drake's room. It takes a couple of deep breaths and a few minutes to get my bearings before I can work up the courage to knock on the door.

He opens it, looking tempting as hell, still rumpled from sleep. Rubbing his eyes, he meets my gaze, suddenly fully awake when he sees it's me. "Pagan, hi. Are you okay?"

I blush, my gaze shifting to his lips as I remember the kiss we shared last night. It's all I've been able to think about. Clearing my throat, I hesitantly meet his gaze. "I'm fine. I came to talk to you. Can I come in?"

"Yeah, yeah. Come in." He moves out of the way just enough so I have to brush against him as I pass, sending shivers racing up my spine. "So...."

Knowing I need to just say it and get it over with, I straighten my back, turning to face him. "I'm sorry about rushing off last night. When it comes to men, I have a bad track record. Not that there's been loads of them," I rush out, my face burning.

This seriously isn't going how I panned.

He grins, sitting on the edge of his bed. "So I'm a part of this bad record now?"

What? "What? No! But I work for your parents. I've never, you know, kissed a client's son before."

"Glad to be your first." He winks.

Well at least someone can make light of the situation. "Shut up." I laugh lightly, tucking a strand of hair behind my ear. Knowing I'm doing this wrong, and that there's no easier way to say what I need to say, I decide to just be blunt. I can't possibly make a bigger fool out of myself than I have already. "I just don't want to get hurt."

His smile drops as his expression softens. "Why don't we start over, be friends."

I smile teasingly. "I thought we already were."

"Well, after sharing itching powder, we've reached bestie level."

I laugh harder at him using the word 'bestie'. "I'm glad we're okay. Now I best go downstairs and face the music. Your parents should be back within the hour, and I need to go over some last-minute plans for the engagement party with them."

Meaning the press, who I didn't count on being there, but I don't mention it. It's my job to be prepared for anything. I just wish they could've given me some kind of heads-up.

"I'll walk down with you. Let me just throw on some clothes."

I nod. "I'll just go see if Alison is ready."

He winks at me over his shoulder and I nearly trip over my own feet.

Damn him and his gorgeous wink.

I shake my head and walk out, bumping into a stormy-faced Alison.

"Your ex is a fucking jerk. What the hell did you ever see in him?"

"Woah, hold up. What happened?"

She scoffs, looking back in the direction she came from. "What happened? He tried it on with me and pinched my arse. The jerk spoke to my tits instead of my face. It's insulting."

"Who spoke to your boobs?" Drake asks, walking out of his room.

Alison blushes, looking between us.

"Aaron," I tell him.

He gives me a knowing look. "Looks like that shoebox is going to get a workout."

I grin. "It sure does."

"Well, whatever you do, make sure it hurts. I think I have a bruise on my arse," Alison sneers.

"Don't worry, it will. I'm sure Ada will be up for helping us out."

She smiles, then looks between the two of us again, her lips twitching into a knowing grin. "So what are you two up to?"

Blushing, I give my best friend the best 'shut up' glare I can muster. "Nothing."

"Talking about our life together," Drake answers, somehow straight-faced.

My glare turns his way. "What?"

Alison claps her hands together. "Goody. Now come on. I've gone two nights without proper food. I need to eat."

Without missing a step, Drake places his hand at my lower back, leading me down the hallway behind Alison.

We're quiet as we make our way to the dining room. The minute we walk in, all eyes land on us.

"Hey, Pagan, where did you go last night? You won the game," Jesse says, giving me one of his boyish grins.

I force a smile as I try to come up with a reasonable lie as to why I bailed. "I—"

"I told you she felt sick after I found her last night," Drake jumps in.

I relax, thankful he didn't give them the real reason. I think I would die if he did. I don't want to be fired, not when I'm enjoying my job for the first time in a while. And yes, Drake is mostly to thank for that, and so is his family. They've been welcoming, and a hoot to work with.

"I bet she cheated, really," Aaron grumbles from the end of the table.

I glare his way. "And why would I do that?"

"Ignore him. He's a sour puss because he lost and had to drink that drink." Amelia giggles as she ducks her head from Aaron's glare.

"I think I'm still drunk." He seems irritated, not looking at anyone as he takes a gulp of his water, sweat forming across his forehead as he moves his arms under the table.

Looks like someone still doesn't handle losing very well.

We all sit down at the table, everyone chatting about the fun events of last night, filling Alison in on everything she missed.

"Um, Aaron, what are you doing under the table?" Hannah says, looking nauseated.

He curses, shaking his head as his arm continues to shake. "Nothing. I'm fine."

"I didn't ask if you were okay," she murmurs, resuming eating her food.

Drake and I look at each other, sharing a knowing smile.

"Will you stop moving," Gabriella hisses.

I look up to find her glaring at Angela. "I can't. I'm fucking itchy." She glares down the table to Aaron, and Drake starts to choke on his orange juice.

Aaron's head shoots up, shooting daggers at Angela. "You! This is because of you. I was fine until I fucked you last night."

"You slept with Angela?" Jesse asks, his voice high-pitched as he stares at Aaron with disgust.

"You slept with Aaron?" That comes from Amelia, who looks just as repulsed as the rest of us. The table quietens down, everyone's attention on the two culprits still glaring at each other.

"What do you mean until *you* slept with *me*? I was fine until this morning." Angela's face is stormy and pinched in anger.

He stands up, no longer hiding the fact that he's scratching his balls. "You've given me crabs or something. I can't stop fucking itching."

Angela stands, her face red. "Me? You're the male slut."

"Didn't stop you from dropping your knickers."

"Hey, bro," Jesse starts, standing between the two.

"I was drunk and clearly not thinking straight," she bites back, her face getting redder by the second.

"I was the one who was drunk. *You* took advantage of *me*, probably wanting to spread whatever the hell you've given me," Aaron retorts.

All I see is orange before I realise she just threw a glass of orange juice at him, her high-pitched scream hurting my ears. "You bastard!"

"Why don't we calm down. You probably just had an allergic reaction to something," Amelia says calmly.

"How did she get itchy down there? Did he change into those boxers beforehand or something?" Drake whispers to me as they continue to glare at one another.

"Yeah, to him!" Angela shrieks, pointing accusingly at Aaron as she tries to discreetly scratch her privates.

"More like you," Aaron growls before storming out.

"No idea," I whisper back, watching the two with intrigue.

"I'm going to get myself checked out. God only knows what he's given me," Angela says. She walks a little too close to Harmony as she turns to leave, and when Harmony leans away, Angela screams again in annoyance before storming out of the room behind Aaron.

Everyone pauses, making sure she's gone before we all burst out laughing.

"Oh my God." I lean into Drake, trying to catch my breath.

"I wonder what happened," Jesse says.

"Ada isn't here, so it wasn't her," Amelia adds.

At that, Jesse turns my way with a knowing look and grins. I blush, ducking my head as I try to control my laughter.

~

Holding a cocktail, Ada walks out onto the back patio where Alison and I are going over some of the plans for the engagement party.

"How was your night, Ada?" I ask politely.

"Boring, but I heard yours was a hoot. Angela just came back from the doctor. They said she seems to have had an allergic reaction to something. Apparently the only thing she did different, apart from sleep with that tool, was wear his boxers."

She eyes me like she knows what I've done, so I smile, humouring her. "That explains how she got itchy down there. I put it in his boxers and on his pillows."

She cackles, sitting down beside us. Alison moves her chair closer to me, eyeing Ada warily. "Those pillows didn't get much use. I went snooping as soon as I got back and found them on the floor."

"Should've smothered him with one," Alison grumbles.

Ada eyes her before asking, "What'd he do to you?"

"Besides be a jerk? Pinched my arse and stared at my tits," Alison answers with attitude. I chuckle at my best friend, not bothering to hide my amusement.

"What are you going to do next?"

"First, why did you go snooping?" I ask.

Ada looks around the garden before slipping a piece of paper towards me. I lift it, ready to open it, when she slaps my hand. "Lower it. Don't let anyone see."

My eyes widen as I lower the paper, slipping it open slowly. On it is a password and information on a message app. "What's this?" My eyebrows scrunch together before I look over to Ada, giving her a questioning look.

"It's his phone's password. Download that app and hide it in one of his folders after you've signed him up. He should get facts about dildos and penises for the next six months." She grins, looking around the garden once again.

I don't even bother to ask how she found out his password. All I can do is grin and try to think of a way to get to his phone. I can't wait to see his face when he opens the messages.

"Do they send pictures?" Alison asks.

"Why, you thinking of signing up?"

Alison smirks. "No, but I heard from Amelia this morning that Aaron's a homophobe. Really hates the thought of two men together."

What a fucking dick.

Ada glares, seeming to be thinking something over. "Why my grandson is friends with him, I'll never know."

An idea springs to mind and I chuckle. "I have the perfect idea to go along with the app. I just need to get his phone."

"I've been waiting for you to mention that. He's sleeping at the moment. It's the perfect time to get it."

"He's sleeping at this time?" Alison asks warily, looking at her phone.

"He needed some help, but yes, he's sleeping," Ada says, glaring at Alison.

I chuckle, then jump when Drake steps out, startling me.

"Hello, ladies, Grams." He eyes each of us. "What are you up to?"

"Nothing. It's girl time, so go away," Ada orders, sipping her cocktail.

"Now I need to know." He smiles, sitting down next to me.

I can feel the heat from his body and I blush, shifting in my seat. Ada stares at me for a long moment before grinning ear to ear.

"You don't need to know anything."

"He helped me with the stink bombs and itching powder," I tell her.

She shakes her head, looking disappointed in me. It makes me feel like a child as I sink down in my seat. "Never get a man to do a woman's job."

"Hey! It was me who talked her into it," Drake jumps in.

Her gaze whips my way. "Is that true?"

"Um." She's staring at me with a pissed-off expression. It's kind of scary how intimidating a tiny old lady can be.

Drake laughs, pinching my thigh. "She just needed a little push. So, tell me what you have planned."

I quickly go over Ada's idea and my own. He laughs, nearly falling from his chair. "And he's asleep now? I thought he got up a couple of hours ago, feeling refreshed."

Ada looks guilty now, moving her chair back. "I need to go powder my nose. See you later."

"What did she do?" he asks, watching her waddle inside with a resigned sigh.

"I dread to think," Alison mutters before grabbing the stack of papers. "I'm going to pick up our dresses from Jessica. I'll speak to you later."

Don't you dare leave me with Drake alone!

"Wait, I'll come with you." I rush to stand up, but Drake pulls me back down.

Jerk!

I can't be alone with him. Not after last night. I might kiss him. Again!

"You have other matters to deal with. I've got this." She grins, winking at me before her eyes flicker to Drake knowingly.

She ignores my narrowed gaze and skips off, whistling the wedding march as she does.

"What dresses?"

I jump at the sound of his deep voice, shivers running down my neck at how close he is. "For the casino night. We weren't informed we needed to attend the events. We presumed we would only be needed here when the parties were going on."

He chuckles. "Ahh. Mum wants you to feel like you're one of the family, not that you're here to work. I've not seen her this happy in ages. She really does hate that we've all moved away."

"Where do you live?"

"Not far." He looks up at the house. "I've actually been thinking about moving. I want to start my own practice. But with so many private practices open here in London, it's tough."

I'm actually shocked. The other night when we spoke about his job, he was undecided. "I thought you didn't know what you wanted to do."

He grins, looking at me. "I fibbed a little. I was going to head to South Africa again to volunteer, but I'm thirty-five. I need to start thinking about putting down roots, settling down."

My heart rate picks up, a part of me wishing I could be involved in his settling down. Something about him draws me to him, like he has an invisible rope wrapped around my waist.

"You didn't mention South Africa the other night." I speak softly after seeing the pain that flashed behind his eyes when he mentioned it.

"It's not something I like to bring up. I love my job. Helping kids, people, it's in my blood. It's who I am. I live for it." He scrubs a hand down his face.

"I understand that. I feel the same about event planning." I feel lame for saying it and wince when I do. His job saves lives; he has a purpose, a meaning, and makes a difference in the world. I just plan parties.

He turns, giving me a glimpse of those sexy dimples. "Yeah, you are passionate about your job."

Feeling shy all of a sudden, I duck my head. "I feel like there was a 'but' coming before."

"*But* it was hard. There's only so much you can do for them. The funding and supplies are low. All I wanted to do was save them, make it right, and I couldn't."

"It made you feel powerless," I mutter.

He gazes at me intensely, like he's surprised I get it, and nods. "Yeah."

"It only takes one person to make a difference, Drake. Just going over there changed their lives for the better. You made a difference being there, never forget that."

My breath hitches when he reaches out to cup my jaw, his body turned fully towards me. "Pagan," he whispers, his eyes closing.

"You two, those sleeping tablets won't work all day," Ada shouts.

We jump apart, looking around for her. When I don't see her, I turn to Drake with wide eyes. "Your nan is a freaking ninja."

"I can hear you. And thank you." This time I even look under the table, making Drake chuckle. "Up here." She sounds annoyed.

When I look up, I find her hanging out of the window, waving at us. "She's a nut," I whisper.

"I can read lips too," she shouts.

"Oh my God."

Drake chuckles. "We're coming, Grams."

"Hurry up, then. The only plan I have next is to whack him around the head with something heavy."

She leaves, closing the window behind her. Drake and I move towards the house in a sprint, hoping like hell she doesn't kill him.

One thing I've learnt in my four days here is that Ada doesn't say something she doesn't mean.

Let's hope we make it to him before she gets any more bright ideas.

Chapter Thirteen

*I*t's the night of the casino party, being held at one of the biggest exclusive casinos in town. When Pam said Amelia wanted to do something different, like going to the dogs or horses, I threw the idea of a casino at her. They seemed happy enough to start, but the second I told them it was mob themed and everyone had to dress up, they were excited. So I scored some tickets, enough for everyone, and ordered costumes.

What Alison and I didn't expect was to be invited along. Fortunately, we purchased enough tickets for everyone and a few more since spaces at big events like this are limited. We didn't want anyone to be left out. After searching all over London, Alison thankfully managed to snag us some last-minute costumes.

"You look fantastic. And so hot," she gushes when she walks out of the bathroom, looking like a bombshell herself.

In a tight black and red number with a lacey tassel fringe, she looks a million dollars. Her hair is in curls, making the black feathered headband stand out. She has ruby red lipstick and sexy red stilettos higher than I've ever seen her wear, finishing the look with a feather boa.

My outfit is a little more daring—a corset dress that's cutting off my circulation with black tassels at the fringe. My legs are more covered with fishnet tights and plain black stilettos. Unlike Alison, mine are only two inches. I have a dozen white pearls around my neck that vary in different lengths, and a headband with a white feather on the side. It looks great with the quiff I put the top part of my hair in, leaving the rest down in loose waves.

I grab my white feather boa and turn to Alison, a little unsure. "You sure I look okay?"

For some reason, I want to make a good impression with Drake. I want to appear as desirable and sexy as he makes me feel every time he looks at me. I've been fretting over it all day.

Part of me is self-conscious because of how revealing the dress is, but the other part is just worried Drake won't like it. I've never had to look good for anyone before, so I've found myself putting in a little extra work, hoping it pays off.

"You look incredible, Pagan. I promise."

"Then why do I feel so bloody nervous?"

"Because of the hot doctor?" She smirks.

I don't deny it, but I do roll my eyes. "Let's go," I say, grabbing my clutch.

We both make our way downstairs, where we join everyone in the foyer waiting for the limo to arrive.

"You all look amazing," Alison gushes.

"You do," I agree, eyeing everyone with my own smile. I have a feeling it's going to be a good night.

"Oh my, you two are beautiful." Pam beams, pride in her eyes.

Pam, Gabriella and her friends are wearing dresses similar to mine and Alison's, just different colours. The only one who has something unique is Amelia. She's wearing all white and it suits her, making her perfectly bronze tan stand out.

The men are handsome—except Aaron, since I'm not looking his way. They all have on striped suits in different colours, Jesse's matching Amelia.

When I don't see Drake, I look around the foyer, my mouth waters when I see him on the stairs wearing a black suit with white stripes and a black tie. The black hat with a white band round it makes him even hotter. He's putting a cigar in his pocket so he doesn't notice my gaze, giving me free rein to perv on him.

"You really should wipe your chin," Alison whispers close to my ear.

"Shut up," I whisper back, smiling when Drake looks up, his gaze meeting mine and stunning me into silence.

Everything around me fades away, leaving just the two of us. The look we share has my body hyperaware of how much I want him, need him. By the look in his eyes, he's just as affected by our intense moment.

His jaw goes slack, his eyes taking me in and I can't help but shift on my feet, wondering what he's thinking right now.

He's so hot.

"You look stunning," he tells me when he finally starts to move, walking up to me.

My attention is solely on him, ignoring everyone around us. "So do you. Nice, I mean." I shake my head at sounding like a total idiot and try again. "You look handsome." I let out a breath and relax my shoulders.

I can't take my eyes off him, and he seems to be struggling as well. I'm having the desired effect on him. He has a way of making me feel like the sexiest woman alive, even when I've just woken up and resemble Scary Mary.

All day he's all I've been able to think about. It's been going around in my head over and over, and no matter how many times I try to find reasons why I shouldn't have some fun with him, I can't come up with one that's good enough.

I like him.

It's as simple as that.

After three weeks, I go home. I'll just have to pray I don't grow feelings for him within that time.

"Did you match your outfits?" Aaron asks snidely, breaking our intimate moment.

Turning to him, my face twists in disgust. *Dick.* "No. I only got my outfit this morning, while he ordered his ages ago."

"Yeah right," he chuckles.

"Um, actually, I forgot all about it. Alison picked this up earlier, which is why I'm so late coming down." Drake shrugs, chuckling sheepishly.

My best friend hears her name and looks at Drake, then me, before winking. She totally had some doing in matching our outfits.

Aaron chuckles. "You've got no chance, bro."

My lip curls and I'm about to ask him why when his phone goes off. Drake just glares at Aaron, seeming two seconds away from wringing his neck.

"What the fuck!" he hisses, staring down at his phone in disgust.

Ada chooses that moment to walk up behind him, looking at the screen. "Oh he's a big boy, Aaron. You sure you can handle him?"

He snarls. "I don't know who the hell sent me that alert."

Not seeming bothered by his clear discomfort, Ada grabs his phone. "I didn't know men used dildos on each other. Hey, is that in the shower?"

We burst out laughing, Aaron going red as he glares at us. "I didn't sign up for it. I just keep getting sent best ways to use a dildo."

"How was the shower tip?" Ada asks, her face serious as she hands him back his phone.

I'm surprised we don't see steam coming out of his ears as he snatches it and storms off towards Jesse.

I laugh harder once he leaves, then turn to Ada. "How did you do that with a straight face?"

"Yeah, Grams, I've drawn blood from biting my lip."

I pout, turning to Drake. "You poor baby."

He grins down at me, tapping my nose with his index finger. "Ah, you gonna kiss it better later?"

I blush, then realise how far I've leant into Drake and step away. "Ha ha. So, Ada, tell us."

She shrugs, pulling her hat to the side. Yes, out of all us women, Ada is the only one not in a dress. Instead, she has a suit on with suspenders. She actually looks pretty cool.

"Oh I was too interested in finding out what app you gave him. I never knew you could get a dildo specially made for the shower like that," she says thoughtfully. "I wonder where you can get one."

Drake groans, turning green as he shouts, "Grams! No, just no."

"Come on, everyone, the limo is here," Adam calls.

"I think I'm going to be sick," Drake mutters, cursing under his breath.

"Come on, you big baby." I grab his arm and pull him away.

As we walk out of the manor, I hear Aaron betting Jesse that he wins more money and an idea occurs. "We really need to make sure we win more money than him."

"Don't look at me, I'm shit at poker." Drake grins, placing a hand at the bottom of my back.

"No worries," Alison says, walking up beside us. "I'm a pro. Watch this." She laughs, calling Aaron's name.

He turns back, smirking flirtatiously at Alison as his eyes skim over her outfit. "You want to ride next to me?"

Gag! What a sleaze.

She tries to cover her disgust the best she can, but her lip still curls. "No. I want in on your wager with Jesse. Whoever wins the most money gets to keep the others' winnings too."

He grins. "And what makes you think you'll win?"

She shrugs, not seeming bothered. "Someone needs to put you in your place."

He frowns. "All right, but don't cry when I take all your money."

"I won't be the one crying," she sings, moving to get in the car.

"Good luck," Drake says, slapping Aaron on the shoulder.

And he needs all the luck he can get. There's a reason my family won't play willingly with her.

The place is packed when we arrive. Drake steers us off to the bar while everyone starts looking around, talking amongst themselves. Jesse bailed out of the bet in the limo once he realised he was about to get duped by a girl. Aaron, on the other hand, couldn't back down, goading Alison the whole journey.

Second mistake he's made tonight.

I knew why she propositioned him too. She wanted him out of my way so I could enjoy the night without having him coming on to me. I also think she's cottoned on to the fact that I'm willing to give Drake a try. We're both willing adults, after all, and share a mutual intense attraction.

And she really is good at poker, so she gets the bonus of wiping Aaron's smug smirk off his face. Not even my dad or brothers have been able to get the upper hand when it comes to her or Brooke. Every time we have a poker night, it always ends up with the two of them while the rest of us are left to get sloppy drunk.

"What would you like to drink?" Drake asks, grabbing his wallet.

"I'll get these." He looks at me like I've offended him and I hold my hands up, giving in. "I'll have a vodka, lime and lemonade."

He winks and puts in our order before turning back to me. "You really do look beautiful tonight."

My gaze softens before I fall into him as someone bumps into me from behind. He pulls me to him, eyes searching my face.

"Thank you," I whisper, my eyes locking on his lips.

"What do you mean you haven't got sherry," Ada yells and we pull apart, looking down the bar for her.

Adam and Pam try to calm her down, and eventually she gives in and takes whatever drink she's offered.

I smile. "She really is a character."

"She's up to something. Sherry isn't her choice of drink—brandy is. Sherry's what she drinks for a nightcap."

I look at Ada again and don't notice anything different. "How do you get all that from what drink she's chosen?"

"You know the saying 'brandy makes you randy'?"

I raise my eyebrow and answer slowly. "Yeah."

"She takes that to a whole new meaning."

"Ew." I hit his chest, laughing lightly.

"I'm serious. She's up to something, and whatever it is, it isn't going to be good if she has brandy."

"We'll keep an eye on her."

He scoffs and I eye him questioningly. "I'm having a hard time keeping my eyes off you and you expect me to watch out for Grams? You're crazy."

"Can't keep your eyes off me, huh?" I flirt, running my finger down his chest.

His eyes dilate, darkening, and his hand on my hip tightens. "You know what you do to me."

His rich, deep voice has me wet between the legs. "Why don't you show me?"

He seems surprised by my bluntness for a second, then smirks devilishly down at me, pulling me even closer.

"It will be my pleasure."

His head lowers and my heart races, anticipating the kiss, hoping it's as good as I remember.

"Are you two going to stand around here all night? Come on, Pagan, I need my lucky charm," Aaron interrupts, and a frustrated growl escapes Drake.

I scoff, wishing we'd left him at the manor.

"And why would we want to watch you lose all night?" Drake grits out, looking annoyed.

"I don't care what you do. I'm talking to Pagan."

Drake grins at Aaron and then looks down at me, pulling me to his side. "And what would you like to do?"

"I'd rather watch paint dry than go with you."

Aaron thinks I'm talking to Drake because he grins, even though my eyes are on him. Drake chuckles.

"Come on, then. I need you, babe."

"Aaron, I was talking to you. Go away. Drake and I have plans."

He looks genuinely confused as to why I would have plans with Drake and not him. "Doing what?"

"Something you're not." Drake hands me my drink. With one last glance at Aaron, we both leave him standing there looking lost and utterly confused.

I chuckle once we're out of reach. "He never was the brightest bulb in the box. I don't know how he became a lawyer. My mum and dad were always sure he'd be a sales rep."

Chuckling, Drake steers me to some high-tech-looking machines. "Let's forget about him. How about you and me have our own little bet tonight."

Intrigued, I eye him up and down, a small smile on my lips. "And what would this bet entail?"

"Whoever wins gets to order the other one around for the day next Saturday."

"I'm not good with taking orders," I immediately tell him.

It's my family's fault for always giving in to my demands. I was the only girl and they doted on me. But once I started school and tried to join after-school activities, it became clear that I couldn't follow the rules unless I was the one giving them. Ever since then, I knew my job would consist of me issuing orders.

He doesn't look surprised. "I can see that. Okay, how about I get to take you out next Saturday?"

"Who says you're gonna win?" I grin, leaning closer.

He laughs, his eyes crinkling at the corners. "If I do, I get to take you out next Saturday. If you win, you get to do something of your choosing. How's that?"

I pretend to think about it for a second. Either way I win because I'll get to spend time with him. "Okay, deal." I hold my hand out to shake on it, but instead he pulls me in to him. I fall easily, his breath fanning my face as I look up at him.

"I'm going to enjoy winning," he growls.

If I wasn't turned on before, I am now.

"And I'll enjoy either." I wink and before I know it, I'm leaning up on my toes and kissing him. The kiss deepens and he wraps his arms around me, holding me tightly. I moan into his mouth, loving the feel of his lips on mine.

God, he can kiss.

∼

After our heated kiss, Drake and I play roulette. It's actually pretty straight forward. You place a bet on a number, and on black or red, as many times as you want. Drake went all professional on me, taking his time on what bets to place. Me? I put my money on whatever my index finger picked out.

At first I was winning, my money stash coming up to a hundred quid.

But my luck soon ran out, and now Drake is in the lead by four hundred quid.

"I give up. You win," I pout. I've lost another fifty quid, thinking if I bet bigger, I'll win bigger. No such luck. I only have two-fifty left and he has six-fifty.

His deep chuckle vibrates down my back as he leans over, printing our winnings to collect at the cashier counter. "Come on, let's go collect."

Looking at the time, I remind Drake, "The limo is picking us up in twenty minutes. We better round everyone up."

"Do you ever not work?" he asks, grinning.

"Hmm." I pretend to think about it. "When I sleep." But even then I dream about work. It's always on my mind, wondering if I ordered the right place settings, or booked the DJ. All except for last night, as my mind was preoccupied with the man in front of me. It wouldn't let me think, let alone dream of anything else.

He kisses the tip of my nose, chuckling. "All right. We'll go get everyone. I'm dying to see who won the bet."

It's my turn to grin. "My money's on Alison."

"You need to stop betting your money," he replies dryly, and I smack his arm.

We collect our winnings and make our way over to the poker tables, noticing a huge crowd surrounding a certain one.

"That has to be them," Drake says, rising onto his toes to look over people's heads. "Yeah."

We push through the crowd to find Alison on one side of the table and Aaron on the other. He's sweating profusely, his jaw ticking as he stares down at his cards. Alison looks relaxed, grinning widely across the table at Aaron, goading him.

Ah, I do love my best friend. She really knows how to work them till they're practically pissing their pants.

I step forward, ready to ask how she's doing, even though the chips piled next her are enough explanation, but Ada stops me.

"Don't interrupt. Anyone converses with the opponents and they're automatically disqualified."

"Why?" I scoff, thinking how ridiculous that is. She's my friend.

"Because Aaron said Pam and I were telling Alison what cards he had, accusing her of cheating."

"Were you?" Drake asks, not ashamed to call her out.

"Lord, no. We were just seeing how much she was going to take him for. I was trying to get a cut."

"How? You're not playing," I remind her, giggling.

"I offered to get back at him for the whole arse-pinching incident, but before she could give me an answer, he told everyone to back off."

"What was Mum doing talking to her?" Drake asks.

Ada rolls her eyes. "Warning her not to negotiate with me."

A bubble of laughter bursts free and everyone's eyes land on me. Alison waves, winking at me, and I give her a thumbs up.

"Hey, you're disqualified," Aaron shouts. The caller rolls his eyes, leaning back in his tall chair. He seems annoyed as he narrows his eyes on Aaron. Not that I blame him. He's had to deal with him for however long they've been here.

"How? I didn't talk to her," Alison growls, leaning forwards on the table.

"She gave you a thumbs up. Probably telling you to play your hand."

"I can't even see your cards, you arsehole. I'm over here," I tell him.

"How about you come sit over here on my lap where I can see you?"

"How about you just finish the game so we can go home?" Drake growls, glaring at Aaron.

Aaron is the one to show his cards first. As soon as he does, Alison stands, screaming in glee. "Read 'em and weep."

I laugh, seeing she has a full house. Aaron curses, swiping the cards across the table. Ignoring him, I rush over to Alison and hug her. "Congratulations."

"Thank you. It was worth the miserable four hours I just spent with him." She grins.

"How much did you win?" Drake asks.

"From a rough calculation, I'd say three grand. I barely touched the hundred I started with."

I smile, proud of my friend. Drake whistles and nods, seemingly impressed. "Wow."

"She only won because I took it easy on her. Ain't that right, babe. I

let her win so she could go buy some nice kinky underwear just for me."
Aaron grins.

We all glare at him as Ada mutters something under her breath, walking away.

"Get lost," Alison tells him, too smug to let him ruin her good mood.

We move away, leaving Aaron to down whatever he's drinking, and turn to Pam and Adam. "Hey, guys, the limo driver will be outside in five minutes. I'm going to round everyone up and get them to meet you outside. Is that okay?"

"That's fine. We've had such a good time. Thank you for organising this," Pam gushes, leaning further into Adam.

"Where have you two been all night?" Drake asks.

"We played a few tables, but then I took your mother in the room next door and showed her how to dance," Adam tells him.

We all smile as a dreamy expression crosses her face before she kisses Adam on the cheek.

"Gross. I'll help Pagan. Why don't you get Alison's winnings with her and make sure that douche doesn't try to get them back."

"He wouldn't," Alison gasps, clutching her chips closer.

Adam looks to his son, then back to Alison. "Oh he probably will. He'll most likely challenge you to a drinking game or something. That boy hates losing."

We watch them lead Alison over to the cashier counter before turning to find everyone else. Before we do, Drake pulls me against him.

"I know what I want to do first next Saturday."

"And what's that?" I ask breathlessly.

"Apart from worship your gorgeous body, I'd like to take you somewhere. A surprise."

My body heats and I continue to gaze at him, hoping I'm doing the right thing by pursuing this.

It *can't* last.

It *won't* last.

I just have to remind myself of that.

"Okay." I nod, taking his hand.

Chapter Fourteen

The next morning, we're all sitting down in the garden room with the windows open, waiting for breakfast to arrive, when a male roar rattles the house.

No joke. I literally felt the floor shaking beneath me.

"What on earth?" Pam gasps, holding her hand to her chest.

"Jesse!" Aaron roars from somewhere inside the house. "Jesse!"

"Oh God," Amelia murmurs, looking at Jesse with wide eyes. "What have you done?"

"Nothing," he says, then turns to Drake and me with curious eyes. I shrug, looking away. I may have done some crazy shit while I've been here, but I have no idea what has his panties in a twist this morning.

"He can't be that sore over losing last night." Alison giggles as we hear him shout again, closer this time.

The door slams open and, clad in nothing but a pair of boxers, a stormy-faced Aaron forces his way into the room.

I gasp, trying to smother my laughter when I see Ada behind him wearing only a dressing gown, a huge grin on her face. Her gaze meets mine and she winks.

"Mother, what's going on? Why are you wearing a guest dressing gown? Where's your *Game of Thrones* one?"

"Ask Aaron," Ada says, her eyes raking over him seductively.

Aaron shudders, moving away from her. "You need to sort your grams out. She... she—"

"We had a fantastic night together." Ada beams, moving closer to a pale Aaron.

Shocked doesn't begin to cover what I feel right now. Drake chokes on the fruit he was munching on. Adam stands up, face full of fury, and Pam has tears in her eyes, though I'm unsure whether they're happy or sad; it's touch-and-go with this family.

Jesse and Amelia stare open-mouthed, and Gabriella, who only arrived a short moment ago, bursts out laughing, high-fiving her nan as she passes.

"You slept with my mother?" Adam roars, slamming his fist down on the table

"We didn't," Aaron rushes out, wisely taking a step back.

"You don't even remember our night of lovemaking." Ada sniffles.

"This is a joke, right?" I whisper to Drake.

He curses, shaking his head as he places it between his hands. "I don't know. I really don't know. This is Grams. Anything could happen."

I laugh, but the look he gives me stops me short. "Sorry."

"This is better than *Big Brother*," Alison chimes in, sipping her morning coffee.

"We didn't do anything," Aaron yells, his voice high-pitched.

"Oh, I could tell you where his birthmark is," Ada whisper-yells to the room, sitting down.

Aaron's face is a picture and I start to laugh, bringing his stormy glare my way. "You! This is all your fault."

"Mine?" I ask innocently. "How? I didn't do anything. You're the one who slept with her."

"For the last time, I didn't sleep with her," he roars before looking down at me. "Nothing like this ever happened to me before you turned up."

"It's called karma," Alison sings.

"Are you saying you regret our passionate lovemaking?" Ada asks. For a quick moment, I actually believe her, but then I look closer and notice her lips twitch.

Aaron looks like he's about to be sick.

"We didn't have sex," he thunders, throwing his hands up before he storms out of the room, everyone watching. As soon as the door slams shut, you could hear a pin drop as everyone turns to stare at Ada.

She seems none the wiser as she pours herself a cup of coffee. When she finally notices, she grins. "What?"

"Mother, is what he's saying true?"

Ada rolls her eyes, looking at everyone around the table. "He's not my type, Pammy. You know that. I just made him believe we slept together."

"And why would you do that?" Adam asks, putting his cup down, looking resigned as he sits back.

I grin behind mine and Drake pinches my side. "It's not funny. Don't encourage her. I nearly had a heart attack."

"It's fine. You're a doctor," I whisper back. He stares at my lips for a few seconds before shaking his head, grinning.

"You're lucky you're cute."

"Mother, answer him," Pam implores.

"I was bored. And he's a cheating jackass. And I didn't like the way he spoke to *my* Alison last night at the casino. I nursed that girl back to health, sat with her through sickness and diarrhoea, and he had the nerve to be rude to her."

"She didn't," Alison announces to the table, bright red.

I laugh, earning an elbow from her. "Sorry," I wheeze.

"So you slept in the same bed as him?" Jesse asks, seeming more amused now than annoyed.

"Do I look like I want to be near him for that long? Of course I didn't. I set my alarm for seven this morning and snuck into his room wearing a bikini," she says, then turns to Amelia. "I'll return it after it's been washed, dear."

Amelia coughs, waving her hand. "Keep it."

"Thanks." Ada smiles. "So anyway, I was in his bed for, like, two seconds before he woke up. He had his arms around me, hand on my boob and everything," she cackles.

"You put his hand on your boob?" Pam screeches, standing up. She looks mortified as she stares at her mother like a stranger.

"No, of course I didn't. He did. Got a good feel too. Another second and I was ready to knee his balls."

"Mother," Pam scolds.

"Well, this has been fun, but I need to get out of this bikini. It's riding right up my—"

"Mother!" Pam yells, covering her ears.

Ada cackles again, getting up from her chair and leaving the room. Poor Pam drops to her seat, her head in her hands as Adam tries to console her.

"It's fine, love."

"She needs to be in a home. Around people her own age," she cries.

"We tried that, dear. They kicked her out."

Pam nods, holding on to her husband before turning to Alison and me. "I'm so sorry you've been subjected to this craziness. She's normally...." She tries to find the right words but sighs, staring straight at us. "She's always like this. We just thought with the wedding around the corner, she would calm down."

"It's fine. I'm actually enjoying myself," I tell her. Everyone looks at me like I'm crazy and I shrug, grinning. "Hey, he did leave me when I was younger for a girl he cheated on me with and got pregnant."

Speaking of, I haven't heard Aaron or anyone else mention his kid. I wonder what happened there. Not that I'm going to ask and make it seem like I care, of course.

"Fair point," Pam says, taking a sip of coffee with shaky hands.

Emily takes that moment to walk in with a huge grin on her face. "Good morning, everyone. Breakfast is served."

"I need you to put those candles on tables one and four, and make sure you set up an extra table for the press. Marcus, can you meet Norman outside? He needs help bringing in the champagne fountain and setting it up in the centre of the room. Jane, change those napkins. There are some teal-coloured ones in a box in the kitchen. It's marked."

Everyone scrambles away and I move over to the main table, rearranging the flowers for what feels like the millionth time. They originally chose a big bouquet, but with the size, it's just going to block their view, so I've been trimming them down all day, never satisfied with the length.

"There's going to be nothing left if you keep hacking at them," Alison giggles.

My phone rings and Alison grins. It hasn't stopped all day. "Hold that thought," I tell her. "Hello?"

"It's Shane. We have a Grace Morgan here."

"Ah, send her up. She's bringing our desserts. Thanks, Shane."

Ending the call, I wipe my forehead, turning to Alison. "Did you get everyone their outfits?"

"Yes. I've had to make a few alterations to Angela's. She wanted it tighter."

I roll my eyes. "Why does that not surprise me?"

"No, no, no, no. That colour is all wrong. And what happened to those flowers?" I hear screeched from behind me. I turn, finding Amelia scurrying after an older woman, her face flushed and pinched tightly. She mouths "Sorry" as they walk up to me.

"This all looks cheap, Amelia. It just won't do."

I look to the older lady, trying not to be offended. "Hi, I'm Pagan." I turn to Amelia. "Is there something you wanted me to change?"

"No. Everything is beautiful. This is my mum, Sharon."

"Nice to meet you, Sharon." I hold my hand out, but she gasps, glaring behind me. We all look to find them putting up some twinkle lights.

"No! Just no! Do you want the newspapers to think you're cheap? What will people say about me after they see this?"

"Mum," Amelia moans softly, shame crossing her face.

Just then another woman walks in, similar to Sharon, only she doesn't seem to have the plastic look.

"Sharon, stop going on about everything and let Amelia go get ready for her guests. This isn't your wedding."

"God, no. It wouldn't be this tasteless."

I'm trying my hardest not to be offended, I really am, but the place looks freaking amazing. My team have worked their arses off all day to get ready for tonight's press release and engagement party.

"Hi, I'm Maggie, Amelia's aunt. You can call me aunt Mags. You've done a wonderful job."

I like her.

I smile warmly, remembering Drake's comment about the two sisters. She really is as nice as Amelia. I wonder if Amelia and Angela were swapped at birth. It's not like it's never happened before.

"I'm Pagan, and this is my best friend and colleague, Alison."

"Nice to meet you both."

"You too," Alison says.

"Why don't you go get ready while I show Sharon and Maggie to the garden room? Pam is serving tea for our early arrivals," I offer, and Amelia smiles gratefully.

"I think I should go with my daughter."

Amelia looks horrified at the thought so I step in, gesturing for her to follow me. "And pass up on the rich tea Emily's serving? I hear it's the best you could buy."

"Well now I have to try this tea," she mutters, sounding put out.

Amelia mouths "Thank you" before rushing out of the room. I'll have to remind myself to take up an alcoholic drink when I go to get ready.

Stepping inside the garden room, Drake, Adam and Pam are sitting with Jesse and another man I've not met yet.

"I told her not to invite him," Sharon hisses to Maggie.

"He's her father, Sharon. And like I said, this is not your wedding. And where is your new husband?"

"He's attending an important business meeting," she replies snottily, glaring holes into Amelia's dad, Eric.

Everyone exchanges pleasantries—well, as pleasant as they can be with Sharon constantly putting something or someone down. Her snide remarks are tiresome.

I leave them to it for a bit to make sure everything is going to plan, but when Emily found me an hour ago, I came back. Apparently they need a peacekeeper, and I fit that role perfectly.

I've also noticed how close Eric and Maggie are. They've exchanged light touches, laughing at each other's jokes, and I've even heard him flirt a time or two in the hour I've been in here with her.

"You've noticed the chemistry too?" Alison whispers, finishing her tea.

I smile behind my cup. "Yeah."

Drake smiles as he walks up to me after finally getting away from his brother and dad. "Hey, shouldn't you be getting ready?"

I glance at my watch and panic. "Oh no! Guests will be arriving soon. I need to hurry up."

"Your dress is hanging up behind your door. I've put your make-up out, along with curlers, and your shoes are at the end of your bed. You've got time to shower, so don't panic."

Drake laughs, looking between us. "Are you married?"

Alison laughs. "May as well be. She wouldn't eat or sleep if I didn't remind her. She's good at organising everyone else's lives, but when it comes to her own... no clue."

"I do too," I argue, turning to glare at my best friend.

"You don't."

"I've listened to enough arguing for one day. Let's get you upstairs. I need to get my suit on too." Drake grins, winking at me.

I blush, badly wanting to kiss him right now, but we agreed last night at the casino that we would keep this on the down-low.

"Don't let me stop you. Just don't take too long in the shower, she still has work to do," Alison says, walking away giggling.

"Remind me why I'm her friend," I order Drake, my face heating.

"She does have a point."

Rolling my eyes, I shove his shoulder and step away. "You, Mr Donovan, are a very rude man. I'm going to get ready, and you...," I start seductively, running my finger down his chest. He gives me a heated stare, smirking like he's won a bet. "Can get dressed yourself."

I laugh when his jaw drops and step around him.

"You're an evil woman, Pagan Salvatore."

I laugh, heading up the stairs. Now I just have to make sure I get through tonight without jumping him, because the image of him in the shower has me seriously turned on.

∾

By the end of the night, my feet are killing me. The caterers and waiters have cleaned up and left, and everyone is now tucked up in bed.

The night went without any hitches. Even Angela and Sharon seemed to be on their best behaviour, minus their snide comments. Luckily no one paid them any attention, going out of their way to stay clear.

Now I'm meeting Drake for a rendezvous in the back garden. Looking around, I take off my black stilettos as I search for him.

A noise to my left startles me and I jump, my hand going to my chest. "Drake, you freaking scared me."

He laughs, holding up two glasses and a bottle of champagne. "Sorry, I couldn't help it. Come on, I'll take you to Mum's secret garden. It's my favourite place."

"So, you aren't going to take me out into the woods and murder me?"

He chuckles, shaking his head at me. "Nah. It would be such a waste."

My body heats at the intensity in his eyes as they rake over my body. Shivers break out across my skin, butterflies twirl in my stomach and my heart beats wildly.

"Lead the way." I try to keep the nervous shake out of my voice. It doesn't work, but thankfully Drake doesn't seem to notice.

We walk side by side towards the right of the property, away from the manor and the guest house.

"I didn't see a secret garden in the newspaper article your mum did."

He looks over, his eyebrow raised. "You read that?"

I blush. "I looked it over last night when we got back. Alison mentioned it before, so I thought I'd check it out. It was nothing like I thought it would be. It had so much information on the history of the manor. It was incredible."

He nods. "She kept getting hounded for exclusive interviews and photos of the manor. It has a lot of history, but no one wanted to really focus on it. So when a good friend of Mum's asked if she could do a back-story on the home, Mum agreed. But she didn't want her garden to be revealed. Can you remember me telling you everyone who's owned the manor added their own impression?"

"Yeah."

"Well, years ago, Dad added the security building on the side, so Mum wanted to add her own personal touch and decided on a garden. But the place holds more meaning for her. Our grandparents' ashes are buried here. She didn't want that to be put in a paper, so her friend kept the whole garden out."

We walk up a stoned path lined with flowers on either side as we come to an ivory archway.

I gasp when we walk inside. I know nothing about flowers, but I don't think it's necessary to admire the beauty. In the middle is a statue of two angels, each with a bow and arrow in their hands, surrounded by a small fountain.

"This is beautiful," I whisper, turning to take in all my surroundings. It's practically glowing with coloured flowers, the nature of it spectacular and well taken care of.

"It is. That's where our grandparents' ashes are buried."

He directs me over to another stone angel, this one weeping with her head down. Buried into the floor below are three marble markers, names and dates scrolled in gold italic writing outlining how much they were beloved. A stone bench sits to the side, giving a perfect view of the burials.

"No wonder your mum wanted to keep this private. This is more precious than a graveyard. It's intimate, personal. This place is special," I tell him softly.

"It is," he says just as softly before taking my hand in his. He pulls me down a path lined high with perfectly trimmed bushes. It goes off in other directions once we reach another circle, this one with more flowers, more statues and a bench or two.

He takes me left. "Are you sure you're not going to kill me?"

He laughs. "No. Trust me, you'll love this place."

"What makes it so special?"

He looks at me, seeming to contemplate whether to tell me or not. He stops and I stare past him to see what has to be the most breathtaking view I have ever seen.

Cabin Lakes has a lot of views, all of them spectacular, but if I could paint, I would frame this picture and hang it up in my living room.

It's meant to be treasured.

A large oak tree sits next to a small pond, covered with hanging lanterns, wild flowers surrounding the area. The forest sits just beyond that, and with the full moon high in the sky and the glow reflecting off the water, it looks magical.

"Oh my God. This... wow, this is amazing." And then I see the picnic blanket laid on the grass next to the large tree, a basket next to it. Twinkly lights hang off the tree and different-sized lanterns are placed around the blanket, giving more of a soft glow to the dark night. "You did all this? For me?" I ask, choking up.

He clears his throat. "Yeah. You deserve it after the work you've put in."

When I see his unsure expression, I decide to tease him. "And to score points, right?"

He laughs deeply, walking me over to the blanket. "I'll never tell. Sit."

I take a seat, chuckling when I see he's even brought some cushions to lean against the tree. "You thought of everything."

"I did."

I sigh contentedly when I lean back against the tree, my eyes closing briefly. The cool breeze is welcome since the day's been scorching hot.

"Are you going to tell me why this place is so special?"

"My grandfather used to bring me out here all the time. The pond has a stream that runs into it, so fish always end up in here. We'd fish, not really catching anything, but I think that was the point. It taught me patience, to relax, to have a steady hand."

"I can see why he'd want to teach a young boy that. My brothers drove my mum crazy." We're quiet for a moment, but I find the courage to ask what's been on my mind. "Earlier, when I asked you what made the place so special, you seemed reluctant to answer. You also spoke in past tense."

He sighs, sitting back next to me and handing me a glass of champagne. "You noticed that, huh?"

"I notice everything," I admit. There's no point denying it.

He chuckles before he turns serious, his expression hard. "When I was twenty-five, I asked my long-term girlfriend, Leanne, to marry me here."

Okay, I was so not expecting that.

I swallow down the hurt and jealousy I shouldn't be feeling, hoping my voice doesn't betray me when I ask, "What happened?"

"She said yes, but a few months later, I caught her cheating on me. We'd been together for years. She's the daughter of a close friend of the family. We grew up together."

"You loved her." I say it as a statement, because I can hear the hurt in his voice and the resentment he holds towards her.

"That's the thing, I don't think I did. It's like you and Aaron—we were young. It didn't help that our parents kept pushing us together. Don't get me wrong, I did love her, just not the way a man is supposed to love the woman he's going to spend the rest of his life with. And yeah, walking in on her screwing my best friend sucked, but I didn't really feel anything. I was just angry. I felt betrayed by my best friend."

I'm confused. "Not to be blunt or anything, but why did you ask her to marry you?"

He laughs but there's no humour there. He gulps his champagne down and turns to me. I take a sip of mine, seeing the hurt in his eyes. I have a feeling whatever he's going to say next isn't going to be good. "Because a few weeks before, I found a pregnancy test in the bathroom bin. I assumed it was mine even though I was always careful. So I bought a ring and proposed."

"She didn't even tell you the baby wasn't yours?"

"No. I don't think she would've said anything had I not caught them in bed together."

"And with your best friend?"

"Yes." He scrubs a hand down his face. "I want kids. Always have. I think that's what hurt me the most."

Seeing he clearly doesn't want to talk about it, I decide to change the subject. "So, Angela and Aaron, huh?"

He laughs loudly and the sound echoes in the distance, making me smile. "He doesn't know it was itching powder yet. They think they had a reaction to his detergent."

"His detergent?" I ask.

"Angela put on his boxers."

I laugh, holding my stomach. "Oh my God. I would've thought that was beneath her."

"I know. And he's getting pretty pissed about those messages and pictures being sent to his phone."

I giggle. "He'll have to get a new phone and number because I have no idea how to unsubscribe—not that I want to. He can keep suffering."

"I'm still pissed about my car. Every time I see his, I want to egg it. He brings out the child in me."

We sit back on the blanket, gazing across the lake. The stars are bright in the sky and I can't look away from the magnificent beauty.

"I don't think there's anything in the box we could use on the car," I tell him, thinking it over.

He hums under his breath. "Maybe Grams has something up her sleeve. I can't let that shit slide. It's my car."

Boys and their toys.

An idea occurs and I grin. "I have an idea, but I'll need to get some supplies first. For now, I want you to kiss me."

I hear his intake of breath at the demand.

"I'm not one to say no to a beautiful woman." When I turn to him, his eyes are smouldering, burning into me with a dying need.

"So don't," I whisper.

His eyes dilate and slowly, so very slowly, he brings his lips to mine.

And I'm in heaven.

Then and there, the walls I promised would stay firmly up around Drake start to tumble down.

We spend the rest of the night in each other's arms, our lips and hands getting to know one another intimately.

Walking away after the three weeks are up is going to be hard.

Chapter Fifteen

*I*t's a few days after mine and Drake's 'date' by the pond, and we've tried to spend as much time as possible together. However, he got called into work yesterday afternoon, right before we planned to take a dip in the pool. There'd been a pile-up on the motorway, so they needed every available doctor.

It gave me time to collect what I needed for our next prank on Aaron. I've traipsed across London, heading into every stationary shop there is to get what we needed.

But before we can carry out our prank, we need to get through today's pool party. There's no way we can do it before or during, since there will be too many guests around to see. I don't want to get caught. I'm actually enjoying torturing him.

"Hey, Pagan, we have a problem."

My head snaps up at the urgent need in Alison's voice as she rushes over to me. "What's wrong?"

"I just got off the phone with the cocktail waiter. He's sick, and we don't have anyone down as a plan B."

I scrub my hands down my face and lean back in the sunlounger.

"And he didn't think to call to give us a little warning?" I bite out, wanting to wring his neck.

She shakes her head, sitting on the bench next to me. "I made a note on your calendar to leave a bad review on his website. He didn't even have anyone to recommend or another colleague to come help."

My laptop is already open next to me on a small table, so I pick it up and start scrolling through my emails, seeing if anyone else I contacted regarding the cocktails is available.

"Let me call a few people. Amelia was really adamant about having a cocktail waiter. Apparently a friend of hers hired one for a Halloween party last year and she loved it. They do loads of crazy stuff while making them or something."

"You sure? I don't mind looking for you."

"No, it's fine. Did you get the bikini for Amelia?" I ask, a smirk forming when I think of Ada wearing the one Amelia originally planned to wear.

She giggles. "Yes. She's actually grateful Ada pinched hers. She loves this one-piece suit I got better."

Which reminds me. "Which one did you pack for me?" My voice is wary as I eye my best friend sceptically. I have a drawer-full, but knowing Alison, she picked the skimpiest one I own.

"I think it was the red one," she says, then gets up, avoiding my eyes.

"Alison?" I drag out.

"I'll let you get on with the cocktail bloke. If you can't, I'm sure it'll be okay. We have two hours before the party. Oh look, Ada's—oh my God."

I glance over to the back door, my eyes bugging out of my head when Ada walks out wearing a white bikini, the bottoms a little too tight.

"Holy crap!"

"Girls, just who I was looking for. Couldn't find me cossie, so I dug this one back out. How nice is Amelia for giving it to me?"

"I'm going," Alison rushes out, struggling not to laugh.

"She's... one in a million," I tell her with a tight smile.

"Even pushes these babies up," Ada cackles, grabbing her boobs. *God, please no more.* "They've been hanging south for so long, I forgot—"

"Where's Pam?" I interrupt.

"She should be out in a minute. But I wanted to catch you before," she says seriously, taking a seat in the sunlounger across from me.

"What did you want to talk about?" I ask, sitting straighter now.

"Paintball tomorrow. I want in."

Oh crap!

"How did you—"

"I have my sources. So?"

Ah, the itinerary she somehow emailed to herself from Alison's laptop when she was sick.

"I think Jesse and Amelia just wanted it to be friends." I choose to tread carefully, not wanting to upset her. Lord knows what would happen to me if I got on her bad side. I shudder at the thought.

She sighs, seeming disappointed. "They won't know I'm there. I'll tell the instructor I'm late to the party or something. I'm going to be old soon. I need to get these things done before I pass."

She's old now.

She bats her eyes at me and I crumble. "Okay. But if anyone finds out you're there, do not implicate me in anyway. I actually love this job."

"Why wouldn't you? We're awesome. But now that I have you, can I ask, what are your intentions with my grandson?"

I choke, staring at her in horror. "I... we—we're friends."

She grins. "I know, I can tell how good of a friend you are. But that's not what I'm asking and you know it."

Sighing, I reach for my drink, taking a sip. "I don't know. It's complicated."

"How?"

Ever so blunt.

"I don't have a good record when it comes to men. I have a hard time trusting them, and myself, anymore. I've hurt a lot of people." Guilt hits me like it does every time I think of the mistakes I made, the pain I caused people.

"I can tell there's a story there. Do you want to talk about it?"

My first reaction is to change the subject, but a part of me wants to finally talk to someone. "You know all about Aaron," I tell her and she scoffs. "The second wasn't a guy I was dating, because well, I never dated after Aaron. He hurt me too much. But we used to do events supporting different charities for a high-end company located near us. There were some really sleazy blokes there, but one, Jordan, was a real dick. He cornered me in the bathroom and wouldn't take no for an answer. He just kept pushing. My twin brother, Sid, heard the commotion on the way to the bathroom and came in and pulled him away. But because I'm stupid, and because I didn't want my dad to lose the business their company brought in, I waved it off, saying he was just drunk. He was my second big mistake, and a massive factor in why I don't trust men or myself."

My throat is dry and I can't bring myself to look at Ada. "You should've told someone, girl. Men like that need their balls chopped off. But you need to remember that not all men are like that."

"I know. I have four men in my life who prove that to me every day. My dad is my hero, and my twin, he's my other half. My older brother, Dean, is my best friend, and my sister-in-law's granddad is like one to me too. But want to know the worst thing about what happened to me?"

"What?" Her voice is soft, and I realise she truly wants to know, that she's interested in what I have to say and cares.

"He did it again to my sister-in-law, but he got further with her. Not much further, but does it really matter? She'd been going through something at the time and it made everything much worse for her. I keep telling myself that if I had just told the truth, she wouldn't have gone through that herself. But it wasn't even the worst thing I did to her. I owe her everything. I nearly had her killed." I'm rambling now, telling her more than I meant to as my eyes water.

I've carried around this huge guilt for so long that saying it out loud doesn't make it any easier to deal with. I've spoken to Lola about it and she doesn't blame me, but I blame myself enough for the both of us.

"Hey, you don't need to talk about any of this." She pats my hand, her eyes soft, full of concern and sadness.

"It's actually a change for me. I don't like talking about it, but I don't mind."

"Go on, then." She sits forwards to hear better, enclosing her hand around mine. As much as I love the kind gesture, I wish she hadn't, because her boobs nearly spill out of her bikini, giving me an eyeful.

"After that night, I tried my hardest to make it up to her. I didn't know about her past or what she was going through. Then one night we went out to celebrate our businesses starting and I met a guy. He was handsome, charming and he made me feel like I mattered. I hadn't felt that way in a long time. And I knew enough was enough. I took a chance on him." I swallow, finding it hard to talk about.

When I met Rick outside the toilets of the club we were at, I was enthralled. He knew all the right things to say to me, and I lapped it up like a kitten with milk.

"What happened?" Ada asks softly, concern in her voice.

I laugh harshly, tears burning my eyes. "He was her ex. Her *abusive* ex. He used me to get to her, and it worked. He kidnapped her, nearly killing her and my unborn niece in the process."

Ada gasps, sitting back in her chair. Her eyes brim with tears and I watch as she struggles to hold them back.

"So you see, it's complicated. Not only do I not trust easily, but I always end up picking the wrong men. And I know deep down in my bones that Drake is nothing like them, but he could still hurt me nonetheless."

"Oh, girl, you're a bloody walking TV show. My Drake looks at you like you hung the moon. I only asked because he's been hurt before too by some little trollop. I didn't want to see it happen again because... well, I kind of like you."

I wipe my eyes and laugh. "Thank you. But I don't plan on hurting Drake, I promise. If anything, it would be the other way around."

"Trust me, girl, with the way you look and the kindness in that big heart of yours, it would be you doing the heart breaking. Those men were just a blip. Your sister-in-law is happy now. I've heard you talk about her. It's time you started to let yourself be too. Plus, London is a great place to relocate." She grins.

My eyes bug out, making her laugh harder. "I think you're getting ahead of yourself."

"Talk to him, make sure you both know where you stand. Now I need to go give the boys a heart attack, then get out of this dreadful thing before I die. It's a torture device."

I laugh, clutching my belly. "You're wearing that to scare the boys?"

"Why else would I torture myself like this? It'll be worth it." She winks, then gets up and walks over to me. "You're special, Pagan. It's why I picked you. You just need to believe it yourself."

Picked me? What's that supposed to mean?

She's already walking off and heading inside. I lean back, wondering what she meant, but with Ada, it could mean anything.

With my mind on Lola, I pick up my phone and call her, needing to hear her voice.

"Hey! We miss you," she yells excitedly down the phone as soon as she answers. I immediately feel like shit for not calling them sooner.

"Hey," I reply softly.

"What's wrong?" she asks, serious now. "Dean, go away. No! *I'm* talking to her."

I laugh when I hear my brother grunt, a sign he's given in to his wife like he always does, no matter how much he pretends otherwise.

"I'm fine."

"Please don't lie to me. Especially when I can't poke you in the eye."

She would.

I cringe at the memory of the black eye she once gave me. I got funny looks for weeks. Even had a few regulars at Lola's ask if I needed someone to talk to.

"I was just thinking about you, about everything. I wanted you to know how much I love you. You're more than just Dean's wife—you're my sister and best friend."

I hear her choke on a sob and my brother's voice comes on the line. "Why are you upsetting my wife? Are you okay? Do I need to come get you?"

I sniffle. "No. I'm sorry, I just—"

"It's just my hormones," I hear Lola tell Dean before the phone rustles. "You're my family too," Lola says, and she shoos Dean away, making me laugh. "But what brought this on?"

"Long story, one I plan on telling you when I have more time. I just wanted you to know. And that I'm sorry for everything that happened."

She knows what I mean because she sighs, sounding sad. "You have nothing to apologise for. I keep telling you that. Nothing was your fault. I've never blamed you and I never will. I love you. But whatever has you thinking of all that stuff, you need to stop. We're fine now. Or is this about something else?"

I wonder if I should tell her, then decide to just go for it. "Am I on speaker?"

"No." The phone goes quiet and I hear her tell Dean she's stepping outside. "I'm in private. Now what's going on?"

I tell her all about Drake, how he makes me feel. I tell her how handsome he is, how funny, and about Aaron being here—who she already knows about. I confided in her one night when we were drunk. It took a lot of tears and three bottles of wine to get through it, but at the end of it all, she was ready to find him and kick his arse. Not that she'd hurt a fly... well, not intentionally.

"He took you to his special spot?" she asks dreamily. "This is so much better than Prince Harry. Brooke is going to throw a fit. She'll want to come out and meet him. What are you going to do now? You sound like you already have feelings for him."

I groan because I think I do. "I don't know. I'll talk to him later tonight, see where we stand."

"Send me a picture. I want to know what he looks like."

I laugh. "I can't send you a picture."

"Yes, you can." Her tone holds no nonsense, and it makes me grin. "How else can Brooke and I check him out?"

"You two are terrible. I can understand Brooke, but you have my brother."

"Yes, I do," she says, and I can hear the smile in her voice. "But you're my sister, and I want to know all about him."

"And check out his abs?"

"Just don't tell Dean."

We both giggle and the earlier memories have now gone, no longer plaguing me. "I love you."

"I love you too."

I smile, loving her to pieces. "I have to go, but I promise to keep in touch. I didn't realise how absent I've been."

"You're working. It's fine. But please keep in touch. We miss you."

"Give a kiss to Cece for me, and say hi to everyone."

"I will. Now go talk to your man. I'm going to calm mine down. I think he's in the bedroom packing, ready to come get you."

I laugh because it sounds about right. "Go on. Tell him I'm fine and was just being sentimental."

"I will."

We hang up and I look down at the phone.

"Pagan, hi."

I turn to Pam and smile, wiping under my eyes. "Hi, Pam. Everything okay?"

"Dear, are you crying? Is this a bad time, because I could come back."

I wave her off. "No, no. I was on the phone to my sister-in-law. We always get like this." It's only a semi-lie, so I don't feel ashamed saying it.

"Are you sure?"

"I'm sure. Now, what did you want to discuss?"

"My mother." She sighs, which causes my lips to twitch. "She's going to come to you. I don't know when or how, but she will, and when she does, she'll want access to the paint bowling tomorrow."

"Paintballing," I giggle. I don't have the heart to tell her Ada's already sought me out. I also don't share I want to know what she has up her sleeve.

"Paintballing. Sorry." She waves her hand, taking a deep breath. "Anyway, she was in the army back in the day and thinks she can still move like a soldier."

"She was in the army?" I ask, surprised.

"Yes. My mother will outlive everyone, I'm sure. But I'd rather she go out with old age and not because she played a part in her demise."

Laughing, I nod. "Ada most certainly will outlive everyone. I've never known anyone with such energy before. If it weren't for her looks, I'd think she was in her twenties."

She chuckles. "Don't I know it. I'm glad we had this chat though. She can be a handful at times, but she means well. Which also brings me to this. She has something planned for that boy Aaron. Whether she comes to you or not, I don't mind. He deserves it. I knew he was a bit of a... well, a skirt-chaser, but I never knew he cheated. It makes sense why we never met his ex-wife."

"Ex-wife?" I don't want to ask, but come on—Aaron and marriage seems a little far-fetched.

She looks around, making sure we're alone before leaning in closer.

"Yeah. He was married to a girl named Lisa. They weren't married long, just enough to have two kids. He doesn't see them though."

If you'd asked me years ago if hearing he got married and had two kids hurt, I would've said yes. I would've felt like I was dying inside. But oddly enough, I feel nothing.

I'm actually disgusted that he has two kids he doesn't see.

What a jerk!

"He doesn't see them?"

"No." She shakes her head, clearly disgusted herself. "I don't know why my son would associate with someone like that, someone with no loyalty or love for family. But my Jesse, he had a few problems at law school with people thinking they were above everything. Aaron helped him out, and I think he feels he owes him somehow. Either way, Aaron's always been good to him. We've never met his children, and no one brings them up."

I'm still mulling over everything, wrapping my head around it all. In the end, I can't make sense of it, so I give up trying. "It seems a shame to bring two kids into the world and not want to see them. I'm actually angry on their behalf."

She nods, agreeing. "He doesn't speak to his parents either. Something went down with them before the divorce. It's why I'm not going to get involved with whatever my mother has planned. I think he needs a little mischief."

I laugh. "Well you can guarantee that with Ada."

"Mum! Mum!" I hear Drake yell, his voice booming across the garden.

Our eyes meet, widening at the sound of pure and utter fear in his voice. We stand, turning towards the doors leading out onto the patio.

"Oh Lord, what's happening?" Pam asks with a shaky voice.

"Mum! Mum!" Jesse shrieks, and he sounds just as horrified. "Grams, please! No!"

We both rush towards the house, heading towards the garden room, where the screaming is coming from. We both stop short when we enter.

I slap a hand over my mouth to smother my laughter. Drake hears and narrows his eyes in my direction.

Sitting in the middle of the table, Ada is sipping her tea, perfectly fine and ignoring the chaos going on around her.

She's also still only wearing a bikini.

"Mother!" Pam gasps.

"Mum, sort her out. I mean it. I'm going to bleach my eyes out and see if I can find something to wipe the last ten minutes from my memory," Jesse yells, still covering his eyes. He walks into the corner of the table, cursing. "Fuck!"

"Language," Pam scolds. "Mother, what are you wearing?"

Ada gives Pam a dry look. "Are you really asking me?"

"Yes!"

"I can't. I need to... I don't know, go drown myself," Drake hisses. "We were happily eating our lunch when she walked in wearing *that*. I feel sick."

Laughing, I dodge his glare and turn to Ada. "I think maybe we should get you dressed."

She winks at me. "I'm just going to go through to the gym, see if Aaron, Jon and Adam would like some refreshments."

"Mother, no!"

"Just be anywhere but *here*," Drake whines, still not looking at his grandmother.

"You've seen this all before. I have what every woman has."

"No, Grams, you don't. I'm scarred for life. I'll never, not ever, get over this."

"Glad my body is that memorable."

"Mother! I think you've damaged my boys enough for one day. Why don't we go choose a nice outfit for the pool party?" Pam speaks to her like she's an unhinged child, and I giggle.

"A snow coat will do," Drake mutters.

Pam and Ada leave, but before they get out of earshot, Pam's panicked voice echoes into the room. "Mother, not the gym, please."

I burst out laughing, clutching my stomach as I try to catch my breath. "I love Grams."

"Makes one of us," Drake mutters.

"It could've been worse. She could've been wearing a thong."

His face turns green as he glares down at me, stepping forward. "That's so not funny."

Taking a step backwards, I shrug, grinning. "True though."

"Run," he mouths, and I squeal, running like my life depends on it.

The minute I get to the staircase, we hear Aaron, Jon and their other friend Toby yelling for help.

Ada steps into the long hallway, her grin wide.

"Fuck. I'm going. Later, gorgeous," Drake curses, slapping my arse before running up the stairs two at a time like he's on fire.

When he's out of sight, I watch Ada saunter towards me, swaying her hips from side to side.

When she reaches me, she holds her hand up for a high five. I palm her hand, still grinning and laughing lightly.

"Ah, this is going to be the best three weeks of my life," she says before heading up the stairs.

Hopefully to get some clothes on. I never want to see that view ever again.

But she has a point. This really is going to be the best three weeks. Not only for her, but for me too.

My smile is wide as I make my way back outside, ready to find the most perfect cocktail maker London has to offer.

Chapter Sixteen

*A*fter another long and successful party yesterday, I'm dying to take the day off. I'm used to my schedule being clear the day after an event to relax, but that's not the case with the Donovans since their schedule is pretty much back to back.

Today I have to go paintballing. The one and only time I've gone, I ended up with bruises the size of a tennis ball all over my body.

Alison comes barging into my room wearing cargo shorts and a green tank top. I want to roll my eyes when I see her green-painted nails and bright green eyeshadow but I don't. I should've known she'd find something to match the occasion—she always does.

Her hair is in two French braids... well, what hair she could fit into a plait. In fact, I think all of us are wearing them in two French braids. But on Alison, it makes her look like a naughty school girl.

"Come on, come on. Put this on. Look at the back!" She turns around, showing me the back of the tank top I had printed for everyone.

The girls have 'Clit, Clit, Splat' written in pink camo and the boys have 'Balls of Steel' written in blue camo.

As cute as our outfits are, it doesn't make me feel any better about getting hit with huge paintballs. I don't think Alison knows what she's gotten herself into either.

I grab the tank top and pull it over my head. "I'm so glad we don't have any parties to attend for another week."

"Why?" she asks. Her eyes scrunch up, the excitement leaving her expression.

"Because, we're—"

"Hey, the bus is here," Drake says, also barging into my room.

I roll my eyes, giving him a dry look. "Come on in."

He ignores me, a slow smirk spreading across his perfectly plumped lips. "Well look at you. Damn!"

Alison grins. "She looks hot, right?"

His eyes heat as he takes in my bare legs. Yes, Alison also bought me a pair of cargo shorts, only mine seem to be a little shorter than hers. I think she did that on purpose. "Oh she looks hot, all right."

"The bus is here," I yell, deflecting their compliments. But the look Drake is giving me has my body heating in places that just aren't appropriate right now.

As we make our way downstairs, I feel his eyes on me. It's the same look he gave me last night when he saw me wearing only a bikini and a sarong, his smouldering gaze burning into me. I was so lost in the intensity I nearly went head first into the pool. Luckily Aaron was standing directly in front of me, ogling some female wearing a barely there bikini, and saved my fall.

He didn't go out of his way to save me, of course. He was just there, and it gave me a pause to steady myself. The same can't be said for Aaron, who ended up in the water.

In all fairness, he did need cooling down based on the drool on his chin.

When we make our way outside, everyone is surrounding Aaron's car. I start giggling to myself before we even see our artwork.

Last night, after everyone had left and the Donovans had long gone to bed, Drake and I carried out our prank.

Which included a lot of Post-it notes.

"Who did this?" Aaron shouts, glaring at each of us accusingly.

A look is shared between everyone before their eyes come to Drake and me. Alison steps aside so she's standing with the group, making sure to give us the same sceptical eye.

Little traitor.

"What?" I gulp, hoping my face isn't as red as it feels with everyone's eyes on me.

Aaron turns our way and glares. "You? Again?"

"What?"

Then he steps through the crowd and a burst of laughter falls past my lips when all the bright-coloured Post-it notes come into view. But what has my laughter bubbling free is the new addition. The front windshield and front bonnet have been completely redone. Covering the front is a giant willy made of pink Post-its with yellow ones surrounding it, helping the giant penis stand out.

Who the hell did that?

I want to slap myself for even asking the question. I know exactly who did it, and wisely, she isn't here to wave us off.

"You did this! I know you did. You're the only one who hates me." Someone scoffs, then covers it up with a cough. "If this is to get my attention, you've got it. I've already told you I want you back."

It's my turn to scoff.

"Aaron, you really are big-headed. I don't want you back now or ever. And I didn't do that to your car," I tell him, pointing to the giant penis. That way I can't be caught in a lie, because I really didn't do it. Although I wish I did. It's pretty genius.

"I know you want me, Pagan. This just proves it."

How did he get that from his car being vandalised?

"No, Aaron, I really don't," I snap, then turn to the group. "Does everyone have everything?" They all nod. "Okay, let's get into the minibus."

～

What I thought would be a couple haystacks and a few wooden blocks turned out to be a huge forest sectioned off into war zones. And I'm saying that lightly since the group that just exited look like they've been in Iraq for the past year. This is nothing like the one I went to.

"I'm not sure about this," I mutter under my breath to Alison.

She grins, her excitement overshadowing my alarm. "Did you bring the box of supplies?"

Scowling, I grumble a "yes" under my breath and walk over to the waiting group. "Guys, listen up," I shout, gaining their attention. "Pam and Adam have bought you a surprise. Inside the changing rooms there is a box. They've had some bibs custom-made. The rest of the clothing should be hung up waiting. The girls' changing rooms are to the left, and boys are to the right. We meet back out here as soon as we're ready, and the instructor will go through rules and safely regulations. Does anyone have any questions?"

"Want to help me into my suit?" Bradley, Drake and Jesse's friend from growing up, flirts.

"I wasn't aware someone needed assistance in changing clothes." I try to remain as polite and professional as possible, but the way Aaron is eyeing him, like he has some claim over me, riles me up. "I can get Butch, the bloke from reception, to assist you."

I turn in that direction when he clears his throat, the guys laughing at his expense. "That won't be necessary. I'll manage."

"Good to hear."

Drake winks before heading in towards the boys' changing rooms. I can't wait to see how the bibs turned out. Usually we'd get one from here, but Pam and Adam wanted to surprise them with their own.

Pam and Adam weren't keen on the names of the teams, but they ordered them anyway. They thought it was a shame our outfits weren't going to be seen.

Bless Alison, she got all excited, telling them she was going to wear her T-shirt and bib when she got home too.

The look of horror on their faces was priceless.

Once we're all dressed and ready, the heat outside has reached its peak. I'm sweating, but nothing could make me take this uniform off. I've seen the bruises you can get with them, so I dread to think what it would be like without adequate clothing.

The instructor goes through the rules, safety procedures, and which areas to stay in. With nine huge sections, other teams are out on the field. There's also a 'dead zone' near the edge of the forest where you go when you're eliminated.

"The girls' base starts here. Boys, you'll come with me and we'll take you over to the boys' base. The flag is hanging in a tree house in the centre of your marked field. As soon as that flag is down and taken back to base, the game is over and that team has won," Garry says.

Everyone nods their understanding and the boys follow the other team leader, Imad, to their post.

"I'm so going to kill Jesse. I want him out first," Amelia giggles.

She's so much fun to be around and has a dirty mind like the rest of us. She's also one of the sweetest people I know.

"I'm hoping I'm hit first. I can see Jon and Toby ganging up on me," Hallie tells us.

I'm with her on that. I have a feeling more than one person on the boys' team is out to gun me down.

Literally.

"They just want in your pants," Gabriella giggles, but I can see the hurt in her tone and wonder if she has a crush on either Jon or Toby.

My money's on Toby. He's always staring at her when she isn't looking, and I've noticed them whispering to each other a time or two.

A horn whistles, letting us know the game has started, and we pile into the forest in pairs at full speed, making sure to keep low.

After a few minutes, I'm hitting the floor and looking around for my fellow teammates. Alison has disappeared and I can't see anyone else. Footsteps rustle close by, which has me lifting my head from the pile of rusty leaves I'm lying on. I'm about to get hit in the face when, out of nowhere, a person wearing a pink army suit with 'Ball Buster' written on the back comes rolling out from the small hill nearby. They shoot whoever was about to hit me, aiming at their nuts. I cringe as one of the lads falls down to the floor in pain.

"You saved me," I whisper, staring up at them in awe.

They lift their protective mask and I gasp.

Oh my Lord.

Save my soul.

"Ada? What on earth?"

"We don't have time. Troops are closing in on us. We need to move," she tells me sharply. I get a glimpse of the army paint smeared across her face before she pulls the mask back down.

I rush to my feet, not arguing with her. The woman just saved me from having a bruise the size of an orange on my face. I'm safer with her.

I think.

I've officially gone crazy.

If you had asked me a week ago if I felt safe with Ada, I would've looked on in horror and told you 'no' vehemently. Yet here I am, my life in her hands.

She rolls down an embankment, landing in a crouch with one knee to the floor, gesturing for me to follow.

I think about it for a second. *Why the hell not? If she can do it....*

My vision of flowing gracefully, like Ada, down the small bank is short-lived. Instead I land hard on a rock, get twigs and God knows what else stuck in my hair, and my cargo pants ride up my arse, giving me the most painful wedgie I've ever had.

I land with a thud, my head throbbing. My focus is shaky and I take a minute to get my bearings. When I do, Ada is gone.

Scared, I crouch low and find her to my left, army-crawling towards a large fallen tree trunk.

Now what is she doing?

Seconds after the thought comes to mind, her gun is blasting out balls of paint, aiming at someone in the crotch area. This time, the male roar is filled with sheer agony. I'm pretty sure it's Toby, but it's muffled behind his mask. He falls backwards, his body still, unmoving. I'm worried she may have killed him.

Then I see quick movement to my right and panic. Standing, I charge up another little embankment and dive into a pile of leaves, all the while shooting aimlessly at whoever was charging my way.

I hear a panicked male scream and roll out of the leaves, aiming anywhere and everywhere.

The screams register and I squeal with glee when I hear it's Aaron. For good measure, I try to aim for his nuts. I miss and end up running out of paintballs.

When Ada comes army-crawling over to me, she holds her gun up like a professional sniper and shoots him clean in the nuts four times before she moves on. Probably because he collapses, his eyes rolling in the back of his head.

I follow willingly, wishing Drake or Alison was nearby so they could see me right now.

Hell, if only my family could see me right now.

The tree house comes into view and I look around warily. Immediately, my head is shoved back down into the dirt and I groan in pain.

"Shit, my grandson has the flag," Ada whispers before turning to me. "This is where I leave you and bid you farewell, my child. I can go no further in this war. You have to go by yourself."

Panicked, I grab her arm, not wanting her to leave. "Don't go. I need you."

She strokes my mask as if she's running a hand down my face. I close my eyes, tears pricking my eyes.

"You need to be brave. Here, take my gun and go get that fucker." She starts crawling away but just as suddenly, she turns and comes back to me. My hope at surviving this is restored. "Don't go for the nuts. I may not be ready for a great-grandchild just yet, but I do want them eventually."

My mouth is agape as I watch her leave.

Great-grandchildren? Is that all she can think about when I've been shoved to a certain death? Bitter and angry, I turn to the scene in front of me with a new determination.

A battle roar erupts from my chest as I charge full speed towards Drake. He slowly turns from where he was hiding behind the tree, his eyes widening behind the mask. In slow motion, I watch as his finger presses down on the trigger.

I'm certain I'm about to be splatted, but when his gun makes no sound, I grin evilly behind my mask and shoot, my finger pressing down again and again until I've run out of paintballs.

He grunts as he falls to his knees, and as quickly as I can, I snatch the flag out his hand.

"Why?" he croaks, looking wounded.

"I'm the 'Clit, Clit, Splat' machine," I tell him, then turn back to the girls' base.

141

I run until I'm out of breath. When I reach the clearing where a little hutch is, I scream in triumph.

Everyone but Drake is in the 'Dead Zone'. All the men but Jesse—who's sitting on the bench with the rest of the girls—are curled up on the floor, blue ice packs pressed against their groins.

I grin, waving the flag above my head. "We won."

The girls jump up, their excited screams echoing around the forest. The men groan but I ignore them as my best friend walks up to me. She searches my face, grinning ear to ear.

"Please tell me Ball Buster wasn't Ada," she whispers, then glances around to make sure no one heard her.

"I'll never tell." I wink, making her laugh, and we walk over the group. Each girl jumps on me, congratulating me.

"You rock," Amelia says. "Jesse has to be my slave for a week now."

"I would've been you're slave anyway." He winks.

That's too cute.

"What I don't get is why everyone but you didn't get hit in the nuts." Harmony grins, then eyes something behind me. "Or your brother."

"Yeah, funny that," Aaron whines, groaning in pain.

I laugh and shrug.

"I can't believe you got me," Drake rumbles from behind me and I turn, a spring to my step as I eye him.

I'm so high on adrenaline. I could totally do this again.

With Ada of course.

"Ah, is someone sore they lost to a girl?"

He narrows his eyes, then pulls me against him. Everyone's gone on to talk about the men's nuts to mind us any. "I'm pretty sure I saw a fucking ninja out in those woods. Jon was the first to go down. One minute he was on lookout, and the next, he was on the floor screaming in agony. I saw someone climb a fucking tree and swing over to the next, getting away."

I laugh, wondering where the hell Ada learnt this shit from. And how she has the energy.

"No way." I avert my gaze a little so he can't see I'm hiding something. All I need is for them to disqualify us for having an extra member.

"And Bradley, I'm pretty fucking sure I shed a tear when the poor fucker got hit."

I laugh harder, shaking my head. "You're so dramatic."

"No I'm not. Toby got so scared he played dead." He shudders, looking over the men cowering in pain with pity.

We pull apart and a first aider walks over, heading to Aaron. "We need you to sign the incident book before you leave, sir."

Aaron glares at the young man but takes the book from his hand.

"What happened?" I ask, trying to hide my smirk.

Alison answers, not bothering to hide hers. "Seems the hit to the nuts was pretty hard. He passed out and Steve, the first aider, had to go get him. When we heard his scream cut off, the instructors got a little worried, especially with so many casualties stumbling out of the woods."

"This is the best day ever." I grin, barely holding my scream of joy inside.

"Jesse, I love you like a brother, but I'm gonna give tonight a miss. I need to ice my balls," Bradley says, groaning as he gets up.

Jesse helps Jon lift Aaron to his feet, letting him rest on their shoulders. "I think tonight we should just go home, order takeout, and crash and watch a movie."

"I think I need to go to the hospital. I swear my balls are swelling," Aaron hisses, limping.

"At least now they'll resemble real balls," Gabriella sings, giggling at the daggers Aaron sends her way.

"What do you say? Want to watch a movie with me, leave this lot to fend for themselves?" Drake whispers, and a shiver runs up my spine.

My gaze shifts his way and as seductively as I can muster—what with sweat and dirt caked on my face and in my hair—I lean up and whisper. "Are you trying to get me alone, Drake Donovan?"

"Please don't call me that," he groans, adjusting his pants. "But if you must know, yes."

I wink, then lean up and run my lips across his ear, biting the lobe before pulling back. "Then yes, I'd *love* to watch a film with you."

Chapter Seventeen

*T*he gang changed their mind about going straight home and dragged us all to a local restaurant near the manor for a bite to eat instead.

Now I'm back, showered and changed into some comfy pyjamas, wondering if Drake would mind if I crashed during the film. My body is aching all over, and I'm beyond exhausted now that the adrenaline's worn off.

But before I meet up with Drake, I have an old lady to interrogate. No one's seen her since we got back. Pam told us that, after we left, Ada went to lie down, claiming she felt under the weather. They haven't seen her since. I know better. How someone so tiny can be so fierce and energetic still surprises me. I can't wait to tell Dad all about her. Before I leave, I need to get some video evidence or he'll never believe me.

Alison steps out of the room, looking fresh but just as exhausted as me.

"Hey, how are you feeling?" I ask.

"Like my bruises have bruises and are having a rave," she moans.

I laugh, although I feel a little sympathy towards her. I've felt the after-effects of paintballing once before and, according to them, they had it rough out there.

"I know your pain, but unlike yours, mine were self-inflicted." I've already told her how I got my bruises. I have one on the back of my right shoulder, and my legs and knees are covered in them. It's just another reminder to never go paintballing again.

"It's not funny! Look at this." She lifts up her shorts, showing me the large apple-size bruise on her thigh. I wince. "And I've some on my back, one on my bum and another on my ribs. I wouldn't be surprised if I've broken one or two."

"Oh, dear. I did tell you it was lethal."

She waves me off, dropping her shorts. "It'll be fine. I'm going to see if Emily has some painkillers and a cold press. And if I'm really lucky, they'll have alcohol in the movie theatre."

I pull her in for a hug and cringe when she hisses. "Easy there, tiger. Did you not hear me say my bruises have bruises?"

"Sorry."

She grins when we pull apart, eyeing me up and down. "You're wearing that to meet Drake?"

I look down at my sleep shorts and tank top and give her a look. "Yeah, why?"

"Meh." She shrugs, her lips twisting in amusement. "Just asking."

Maybe it is a bit revealing, but it's too hot to wear anything else.

"I'm going to change."

"I'm joking." She laughs, pulling me down the hallway. "You look fine. Have fun. The others think you're having an early night. I heard Drake informing them on my way up." I grin, my excitement forgoing my exhaustion over hearing I'll have him all to myself. "You like him."

This time I smile, and sure I have stars in my eyes and am glowing. "I really do. But we spoke yesterday about whatever this is between us and, although he didn't offer much since I spoke over him, I think we agreed to keep this as a casual thing, then let it end peacefully when I have to leave."

She looks doubtful. "Okay. I'm just glad you're getting some."

I gasp. "I... I mean, we haven't, you know—" She laughs and I pout. "It's not funny."

"It is. You look so cute all flustered. Go enjoy your night. I need to tend to my wounds."

I nod, hugging her lightly this time before saying goodnight.

I'm walking up the second set of stairs on the right side of the house when I look up to find Aaron hobbling down the hallway, grimacing.

He looks like a distraught penguin.

"Pagan, were you coming to see me?"

"No." I move to step around him but he grips my bicep, stopping me. "Can we talk?"

"I have nothing to say to you, Aaron, so just leave me alone, please. I have a job to do here, and I don't want you jeopardising it."

"Look, let me just say what I need to say and then you can go, okay?"

"Hurry up. You have a minute," I huff.

"I know I'm a hard person to get over, Pagan, but can we just be civil to each other?"

Now I want to smack his baby face.

"You have a minute and you want to start with that? Because I hate to break it to you, Aaron, but I have every right to hate you. I don't care if it happened years ago or yesterday, what you did was fucking shitty. I was over you a long time ago, and you weren't that special to begin with. I was naïve to even think you were."

"You don't mean that, babe. You loved me. You still do. I can see it in the way you look at me and the way you act."

And again, I want to smack his baby face. And knee him in the balls.

"Yes, Aaron, I do. And I don't love you. I never did. I just thought I did. And I'm not saying this to hurt you. I'm telling you because it's the truth. And if I'm looking at you, which I highly doubt it, it's because you disgust me. You're a pig, and a part of me wants to believe you were never like this, but you were. I was just stupid to think otherwise. Now if you don't mind, I have things to do."

"I don't understand, Pagan. I really don't. I know I hurt you, but you must want to see where we can take this. I feel it between us still. The moment I laid eyes on you, I wanted you to be mine again."

My eyes narrow and I step forward, poking him in the chest. He winces, hissing. "Listen here, buddy. Nothing, and I mean *nothing*, is going to happen. There is fuck all between us, nothing but stale air. And just so you know, I'm not property, I'm a person. And you had me once, but you still found your way between another girl's legs."

"Are we really going there again?" he asks, clearly frustrated.

"Again? You never even gave me a chance to mention it the first time. Just leave me alone, Aaron. And I'd highly recommend you seek medical assistance, because you have a deluded mind."

"Honey bunches," Ada coos loudly. I look behind Aaron to find her strutting down the hallway wearing her famous *Game of Thrones* dressing gown and fluffy white cat slippers.

Aaron groans, cursing under his breath.

"Hi, Ada, how was your day?" I call sweetly.

"Oh, I had the poops earlier, but all is good. How was your day?" She winks as she steps closer, smacking Aaron on the arse.

He yelps, nearly falling to his knees before he uses the wall for balance. I laugh under my breath and high-five Ada whilst he isn't looking.

"Oh brilliant. Eye opening," I tell her, grinning wickedly.

"Experiences like paintballing can do that to you. And what's up, my man? You ready for round two?" She winks at me, fingering the robe at her chest as she eyes him suggestively.

Aaron looks ready to hurl, making me love Ada all the more.

"I need to go," he rushes out. "I'm sorry I have to rush off, Pagan, but I'll make it up to you."

"*Please* don't."

"See you."

He gives Ada one last look before rushing off. Once he's out of sight, we turn to each other and burst out laughing.

"I heard he passed out, the pansy."

I giggle. "He did. No one knows it was you. They think it was me, even though I kept telling them it wasn't. I'm pretty sure Drake believes he saw a real-life ninja."

Ada cackles. "Oh, his face was priceless. I have it all recorded."

"You recorded it?" I ask, shocked. "How?"

"I have my own gear, and it has a camera installed in the helmet. I'll make a copy and send it to your email."

147

"Definitely." I grin. My dad is so going to love this. "I'll text you my email later."

She waves me off. "Already have it. I must be off. I have dinner with Pam and Adam. We're going to scare the kids after."

"Scare the kids?"

What kids?

"Jesse mentioned they were watching a horror movie, so Pam and I had an idea. We have some Halloween masks that will scare the daylights out of them."

Laughing, I grab the wall for support. "You're evil."

She shrugs. "It'll toughen them up. We mostly want to scare Angela though."

"Why?" I ask, still laughing.

"Emily made her lunch earlier and because it wasn't to her standards, Angela threw the hissy fit to end all hissy fits. Me? I would've tanned her hide, but my poor Emily was scared out of her mind."

I want in on what she has planned. "Why on earth would she do that to poor Emily? She's tiny and the kindest person to everyone, even when they're rude. Has she informed Pam?"

"It was Pam who came to me. Luckily I'd just come out of the bathroom and changed out of my gear when she walked in. It was a close call. My Pam doesn't like conflict. She's always been kind-hearted, ever since she was a baby. Sometimes, something will push her to the brink, but with the wedding so close, she doesn't want anything to ruin it. She's worried Angela will take it out on Amelia, so she called in the big guns."

"I thought she asked you for help?" I ask, dumbfounded.

She gives me a dry look. "I am the big gun."

I grin. "But scaring the others doesn't seem fair. She needs something done to her. In fact, I have an idea. They're all meeting for drinks in the garden room, aren't they?"

She eyes me warily. "Yeah, they are. Why?"

"Go find Angela. Tell her they're meeting outside. Drake's roof is above the patio."

"I'm not following. What are *you* going to do?"

She says it like I'm a measly child. I grin. "You gave me a box, remem-

148

ber? I've got bangers and water balloons left. I'm going to fill them with flour and water."

She grins, her eyes sparkling. "Oh my. Let me get Pam in on this. You go get the supplies and I'll meet you upstairs in thirty minutes."

❧

"I'm not sure about this," Pam whispers, looking over the side of the balcony once again.

Drake chuckles, winking at me. "Mum, she's never going to know it was us. I promise."

"But it's mean, isn't it?"

Ada scoffs, bringing the last of the balloons inside. She insisted on filling them up, I've suddenly realised why—she's filled them with dye of some sort. I don't say anything, knowing Pam will back out if she knows about it. When I eye the bags of flour, I have to bite my lip from asking her what she has planned.

"Pammy, do you remember the look on Emily's face? The tears that ran down her cheeks and how distraught she was to have her first complaint? Are you going to let her down, let the team down, for some uppity little wench?"

I watch in amazement as Pam's back straightens and her shoulders roll back. A look of determination takes over her face as she crosses the small balcony to the bucket of water bombs. She grabs one, then looks at her mother with all seriousness. "I can do this. Nobody messes with my staff and lives to tell the tale. Emily's been good to us. She helped raise my sons. How dare she insult her."

"That's the spirit," Ada cheers, grabbing a few of her own.

Drake moves closer. "Um, Grams, are they—"

"Shush now, my boy. It's grown-up time," Ada snaps, gazing over the edge.

"But I think you've filled them—"

"I said shush. I think I hear her coming."

"How?" Pam whispers, looking to her mother.

"Instincts."

149

Drake and I stare at each other before finally giving in and shrugging. We carry the bombs over to the wall and take our own balloons.

"Here, you do these. I'll do the bombs," I tell him, handing him the bangers.

"No, I'll do the bombs. I have better aim."

He tries to take the bomb off me but I pull it back, frowning. "No, I'll do it. I want to, please."

"No, I'll do it. You'll completely miss and it'll be a waste of a bomb."

We play tug of war on the balloon before it bursts, landing mostly on Drake's clean shirt and my feet. I gasp, covering the giggle with my hand.

He narrows his eyes on me. "Seriously?"

"Sorry?"

"You don't look it," he states dryly.

I wink. "Really."

His lips twist into amusement and he shakes his head. "Cute. You're fucking cute. Let's just do them together, okay?"

"Okay, here."

He grins, taking them from me, and I fight hard not to laugh at the sight of him.

"On three," Ada orders sternly, a bomb in one hand and a bag of flour in the other. I giggle, earning a glare from her. "One, two, three."

We all stand up and Pam, being Pam, screams as she throws her balloon down. Angela's eyes widen, but before she can move, the ground around her is popping from the bangers, making her jump and scream. And when the first balloon hits, her wails turn into screeches of horror before she's choking on flour.

Her hair is matted down the front of her face, covered in blue, green, yellow and red dye mixed with flour. Ada doesn't give her chance to recover before she's aiming more bombs her way. We all follow and, to my amusement, Pam's giggling like a schoolgirl, throwing more and more until we run out. I'm about to throw the last of the bangers, but heads popping out from the side door grab my attention. As one, they all look up, and a startled scream escapes me before I dive to the floor.

The floor isn't what I land on though—it's Drake. He grins up at me, his eyes glowing. "Miss me?"

"They're outside," I whisper-hiss, wiggling.

He groans. "Don't move on me like that with my mother and Grams about."

Since he sounds pained, I do it again, giggling at his expression. "Sorry."

"We have to go. We need to get downstairs so we don't get accused," Ada orders.

Still lying on Drake, I turn their way, Drake following with narrowed eyes.

"So you're going to lay the blame on us?"

Ada looks at me like I'm stupid. "If you knew what was good for you, you'd run too. But you look comfy." Then she grins, winking at me.

"Shit. We need to go," Drake says as Angela screams that she's going to kill whoever's up here.

My eyes widen and I burst into laughter before struggling to get up. "Grab the film. We can watch it in your room."

"If you wanted in my bed so badly, you should've just asked me, sweetheart."

I growl, then point to my left. "They abandoned us. We need to go and make it look like we had nothing to do with it."

He frowns, noticing they've gone for the first time, then looks down. "I have dye all over my shirt," he screeches, sounding like a girl.

Clutching my belly from laughing so hard, I try to tell him it's fine, but it's not. Not only does he have it on his shirt, but I have it on my knees and toes. There's no way we'll get away with it if they see us.

"Grab the drinks from the fridge and some snacks, quick," he rushes out.

He doesn't bother to look at what films he grabs before we both head downstairs. We barely make it to his door when we hear everyone running up the stairs after Angela, who's screaming like a banshee.

The door slams shut behind us and all I can hear is our heavy breathing. Drake's phone going off breaks through the silence and he walks over to his bed, picking it up. He grins before typing back.

"What?" I ask, walking over.

"Jesse took a picture of Angela and posted it on his Facebook. He tagged me in it." He laughs, still typing away.

I take the phone from him. My laugh is loud and hard, and a snort escapes. In the photo, Angela's covered in red dye and flour, but it's the furious expression on her face that has me doubling over. It's mid-scream, and I can actually see the veins in her neck and temples, she's that mad.

"Oh my God. I can't breathe," I wheeze.

He's laughing too as he pulls me down onto the bed, laying us back before manoeuvring so he's draped over me, keeping his weight off me. "This has been the best week of my life. And it's all because of you."

My laughter fades and a shy smile reaches my lips as I blush. "Thank you. It's been mine too. Thank you."

His smile is warm as he reaches out, tucking a strand of hair behind my ear. In a blink, his lips are seductively brushing against mine, once, twice, before he pulls back, staring down at me longingly. Unable to help myself, I wrap my hands around his neck, pulling his lips down to mine.

I thread my fingers through his short hair, pressing my body closer, desperate for more. He drops his weight on me and I welcome it, loving the feel of his hard body pressing between my thighs.

This is a kiss most women fantasise about having, and I have no doubt that Drake is one of only a few men who can pull it off.

I want more—no, need more. I need *him*.

I'm about to open my mouth to tell him just that when the door bursts open and a throat clears.

We pull apart and turn to the door, my cheeks heating at Jesse's amused expression as he leans against the doorframe.

"Sorry to interrupt your... um... whatever this is." He grins, gesturing to our very compromising position. I quickly jump up from the bed, hoping I don't look guilty.

"We... I—"

"Go away," Drake snaps, saving me from embarrassing myself further.

"Love to, but Angela is on a mission for your balls. She's two seconds away from finding out the attic is yours and will be on her way here. I came to warn you."

"Why would she care if the attic's mine?" Drake asks, sounding casual. My face heats further and I have to gaze down at the floor to hide my smirk.

"Well, can you believe she got attacked by dye bombs and flour? She's currently covered in it from head to toe. She just had a facial, massage, and other things done, so she's seriously pissed."

"And what does that have to do with me?"

Jesse clears his throat, eyeing Drake up and down, and starts chuckling. "Bro, you're covered in fucking dye."

He looks down. "Shit."

"Drake Donovan!" Angela screams from down the hallway.

Drake and I turn to each other with wide eyes. He launches himself at me, whipping his shirt off on the way before grabbing me around the waist and throwing me over his shoulder.

"Drake!" I yell, slapping his bare, muscled back. "Put me down."

"No." I watch as he kicks his top under the bed before throwing me in it.

"What are you doing?"

Instead of answering, he jumps on top of me and pulls the covers over us before slamming his lips down on mine in a hungry kiss. I try to pull away but he growls deep in his throat, stopping me.

"Ew, gross," Angela hisses. I try to shift but Drake pins me in place, continuing his assault.

"Do you mind?" Drake asks casually, looking over his shoulder. "I'm busy."

I punch his shoulder. "Drake!"

"Clearly, and with the help," she replies snottily. "And Jesse, does Amelia know you like to watch your brother fornicate with the help?"

"Fornicate?" Jesse chokes out.

"Fornicate," I mouth to Drake, who's trying to hold back his laughter.

"Whatever," Angela huffs. "I'll get to the bottom of this. Obviously Drake didn't do this to me."

I listen to her footsteps fade away before glaring at Drake. "Really? You manhandled me into bed so she wouldn't question you?"

"It worked, didn't it?" His gaze shifts to my lips. "And you needed to cover your legs."

I shake my head, ready to hand him his balls, but footsteps coming towards the room stop me. I start to squirm underneath him, praying they don't walk in. "Oh my God, move. People are coming."

"Stop squirming, you're making it—"

"Hard?" Jesse chokes out, laughing.

Drake ignores him, as do I. "Get off me."

"But we were having so much fun." He smirks down at me, his dark eyelashes fanning his cheeks.

My eyes narrow. "Arsehole." I pinch his nipple, making him curse.

"Aw, we're having a sleepover," Amelia squeals as she and the others pile into the room.

Having no choice but to let me push him off, Drake falls to the floor as Alison eyes me, grinning and mouthing "Hot" with a wink.

"We're not having a sleepover," Drake growls, clearly frustrated.

"But you have the movies and snacks," Amelia points out just as Gabriella and Harmony drag two beanbags into the room.

"Movie time," Gabriella squeals, flopping down.

Alison comes to sit next to me on the bed as Drake takes the other side, pouting. But as I look around the room at the people I now call friends, I can't find it in me to complain. I've grown close to each and every one of them.

Though I had been excited about enjoying a night alone with Drake.

Maybe tomorrow.

"We'll pick up where we left off later," he whispers, dropping back against his pillows with a sigh.

I smile, hoping he keeps that promise.

Chapter Eighteen

The night before last, Drake woke me at three in the morning after a night of watching dreadful horror movies with the others, having been called into work. I presumed he was in for the day, but when he still hadn't returned to the manor two days later, I was beginning to worry.

"Hey, Ada, can I... um, what are you doing?" I ask, worried about her mental stability.

"Being tortured," she snaps.

"With knitting needles?"

"Yes." Her harsh glare has me moving back a step.

"Um, can I ask why?"

"Because," she drags out, her voice full of sarcasm, "Pammy found my paintballing gun in the shed." I'm shocked to say the least. I thought Ada would cover her tracks better. "I forgot to clean a splatter off my suit."

"Sooo you're knitting because she found your stuff?"

"Not by choice. If I want to go the bachelorette party, I have to show my Pammy that I can do something people my age do. She handed me these." She throws the offending objects on the table next to her. "I'd rather stab my eyeballs with those needles than try to knit again."

"Okay."

She rolls her eyes at me. "Drake said to tell you his battery went. And because he's stuck in the new ways, he just programs a number into his phone and never looks at it again, so he couldn't ring you from another phone. He wanted you to know he'll be back later and to wear something nice."

"Something nice?" I repeat, though I'm relieved that he's okay.

"Don't you have anything nice? I can lend you my—"

"Nope, it's fine," I interrupt. "I'll let you get back to... yeah, I need to go. Speak to you later."

Rushing away, I head upstairs to find Alison before Ada forces me to wear one of her outfits. She's been avoiding Angela since yesterday when they had their dress fitting, and I don't blame her. Angela had been a nightmare, acting like a disobedient child.

"Pagan!"

My groan is audible as I turn around to find Aaron walking towards me. "Aaron."

"We need to talk about the bachelor party," he tells me matter-of-factly.

"We do?" I ask, confused. The bachelor party is already planned. They're going out in the day to watch a tennis tournament—boring, I know—and then they're off to some high-end club where they've rented a private room with a bar. Jesse asked for a live band to play, since they're his favourite, so I can't possibly fathom what could need discussing about it.

"Yes!" he says curtly, the pleading Aaron I've grown accustomed to over the past several days now gone. "You need to book strippers." Stunned, I can only stare as he continues. "None of this pansy band shit."

Snapping out of it, I reply, "No. Jesse asked for the band, so he's getting it. He's the one getting married, not you." I turn to leave but he stops me, grabbing my bicep. *I wish he'd stop doing that.* I turn to him, fire in my eyes. "The next time you put your hands on me, you're going to regret it."

He grins, but it's malicious. "Right. Just do your job. It's what you're hired to do. I expect strippers to be there. I'm paying for the bachelor party, so you'll do as I ask."

"And if I don't?" I bite back, clenching my fists.

He tilts his head to the side, eyeing me up and down. "Then you lose your job. Not only would you have fucked up a direct order, but if Pam and Adam find out you've been fucking their son too...." He shakes his head, clearly disgusted.

My eyes water as I take a step back. "Goodbye, Aaron."

I've been spoken to like crap before, but never, and I mean never, have I been degraded to that level. I've also never been blackmailed before.

I storm into Alison's room. "I'm going to bloody kill him."

"Who?" she asks, moving away from the window.

"Aaron." My temper is boiling, tears of frustration and anger falling down my cheeks as I pace back and forth.

"What did he do now?"

The venom in her voice doesn't surprise me. She hates him just as much as me, since any time they're in the same room he's staring at her boobs.

"Ordering me around and telling me how to do my job," I hiss.

"Huh?" She clearly wasn't expecting that.

"Yeah. Telling me—no, *demanding* I order strippers for the bachelor party. When I said no, that I had already discussed and planned it with Jesse, he said he'd get me fired for fucking up a direct order, and threatened to tell Pam and Adam I'm fucking their son."

"You've slept with Drake?" she shrieks, her face lighting up.

"No," I shriek back, rearing my head back in shock. *Is that all she got out of my little declaration?*

"Oh." She sounds disappointed as she flops down onto the bed before her eyes narrow dangerously. "That egotistic arsehole. I have a mind to go find him and shove his dick down his throat."

I laugh. "I know! I didn't know what to do. I was too stunned over the fact that he wasn't hitting on me to say anything. I just stormed off. Now I wish I'd kneed him in the balls. Better yet, I'm going to order his goddamn strippers. He only said strippers, after all. He didn't specify what gender."

Alison squeals, running to her laptop on the dresser. "I have the perfect idea. You know the people we hired for Amelia's bachelorette party?"

"Yeah," I answer warily as I step up beside her, looking over her shoulder at the screen. Then I grin, wondering how I never thought of this. "But what about the others?"

"Who cares." She shrugs. "They're to blame by default. He's *their* friend."

"Very true. They can all make him suffer further for making them suffer. You're a genius."

"No, *we're* genius. Now, I hear Drake is picking you up at five. Want to go dress shopping?"

"How did you know?"

She smiles. "I have my ways. Now come on."

Bloody Ada.

She's rubbing off on my staff now.

Rolling my eyes, I follow her out of the room, excited to see what Drake has planned for tonight. I just hope it doesn't involve paintballs, crazy grandmas, dye bombs or itching powder.

To miss someone after only knowing them eleven days is madness, but I do. So when Drake steps into the foyer, looking dapper in a suit, I smile wide and run up to him, jumping in his arms.

"Miss me?" His chuckle is deep as he swings me around once before dropping me to my feet. I breathe him in, my smile never dropping.

"Nope. I just knew you missed me, so I thought I'd save you the embarrassment of running and jumping in my arms."

He grins. "Smartarse."

"I try." I shrug, still smiling.

He kisses the tip of my nose before taking my hand in his. "There's a taxi waiting outside."

"Where are we going?"

"It's a surprise."

"What's the surprise?" I prod.

He turns to give me a dry look and I giggle. "Just trust me, okay. You'll love it."

"Oh all right." I sigh, pretending I'm put out when really I'm dancing with excitement.

He chuckles and opens the taxi door for me. I step inside, feeling his eyes on my arse when I do.

Tonight, I decided to wear a white strapped dress to show off my tan. I have a black short-sleeved blazer since it's cooled down, and a black pair of ankle boots. I wasn't sure where we were going, but the dress can be for anything. And since I accessorised the outfit with gold bangles and necklace, I think I look pretty darn good.

Drake is wearing a dark blue shirt with a couple of the top buttons undone, making him look drop-dead sexy. He's mouth-watering at the best of times, but when he dresses up, he's a knockout.

We only travel twenty minutes before the taxi pulls up near the boating docks on the River Thames. A massive boat is docked, passengers milling around and talking, some already walking on the boat. My face must be full of surprise when Drake glances in my direction because he chuckles, taking my hand.

"Come on."

"Are we going for a romantic walk along the river?" I gasp, teasing him.

He's adorable when he frowns. "Um, I—"

I laugh at his expression. "Come on. I've never been on a boat on the River Thames before."

He looks shocked. "You've never been on a boat? But don't you live in Winchester? That's surrounded by water."

"I said I'd never been on a boat on the River Thames, not that I hadn't been on a boat," I giggle.

We walk hand in hand down the wooden platform, smiling at other passengers as we pass. The boat is lit up with round glowing lights around the edge, and on the top and bottom decking are tables with candles flickering.

"Let's get seated. I heard they serve the best steak ever," he tells me, helping me up the steps.

"As long as it's not sushi, I'm good."

He chuckles, moving to my side as we walk up to the hostess stand. "Hi, we have a table booked under Donovan."

The waitress, dressed in a black pencil skirt and black shirt, with the boat's logo on the breast, paired with a white tie, looks Drake up and down, licking her lips suggestively.

My eyes flicker to Drake, waiting for his reaction. From what I've read, if he simply ignores her, he's a keeper, but the second he engages or even shows a hint of approval, it's time to walk away and never look back.

But when I look at Drake, he's doing none of those things. Instead he's smiling down at me, not even registering the girl's flirtation.

"What?" I ask when he doesn't look away.

His eyes are doing that darn sparkling thing, shining brightly at me. It doesn't escape his notice when a sigh—like I always do when he does it—escapes.

"Did I tell you how beautiful you look tonight?"

No, he hadn't, and I melt, grinning like a fool. "No, but thank you. You don't look so bad yourself."

"Not so bad?" He chuckles, winking at me. We both know damn well I think he's hot. My jaw practically hitting the floor when I first saw him said it all.

"Excuse me!" the hostess says rather loudly. I'd forgotten she was even there.

"Sorry," Drake replies, not looking sorry at all.

She smiles coyly at him. "It's fine. Let me show you to your seats. If you need anything, and I mean *anything*, just call me. I'm Clarissa." She grins, practically drooling over him.

If she knew how hot he looked naked, she'd pass out.

"If you and your sister would like to follow me."

I rear back, disgusted she would even have the gall to say something like that in front of me, especially when he was distinctly checking me out not a few seconds ago.

"She is not my sister," he says loudly, looking offended. "What kind of guests do you have on board?"

My cheeks heat, but I swallow the laughter bubbling up my throat. She glances around, horrified. A few guests have stopped talking, staring our way to see what the commotion and hold-up are about. And when a man in a crisp black suit walks briskly our way, I know he's the boss. It's written all over his face.

"I'm—I—" she stutters, but in the end she wisely snaps her mouth shut, her face now red.

"Hello, may I be of assistance?" the burly man asks, his rounded belly sticking out of too-tight trousers.

"I most certainly hope you can. I want to know what kind of boat you're running."

"It's a restaurant on the water, sir."

"Then why did she just accuse my date of being my sister after I'd just been flirting and practically undressing her with my eyes? Hell, look at us. Do we look like siblings?" The manager, who seems more appalled by Drake's outburst than the girl, turns bright red. When he turns his glare Clarissa's way, I feel a tiny bop of sympathy for her. She looks like she's going to get her arse handed to her.

"I didn't—"

"Clarissa, why on earth would you say such a thing? You can clearly see the young couple is in love," he snaps before turning back to us. "I apologise for the misunderstanding. Please take a fifty-percent discount on your meals as an apology."

I'm shocked to say the least, because this place looks expensive.

Drake stands up straighter. "We will. Thank you for your hospitality."

The man seems to relax. "I'll show you to your seats," he tells us, quickly looking at the clipboard Clarissa is holding.

"Donovan," she whispers.

"Ah, follow me."

The man walks ahead and, with a snarl from Clarissa, we walk off. I'm half tempted to turn around and stick my tongue out at her. What did she expect? She was trying to belittle me in front of Drake, knowing full well I was his date.

"You're a mean man, Drake Donovan," I whisper, giggling.

He chuckles, staring down at me lovingly. "Serves her right. She openly flirted, then had the nerve to insinuate that you're my sister."

"I'm too awesome to be related to you."

He shakes his head in amusement. "At least we get a discount. Not that I cared about paying, of course. It's just a bonus."

"Devious man."

He smirks, then turns to the manager who's waiting for us to arrive at our table. We're right next to the edge, overlooking the water, and I gasp at how beautiful it is.

He really does make it hard to keep my feelings at bay when he does things like this.

"It's beautiful," I gush. He pulls my chair out, then pushes it in for me when I take a seat. My smile widens at the chivalrous act. My father does it for my mother all the time, but they're... well, old. I never expected to be treated like a princess. "Thank you so much for bringing me."

"Oh, it's my pleasure." He winks.

~

After having one of the best nights of my life, and what has to be considered the most romantic night I've ever had, or ever known about, I can't seem to keep the smile off my face.

When Drake said he had another surprise for me, I expected him to take me somewhere else, but when we arrived at the manor, I got confused.

Instead of going inside though, he pulled me round the back where a grinning Jeff waited with a bag. He handed it to Drake before bidding us a good night.

Drake didn't stop to exchange pleasantries, just nodded and headed to the right.

When I realised where we were going, my heart began to beat faster. He was taking me to his favourite spot, and to me, that was more special than any gift a man could buy a woman.

"Where are all the lights?" I ask as we near the large oak tree, the same one we sat next to the first time we came here.

"Jeff must've taken them down. I put them up." He passes the oak tree, surprising me, but then I see a large thin garden mattress on the ground. It belongs on one of the sunbathing beds in their little hut. I've been wanting to lounge on it since I first saw it, but I know if I ever lay on it with the heat we've been having, I'll fall asleep.

He throws some blankets onto the mattress and sits down, grinning up at me and holding his hand out. I take it, sitting next to him, still stunned. The night went from romantic to magical.

No one has ever done anything so special for me in my life. Nothing could beat tonight, nothing whatsoever.

"Lie back," he whispers.

"Why?" I ask, looking around but seeing nothing.

He glances at his watch and pulls me down next to him. "Look up."

I do as he says and squeal when the sky fills with fireworks. Not just the crappy ones my brother always seems to get but giant ones, filling the sky in the most spectacular arrangements I've ever seen.

"Oh my God. It's breathtaking."

"Yeah," he replies hoarsely. I shift my head in his direction to find him staring down at me intensely. My heartbeat picks up and I stop breathing.

"Drake," I whisper, right before his lips meet mine.

Hungrily, I kiss him back, pouring everything into the kiss that I know will change my life forever. It's different from the other ones we've shared. It's more intense, demanding, and needy. I'll never be able to get enough of him.

My legs open on their own accord, letting him fit perfectly between my thighs. I gasp when his erection presses against me, whimpering when he pulls away.

He chuckles against my neck before kissing down my collarbone, sliding the thin straps of my dress down for better access.

I moan, breaking out in goosebumps. "Oh God."

His hands finds their way up my body, trailing over every dip and curve before finally cupping my breasts, leaving them aching and begging for more.

When I become restless, Drake keeps his assault up with his talented mouth.

I'm completely lost in the sensations running through me, fuelling a need inside me until it screams to burst free.

That's when I do something I never expected—I push Drake off me.

At first he seems confused, a flicker of worry and hurt flashing in his eyes. His mouth opens when I straddle him, undoing his buttons as I lean down, capturing his mouth with mine. He moans into my mouth, and with one swipe of his tongue I'm lost again, nearly forgetting what my goal is. And that's to have this incredibly sexy, intelligent, funny man inside me.

"Pagan," he hisses, sounding pained, and I realise I'm rubbing myself against him aggressively, desperate to find the friction my body craves.

I want to tell him it's not me, it's my body, but it would be a lie. This is all me. My body has a mind of its own, like it's synced to his somehow and knows what he needs—what *we* need.

"I want you," I whisper against his lips.

"Are you sure?"

"Pretty darn sure."

I squeal as he flips me over, looming over me. He loses his shirt quickly, unbuttoning his trousers but going no further to remove them. I'm worried he's changed his mind, but his fingers running up my bare thighs has my core tightening, begging to be touched.

"I'm going to worship you, Pagan. I'm going to devour every inch of you until you can barely scream my name, and even then I'll keep going," he growls, and in one swift movement he has my dress off, leaving me in only a pair of white lace knickers.

His eyes are fierce, and chest heaving. "Christ, you're so goddamn beautiful."

"Please, Drake."

He quickly kicks off his trousers and boxers, grabbing a condom from his pocket before moving back up my body. "I didn't have this thinking we would—"

I kiss him, shutting him up. "I know."

His gaze burns into me, seeming to reach right into my soul. He looks like he's about to say something but changes his mind as he leans down, kissing me once more with a fiery need.

The rustle of the condom wrapper has me squeezing my thighs together in anticipation. It's been too long since I've been with a man, and back then, Aaron was just a boy. He never made me feel like the world was imploding around me with just a kiss, or made my pulse pick up speed with just one heated look. No, Drake is different, and being with him will be more than I ever dreamt of.

His fingers slide through my folds and he growls. "Fuck, you're so wet."

He positions himself at my core before leaning down and kissing my lips gently. "Are you ready?"

Am I?

It's a loaded question because I've never wanted anything more in my life. On the other hand, am I ready for the heartbreak I know is soon to follow when I have to leave him behind?

"Yes."

The moment he enters me, I know I've fallen in love with him.

And I've only known him eleven days.

Chapter Nineteen

I'm a chicken.

A big, fat, nerdy chicken.

After spending hours under the stars worshipping my body like he promised, and bringing me to five orgasms, Drake and I fell asleep in each other's arms. But when I woke up at four this morning, I looked over at the man I've fallen in love with and got scared.

There's no way in hell he loves me back. Not in eleven days, now twelve. I feel stupid. I promised myself not to let my feelings get involved, but it happened anyway, and now I'm *in love* with a man I can't have.

I'm so beyond stupid.

He looked so peaceful sleeping, the blanket draped across his lower half, showing off his cut abs. I knew then and there that a man like Drake Donovan could never fall for someone like me.

So I ran.

Don't hate me. I did say I was stupid.

I made sure he was covered, and as quietly as I could, I got dressed and went to my room.

Last night was perfect. More than perfect. He took me places I've never been before, made me feel things I've never experienced before. I'll never feel that intensity with another man again, of that I'm certain.

Because he's special. One of a kind. And now I've gone and royally fucked it up by running.

"Hey, we're—why aren't you dressed?" Alison asks, stepping into my room and closing the door behind her.

"I'm not feeling too well," I lie, sniffling for effect.

"Uh-huh," she mutters, clearly not believing me. She sits next to me and asks, "Was he not good in bed?"

"Alison!" I squeal, my face burning.

She grins. "What? I'm your best friend. I can ask these things. I knew he was too good to be true."

"No, he isn't. He's perfect. But I fucked up this morning. I panicked when I woke up, so I... left him sleeping outside.

"You had sex outside?" she shouts in my face, grabbing my shoulders.

I slap her away. "None of your business." She frowns, pouting, but I don't give in. "It was amazing. But I can't go today and face him, not after leaving him there."

"I've not seen him this morning," she says, looking over her shoulder like he'll magically appear. "I can't believe you just left him."

"What do you mean?"

She shrugs. "I had breakfast with Emily this morning. She was teaching me how to bake bread."

I grin, rolling my eyes. "It doesn't matter anyway."

"Why did you run away?" She looks me in the eye. If there's one thing Alison's good at, it's reading people's emotions. "Oh my gosh, you love him?"

I drop my head, sighing. "Yes."

"And why did that scare you?"

"Are you my shrink now?" I snap.

She just grins. "I'd make an awesome shrink."

"No you wouldn't," I mumble. "Now leave me alone. Don't you have somewhere to be?"

"Not for another half hour. Now spill, or I'll have to take action into my own hands and nipple twist you."

"You wouldn't!" I gasp, covering my precious nipples.

"Oh I would, so get talking."

I sigh. "It won't work out. It's been twelve days and I love him? It's utter madness. Who does that? Me, that's who. All I've done is set myself up for heartache."

The pity looks she gives make me want to slap her. Almost. "Have you ever thought the reason you've never dated is because you knew they weren't the one? You took a chance on a guy, Pagan, and it must've been fate because look at you. You can't even look at him without going all googly-eyed on him. And don't even get me started on the coy looks you share when you think no one's looking. If he doesn't love you, I'll eat my hat."

Her words register, but I don't have the energy to keep arguing. One, because I was kept up most of the night being made love to, and second, because I'm emotionally drained. I'm a sensitive person by nature, always have been this way. I let things get to me easily if I'm deeply involved in something. And in a way, Alison's right; my heart hasn't let me love since Aaron, and even that was puppy love. What I feel for Drake is explosive, world-changing and empowering.

"You don't wear hats," I reply sarcastically, to which she rolls her eyes.

There's a knock at the door. Before I have chance to tell them to go away, it opens, revealing a panicked Drake.

"I'm sorry. I knew I fucked up. I should've waited," he rushes out, then actually blushes when he sees I'm not alone. "Oh, hey, Alison."

She grins, getting up. I want to drag her back down and beg her to stay, but she just winks at me before leaving. "Hey. I'll speak to you guys later."

When the door shuts behind her, Drake walks over to me, his steps unsure and slow. For the first time since I met him, he looks uncomfortable.

"Did I rush you? Hurt you? I'm so sorry I messed this up."

Heart melting again. He's just too darn sweet.

"Drake," I whisper, giving him a small smile. "You could never hurt me. I just got a little overwhelmed."

He seems to relax, sitting next to me. "It was intense." He pauses, his soft gaze catching mine. "Pagan... last night was the best night of my life. I, I—"

"Cooey," Ada sings as she walks into my room, stopping whatever Drake was going to say. A part of me wants to thank her, but the other wants to strangle her. "Boy, you need to get going downstairs. You leave in ten minutes."

"Don't you mean *we?*" he asks, eyeing his grandmother's outfit, which is exactly what I've been doing. Instead of the normal racecourse attire where people dress to the nines, Ada is wearing a purple Juicy Couture tracksuit.

"No, I'm staying home with my girl. We have some wedding stuff to do."

We do?

"You're not coming to the races?" he asks. He looks disappointed, and it makes me feel guilty.

"I have a lot to finish." Which isn't a lie. I have some stuff I need to get rid of from Ada's box, and today's perfect since no one will be here.

"Oh. Will you be free when I get back?"

Ada puts her hands on her hips. "Drake, she'll be here when you get back. Now go. You need to explain to your mother why you slept naked in the garden last night. She's worried she might have to call a doctor."

I bite back laughter when his face turns a bright shade of red, his eyes widening in horror. "What?"

"She also said she could've sworn she saw a half-naked woman next to you, but when she went out with more blankets, it was only you there."

Now it's my turn to be horrified. Ada winks at me, which only makes this more mortifying.

"I wondered where the extra blankets came from," he murmurs, almost to himself.

It makes me smile. He looks so boyish when he's deep in thought. It's cute. "Go. I'll be fine. Have fun, and make sure you put a bet down for me."

He smirks. "And what do I get for doing it?"

"Get your mind out of the gutter. I'm standing right here," Ada snaps.

He doesn't even seem embarrassed. "Then go away," he teases.

I gasp. "Drake!"

He shakes his head, cursing. "I'm going. But the moment I'm back, Grams, she's mine."

"Good for you. Now scoot."

I laugh as he walks out, staring longingly at me one last time before shutting the door behind him.

I turn to Ada, smiling. "You don't need to stay back with me."

"Oh I was staying anyway. I'm banned from the horses."

That doesn't surprise me, but I still ask, "Why?"

She scoffs. "Some weasel rigged the race. My horse was clearly in for the win, and some little kid spooked it with a toy snake."

"A toy snake? Are kids allowed at the races?"

"Yeah, I've got the bloody thing in an evidence bag in my room. He waved that thing around like a bloody psychopath."

"That doesn't explain how you got banned." *I hope this isn't going to end with the police.*

"I confronted the kid, and then the manager got involved. We had words, and just when I thought he was coming around to my terms, he called security. It was all a misunderstanding anyway. I was never going to really fill his house with live snakes."

I curl into a ball, laughing harder than I have in ages. "You didn't!"

She chuckles. "I really did, but if Pammy ever asks, I never said anything of the sort. She still thinks to this day that the boy hit me with the snake. I told her I'd never step foot inside the place again after the management refused to do anything."

"And she believed you?" Somehow, I can't see that happening. Pam is more clued in to Ada's ways than she thinks. After all, Pam learnt from the best.

"Of course she does. I had a bruise to prove it."

I laugh. "How on earth did you get a bruise if he never really hit you?"

"I may or may not have shouldered the manager as I was being escorted out. We were on the stairs. He went down and pulled me with him."

Legend.

"Oh, Ada, you've made my day."

"I thought my grandson did that last night."

I didn't think my face could burn any redder. I was wrong. "Let's change the subject. What did you want to do?"

"Alison told me your plan for the bachelor party."

Ah, devious Alison. I'm still unsure whether I should be worried about the close connection the two seemed to be getting.

"Great, isn't it? But I was actually planning on doing something today. You want in?"

"Do pigeons shit?"

I laugh and grab the box she gave me. "Let's do this."

~

This really isn't a good idea.

We could seriously do some damage to Aaron's mental stability.

I can't seem to care.

"Are you sure this is a good idea? Alison said he's pretty wasted. Apparently he's been getting extra male sexual positions messaged to him today."

"Did they include pictures?" Ada asks, stopping what she's doing to look at me.

I grin evilly. "Yes, and went into detail about how good sex is with another male. We might end up giving him a heart attack."

"We've given him a glass of water," she says incredulously.

"It has laxative in," I remind her.

"We're still being nice. I'll even leave a couple of paracetamol next to it."

We've somehow managed to form the shape of a human body, wrapping sheets around pillows and blankets. We even went as far as to get some red food dye to make it look authentic.

This was my idea, but then Ada decided to put laxative in his drink and swap his loo roll for duct tape.

"What shall we do with it before he comes back?" I muse, looking around his room. They're due back any minute, and from what Alison said, he's completely wasted and falling asleep in the back of the car.

"Let's put it in the wardrobe until he comes back. When he passes out, I'll come in and put it in the bed next to him. Did you put the snake in the shower?"

Laughing, I nod. "And the mat I picked up." The bath mat, if you can call it that, turns red when it's wet. The minute he steps out of the shower, he's going to leave red footprints and crap his pants.

"Ah yes, I'll be visiting there once I'm done for the day. My Pammy is going to love them."

Oh no. Now I regret telling her where I got it. It was a slip of the tongue, and I wasn't really thinking.

"I don't think you should—"

"They're here," she tells me, looking out the window.

"Come on." I help her shove the blanket human into the wardrobe before leaving the room, making sure everything is how we found it —sort of.

"Do you think I'll get the blame?" I ask. When I get no answer, I turn, not finding her. "That sneaky old woman."

My phone beeps.

ADA: Can't be seen together.

Yeah right.

More like she doesn't want to be associated with me when I get the blame.

I meet the others at the door, gasping when Jesse and Drake walk in first supporting a passed-out Aaron. He's also sporting a black eye, which Alison failed to mention.

"What happened?" I ask, trying to cover my grin.

"He asked some dude if he could help him with the subscription on his phone," Jesse says, sighing when Aaron starts muttering under his breath.

At my confused expression, Drake explains. "The lad was gay. He thought he'd know about the app or whatever is on his phone because of his sexuality."

"So the lad gave him a black eye?" *There has to be more to the story.*

"No." Jesse's eyes are full of pity as he stares at his friend. "The dude's boyfriend thought he was hitting on him, so he punched him out."

"No!"

"Yes. Then he proceeded to spend the rest of the day getting smashed." Drake's unhappy expression makes me laugh. He seems seconds away from dropping Aaron on the floor, and not because he can't handle the weight.

"Boys, you're back. Where are the others?" Ada asks, glancing behind them.

"Alison's outside paying the taxi. The rest were going to finish their drinks and then follow us. We had to get this one back before he ended up in more trouble."

Ada pops up from out of nowhere. "Ah, I saw you carry him out of the taxi. I've put some water and painkillers on his bedside table for when he wakes up."

Jesse seems surprised before smiling lovingly at his grandma. "Thanks, Grams. That's awfully kind of you."

She waves him off. "More than happy to help my grandson's best friend. Why don't you two take him up and we'll see you in the garden. Such a lovely day."

Such a devious little woman.

~

A few hours later, I'm sitting down with Drake, his family and their friends in the garden enjoying a late-night dinner.

We're discussing the wedding when Jon pipes up, grabbing my attention. "Has anyone seen my best man speech anywhere?"

He's lost the damn thing three times since he's been staying here.

"Jon, I found the latest speech in the kitchen. I emailed you a copy in case you lost it again."

He looks dumbfounded for a second before grinning at me. "You're a legend. Thank you. But, um... how did you get my email address?"

It's my turn to grin now. "I can't reveal my resources, sorry."

Ada gave me strict instructions not to let on to the others that she has all this information on them. She said it's her way of protecting the family. Me? I say it's her way of getting even if they ever try to pull something. Or for her to just have some fun.

"Either way, thank you. I didn't want to have to write the damn thing out again. It was becoming a chore."

"Hey," Jesse yells in mock offence.

"Sorry, bud, but there's only so much I can remember before I just end up with 'To the bride and groom' as my speech."

Everyone laughs at Jesse's expression before they go back to talking about the bachelor party. I don't bother informing Jesse of Aaron's plans; it'll just ruin *my* plans to get even, and I'm sure I can make it up to him.

I'm hoping the England football tickets grant my forgiveness.

Screaming from inside the house echoes outside and everyone drops what they're doing. At first I think it's to look behind me, inside the house, but then I realise they're all staring at me.

"What?" I ask innocently.

"What did you do now?" Ada asks, sounding disgruntled.

I snort, giving her the evil eye. "Nothing, Ada. Whatever do you mean?"

More screaming, this time closer.

"He sounds like he's seen a ghost," Jesse comments.

"Or looked in the mirror," Gabriella chuckles.

"I just want to know how she does it." Harmony grins. "It's entertaining, to say the least."

With mocked outrage, I gasp, holding a hand over my heart. "I have no idea what you're talking about. I'm doing nothing."

"Yeah, yeah," the whole table says, laughing.

That is until Aaron runs out onto the patio, gasping for air. "You... I... there's... oh my God, what did I do?"

He looks pale as a ghost, sweat running down his face. The only colour is from the black eye he's sporting.

"What's wrong?" Pam asks, biting her lip worriedly.

Aaron ignores her, looking to Jesse. "Man, I... there's... I don't know what happened."

"What did you do?" Jesse asks, also concerned now.

"Yeah, what did you do? You look like you've seen a dead body," Ada helpfully comments.

Aaron's face turns a paisley green and he looks ready to be sick. "My room," he chokes out, still standing there.

My lips twitch as I go back to my dinner. It gains Alison's and Amelia's attention and I shrug, stuffing my face with the yummy hamburger Emily cooked up.

"I'll go check it out," Jesse tells the group, and Adam offers to join him. Not wanting to miss out, Drake and Jon get up too, following the men into the house.

Pam must take pity on Aaron because she guides him gently over to the chair. Still completely out of it, he sits down mutely, not looking at anything but his shaking hands.

Ada catches my eye from across the table and winks. I return it, giving her a thumbs up.

This prank couldn't have gone any better.

Not even five minutes later, the men walk outside. The second they see Aaron, they burst out laughing. His head snaps to the sound, looking horrified and truly scared for his well-being.

"Why are you laughing? There's a dead fucking body wrapped in a sheet in my bed," he snaps.

"What?" Amelia gasps.

"Oh no," Alison chuckles.

"This is epic." Gabriella grins.

"This is better than *Love Island*," Harmony whispers.

"It's not a dead fucking body. It's blankets and pillows wrapped in a sheet to make it look like a body," Drake booms, laughing his arse off. He slaps his knee, walking back towards me and taking his seat. "Best one yet," he whispers, his breath close to my ear, and images of him from last night whispering how good I felt come back to me, making me blush.

Aaron shakes his head vehemently. "No, I saw the blood. It was everywhere," he says, voice cracking.

Jesse chuckles, slapping his friend on the back. "My friend, you've been played. It's definitely a bed sheet. Dad's going to dispose of it."

He's not even finished when Adam steps out, cradling the makeshift body in his arms and grinning like a fool. "Pammy, we have to keep this. Imagine what we could do next Halloween."

Aaron whimpers pathetically.

Pam claps giddily. "Oh, Adam, that would be fantastic. Just think of their faces. It's a shame we don't know who designed such a creation or we could get them to make more."

"What am I, chopped liver?" Ada snaps. "A two-year-old could put that together. Leave it to me, Pammy. I'll make the next murder mystery night the best."

"Oh, just marvellous."

"Halloween? Murder mystery?" I whisper to Drake, taking my eyes off the body and Aaron's stunned face.

"Who did it? Why would someone do that to me?" Aaron asks quietly, not looking at anyone.

Everyone ignores him, now talking about Halloween, which is months away.

"Every Halloween, Mum and Dad's friends take turns throwing a Halloween/murder mystery night. Each year it gets more competitive. It's a tradition, and one that can't be missed. Mum's been dying for some new material."

"I don't understand why any of this is happening to me!" Aaron yells, banging his fist on the table.

I ignore him, staring at Drake like he's grown two heads. "But she lives with an evil mastermind. Why doesn't she just ask her?"

He smirks. "Because at the last party, Grams nearly gave dad a heart attack. Luckily it was only indigestion from choking on his food."

"What?"

"I don't deserve any of this, none of it. What have I ever done?" Aaron cries, sounding distraught.

And again, he's ignored.

"Yeah," Drake laughs. "Gave us a right scare. Grams had some make-up artist come in and make her look dead. She even went into the walk-in freezer to cool her body down before sitting in the old rickety chair Mum had hired for decoration and pretended to be dead."

"She didn't!" I gasp.

A phone beeps.

"She did."

Aaron groans. "I can't take any more of these messages. If I wanted to see a fucking cock, I'd look at my own."

"Isn't it hard to see something so small though?" Gabriella pipes in, earning a glare from Aaron.

He throws his hands up in frustration just as his phone beeps with another alert. He looks disgusted before finally smashing the device at his feet, stepping on it.

"I'm going to have nightmares for the rest of my life. This week has been traumatising. In fact, I don't think I'll ever get over it," he cries, throwing himself back down on the chair in a slump.

"Ah, damn. That app was the best prank we had going," I pout.

But one look in Ada's direction tells me she's already on it. She'll have his new passwords as soon as he has a phone.

"Surely it's not that bad," Pam says softly, but her lips twitch, showing she's just as amused as the rest of us.

"Pam, I dreamt of cocks last night," he whispers, mortified.

"I have those dreams all the time," Ada tells him.

The rest of us choke on laughter, unable to hold it in. "Maybe it's the universe's way of telling you something," Gabriella sings. She's really enjoying his discomfort, but then again, she hasn't hidden her dislike for Aaron since I arrived.

"And what's that?" he snaps, glaring at her.

"That you should be gay and leave the female population the hell alone."

He rears back like he's been slapped and gasps. "Take that back."

"No." She grins, sipping her drink.

He looks to Jesse. "Get her to take that back. I'm not gay. I love women."

"But the women just don't love you," Gabriella teases.

"That's not true. Pagan's in love with me, even after all these years."

I snort, disgusted at the smug look he gives Gabriella. "Not in this lifetime or the next."

The group laughs before Aaron turns his attention to me. "When you're finally ready to admit it, I may not be here waiting for you."

My mouth gapes open. "You'll be waiting an awfully long time, buddy."

He snorts as if what I'm saying isn't true. "She loves me."

"Delusional."

"Okay, enough. Let's enjoy the rest of the dinner," Pam says. We all nod at her firm tone, not wanting to argue.

"What shall I do with this?" Adam asks.

"Put Kevin next to Aaron since they're well-acquainted," Ada says, gesturing to the body.

~

Later that night, Drake walks me to my room. As I'm about to open my mouth to explain this morning and why we can't keep doing this, his is on mine.

"Drake," I whimper, unsure whether it's to pull away or to pull him closer.

His kisses are hypnotising, rendering me speechless.

"No more talking. I've missed you," he whispers against my lips, slamming me against the door.

What can I say to that?

When he tugs me up his body, I happily wrap my legs around his waist and kiss him back passionately, leaving us both breathless.

Tomorrow. Tomorrow I'll talk to him.

Tonight it's just us.

Chapter Twenty

Ah, bachelorette parties.

How much I enjoy screaming women, sloppy drunks and annoying screeching—not. Thankfully Amelia didn't want strippers; otherwise, I'd be in twice as much hell right now. I think I'd be okay if I could sit down, relax and enjoy the fun alongside them.

But after one of the band members showed up late, then began to moan over there not being any hot single chicks, I'd had enough. I had a headache forming, and I just wanted to forget tonight altogether.

"I'm sorry about him," Tobias, the lead singer, says.

I smile, blushing at the handsome young musician. He's covered in tattoos and is flaunting a rock-hard body under his tight white T-shirt.

"It's okay.... Um, can you tell him there's no drinking on the job?" I ask, watching as the band member sneaks one of the free drinks from the bar.

I pulled out all the stops for tonight, going as far as to make a backstage for the drag queens to get dressed and for the band to relax. A stage was built with red flowing curtains, making it look like a real show house.

When Amelia explained how she wanted to do something different for the hen party, I hadn't been surprised; so far, the only traditional wedding theme she's had are the vows.

I sat her down and asked her what her most memorable, favourite activity or moment had been, and she told me about a night she spent in Spain. The hotel she was staying at had a drag queen on for entertainment, and she claimed she'd never had as much fun as that night.

So I got to work, giving her what she wanted.

Earlier in the day, she and a small group of girlfriends went to a studio to learn how to pole dance. I stayed back, organising tonight, glad I did when Amelia came back with a bruised arse. Ada came back with stiches on her head after trying to do a manoeuvre someone her age just shouldn't do. The video the girls managed to get was mortifying. I didn't know where to look. Not only was Ada participating, but she was wearing the skimpiest outfit known to women. I'm pretty sure she'd leave strippers blushing.

But seeing her front row centre, hooting at the stage, her injury doesn't seem to be bothering her. She's thoroughly enjoying herself.

Tobias sighs before giving me an apologetic look. "I'll go sort him out. I'm sorry about this."

I watch him go, admiring his jean-clad backside.

He really does have a nice arse.

Tonight wouldn't have been so bad if there weren't over thirty women currently screaming and laughing. But I'm counting my blessings because the spawn of Satan—Amelia's mum—isn't attending. According to Angela, who didn't hold back when she told us, Amelia's mother would rather scratch her eyes out.

Well, her loss, our gain.

She certainly isn't missed, that's for sure, but I could tell Amelia was disappointed deep down. Her mother hasn't been involved in the wedding planning at all, but she doesn't seem to mind voicing her opinion whenever possible.

The song switches to Tina Turner and a smile touches my lips as I watch, laughing when another Tina lookalike steps out, waggling her huge hair around like nobody's business, giving the current one some sass.

Amelia picked well. Everyone is thoroughly having the night of their lives.

The band's up next. I really should go make sure they have everything they need, but I'm too tired from staying up all night with Drake.

Yes, my one last time turned into another night and another six orgasms.

But in my defence, he's really hard to say no to when he kisses me the way he does.

And I miss him—like *really* miss him. He's been gone all day, with not even a text or a phone call to tell me how his day's going.

And I'm becoming that clingy girl who needs to know what her man is doing at all times.

My face scrunches up in horror, knowing I need to get a grip on myself before I do something stupid like tell him I love him.

A door behind me slams shut, startling me. Going to investigate, I'm surprised to see the boys back so soon; they weren't due for another three or four hours. What doesn't surprise me is the thunderous look on Aaron's face as he storms towards the ballroom, making sure to shoulder his way past me.

"Hey," I snap.

Seconds later, he's heading for the stairs, cursing.

The lads are grinning as they walk up to me. "What's up his arse?"

"You, Pagan Salvatore, have made my wedding epic. When Amelia and I planned the three weeks, we did it because we didn't want it to be dull, boring, or original, but this... I'm never going to forget this," Jesse chuckles, walking past me before I have chance to ask why.

Okay, more like ask if they recorded it.

"Hey, you can't go in there. It's the hen party," I yell, but he and his buddies ignore me and walk over to the girls, who are excited to see them.

"Hey, you." Drake's husky voice sends a shiver down my spine.

Turning, I wrap my arms around his waist, smiling up at him. "Hey. Are you drunk?"

"Nope, just happy to see you." He kisses the tip of my nose and my heart flutters. There're so many small things he does that I don't think he knows he does, which only makes it harder to not fall for him.

I tried putting distance between the two of us, but one look from him, one kiss, and I forget why I even suggested it.

I only have six days left, and even if I leave with a broken heart, I'm determined to spend the rest of my time—as much as I have free—with him.

There's one thing I've learnt from life and mostly Lola, and that's to grip life with two hands and never let go. And if you manage to find the love of your life, enjoy every single minute of it. It will never come around twice. And I know that for a fact because no one, and I mean no one, could ever replace the time and moments Drake has blessed me with.

"Miss me?" I tease, earning a sexy growl and kiss from him.

"I should be spanking your arse, but you're lucky the rest of us were left alone."

I feign innocence as I bat my eyelashes up at him. "Whatever do you mean?"

"We were looking forward to the band they had playing, having a few drinks and maybe tying my brother to a lamppost naked. To our surprise, strippers walked out."

I grin, holding back my laughter. "Oh? Not pretty enough?"

He shrugs, smirking. "You can help burn the image of what happened to Aaron out of my mind later with my own personal striptease."

A tingle shoots between my legs and I have to press my thighs together. The look he's giving me says it all—I'll be stripping for him later. And surprisingly, I'm looking forward to it.

"If you say so," I muse. "What happened to Aaron?"

When we booked 'Drags on Tour' for Amelia, we noticed another service they provided. A group of men, transvestites, and some women strip, putting on a dance show and whatnot.

When I emailed them the other day, I didn't expect them to agree to my terms, but thankfully after I told them what a harmless jerk Aaron was, making sure they knew he wouldn't hurt any of their employees with the act, they agreed.

And after one email, a photo of Aaron and their payment, it was all set. What I never got to know was what the act would be like.

"A dominatrix stripper tied him to the chair. He loved it."

Really?

"So what's the problem?" I ask, bummed my plan didn't work.

"Aaron spent nearly the entire act chatting her up. Even managed to score a date. But towards the end of the act, she dropped her skirt." He stops again and I stomp my foot, wanting him to get to the good bits.

"And?"

He grins. "She was a transvestite with a very large appendage."

Laughing, I bend forward, gripping Drake's biceps. "Please tell me you recorded it."

He laughs. "Jon has it all on tape. Apparently their manager pulled him aside when we got there and said it was requested it be recorded."

'Drags on Tour' don't usually let you record their employees, but after he heard Aaron is homophobic, he was happy to.

"What did Aaron do?"

There's a twinkle in his eye. "Nothing. He had to sit, straining in his seat, until the act was over. The staff cleared out before we untied him, but we made sure to get some photos taken before she left, with her on his lap."

He takes out his phone and clicks on his gallery. Swiping through the pictures, my laughter comes freely. They're all standing behind an angry-faced Aaron with wide grins, some even laughing. He has nipple clamps on and angry red marks on his chest, which makes me chuckle. She didn't hold back.

My eyes go to the woman on his lap. She's really beautiful. I can understand why he was so determined to score a date. My eyes flicker to the appendage dangling between the two and laugh.

"My, she's huge."

"That's what we said." He grins.

"Did you have a good night?"

"Yeah, it was ace. All of them were brilliant."

"Oh yeah? Did you get a striptease?"

"Oh yeah." He pulls me closer. "The bloke even told me about his three kids and wife. Jesse invited him to his wedding. Great guy."

My smile widens. "Really?"

"Yeah. He does it for the extra money to support his family, and when Jesse overheard, they got talking. In the end, we all sat back, watched

Aaron's performance and got to know our strippers. Jon even has a date with his."

"Good for him."

"Um, what is Grams drinking?" Drake asks suddenly, looking behind me.

His concern for his grams is incredibly sweet. "Lemonade. She had a fall earlier and banged her head. Don't worry, she's completely fine. The pain medication the doctors gave her can't be taken with alcohol."

"Then why is she swinging her bra around... she just threw it at the lead singer," Drake gasps in horror.

"What?" I spin around and sure enough, a bra is hanging from the mic Tobias is using. "But she isn't drinking."

Pam already warned me the third night we stayed here that Ada can get a little *too* merry after having a drink. And has been known to strip whilst under the influence of whiskey.

"Did you check her bag?" Drake sighs. I turn in time to see him scrub a hand down his face.

Confused, I raise an eyebrow. "Why would I do that?"

He looks at me like I should know. "Because she's Grams. She hides alcohol in her knicker drawer."

I gasp. "She wouldn't do that to me," I tell him quickly. We formed a bond. She loves me. She wouldn't do it.

But as soon as the words leave my mouth, I want to slap myself.

Because of course she would.

"You sure about that?" he asks, doubt filling his voice before he groans.

My attention turns back to Ada and I panic. "I need danger pay for this," I tell him before rushing off to get Ada off the stage.

I mouth an apology to Tobias as I grab her arm. "Come on, Ada. Let's go sit down so they can do their thing."

"They can do it with me. I've been known to shake my booty a time or two."

"Yes, I'm sure you have." I help her down the stairs just as Tobias asks if anyone can sing.

To my horror, Alison, who has the night off, screams my name. "She can sing better than anyone I've ever heard."

And she manages to embarrass me and insult him in the same sentence. Only Alison.

"I really am sorry," I tell Tobias, but he just winks.

"Is that right?" he asks into the mic.

"Yep. Her twin is in a band."

"There are two of you?" Drake asks, and I can hear the smirk in his voice.

Dirty fucker.

I've only told him about my brothers, forgetting to mention Sid's my twin.

Turning around, I smile sweetly up at him. "Yeah, Sid would really love you."

His eyes widen for a second before he chuckles. "Knew you were one of a kind."

And again with the damn heart flutters. He really needs to stop doing that.

"Come on up, Pagan. Show us what you got," Tobias calls.

My eyes widen in horror because I don't sing. Okay, I sing, just not in public or in front of pretty much anyone, ever. I'll never understand how my brother can do it, or stand in front of a classroom full of kids and teach them.

"Oh no, no, no!"

"Go on, show me what you got. Or are you scared?" Drake whispers.

He has no idea.

"I'm not singing."

Everyone starts chanting my name and I look at Drake for help. He just grins, shrugging.

I'm not going to get out of this.

With some luck, and more drink poured into them, they'll forget the whole ordeal in the morning.

"Okay, just... can you go?" I ask Drake. Maybe then I'll be able to get through it without puking.

"Is that what you want?" he asks gently, running his finger down my cheek.

"Please." I sigh with relief, glad he understands, but then he gives me that all-knowing smirk. I narrow my eyes because it can only mean he's up to something.

"Nope. I'm staying for the show." He makes a point of taking a front row seat, grinning like a damn fool. As soon as Ada claps, sitting next to him, he snatches her handbag from her.

She pouts before glaring at me like it's my fault she got caught slipping drink into her lemonade.

"Oh God," I whisper, stepping onto the stage. I walk up to Tobias, glaring at him. He chuckles, shaking his head as he passes me a spare mic. "What do you want me to sing?"

"Do you know 'When I Fall in Love?'"

I do. It's one of my mum's favourites.

I nod, taking the mic, and watch as he signals to his bandmates to start. My heart is beating so wildly, I pray I don't pass out before the song ends.

Or vomit.

The last time I vomited was in school when they made me stand up in front of the entire student body and make a speech on bullying. It was humiliating. Took me *years* to get over the embarrassment.

I'm okay one-on-one, but put me front and centre of something and I'm a nervous ball of energy.

As I sing the words about giving my heart away, my eyes drift to Drake, knowing with everything inside me that I've given him mine completely.

His eyes widen as he watches me, darkening to the point that they look almost demonic. The heat in them surprises me and I duck my head, blushing.

My gaze drifts over everyone else, but when I see their shocked, surprised faces and bright smiles, I look away, my eyes going back to Drake so I don't start falling over my words.

When we reach the part where Tobias and I sing together, I turn to him, closing my eyes as I pour out the soulful words, meaning every single one of them as I think of Drake. Tobias grins, just as surprised as the rest of the group when I open my eyes. He winks before turning to the crowd, using his smooth voice to entice them.

The minute the round of applause almost bursts my eardrums, I want to die of mortification. I smile, pretend to do a little bow and go to step down, but before my foot hits the first step, Drake is there. The heat in his eyes burns through me.

"You are one amazing woman," he whispers hoarsely.

"Drake," I whisper back, affected by the intensity in his voice.

He grabs my hips, his touch igniting the fire inside me that only burns for him.

He throws me over his shoulder and I gasp. "Drake. Everyone is watching."

"I don't care," he tells me, swatting my arse.

Everyone in the room cheers, catcalling and whistling. The music has stopped, the band obviously enjoying my discomfort, so when the door bursts open, slamming against the wall, it echoes around the room.

"There's a snake in my shower!" Aaron screams, to the point I can almost hear tears in his voice.

"There's a snake on my plane." I don't know who shouted it but I burst out laughing, almost forgetting I'm hanging upside down from Drake's shoulders.

He doesn't seem to care about Aaron, or his sheer terror, never mind the fact that there could actually be a snake in his shower.

The minute we're out of the room, he slides me down his body until my legs are wrapped around him and he's kissing me. Aaron is long forgotten.

Drake is my only focus.

I kiss him back, running my fingers through his hair. How he manages to keep walking, not missing a step or falling over, is hot. It proves he has one thing on his mind, and that's to get me to his room safely so he can have his wicked way with me.

It doesn't take us long to get to his bedroom, but I still have most of his shirt buttons undone and have completely messed up his styled hair.

He kicks the door shut behind us, not once removing his lips from mine. He turns us, slamming me against the door as he runs his hand up my thigh, reaching between my legs.

My head drops back against the door and I release an embarrassing moan when his fingers slide easily through my wet slit.

After that, it's all hands, tongues, and a lot of grinding. Sex with Drake is out of this world, and each and every time he's made me feel special, sexy and wanted. But the way he ravages my mouth as he drops me to my feet has my sex clenching, seconds away from exploding.

When he rips the dress from my body, tearing his lips away from mine, I let out a pitiful groan. I don't have to wait long until he's kissing me again, walking me backwards towards his... bathroom.

"Why are we going into the bathroom?" I ask through pants.

He chuckles against my lips, his fingers undoing my bra expertly. "Because I'm going to fuck you in the shower. I need to wash away tonight so that when I wake up, all I smell is you."

My breath hitches at his promised words. His eyes slowly travel down my body and he groans as he takes one breast into his hand. He licks his lips before bending down, devouring me.

"Please," I moan, throwing my head back.

Just when I think he's going to put me out of my misery, he takes my other nipple into his mouth, sucking and nibbling to the point I feel my core tightening. And I know, I just know, he could make me come like this.

But I want him inside me. Where he belongs.

He picks me up, carrying me into the shower and blindly reaching for the taps to turn the water on. The cold water drowns me, though instead of cooling me down, it only ignites the fire inside me.

I grab the pipe behind me as Drake lifts me, wrapping my legs around his body.

"Oh God," I cry out when he thrusts inside me.

He feels good.

So damn good.

He stills inside me, his head going to the crook of my neck as he groans, his hands on my hips tightening.

He needs to move. I *need* him to move. I'm torn between screaming out in frustration and screaming at him to move.

"Drake, please." I'm not ashamed to beg.

"Hold on tight," he grits out, pulling out until the tip is at my entrance before slamming back inside me.

I hold on to his shoulders, my nails digging in as I continue to cry out in pleasure. Sex with Aaron was boring, dull, but with Drake, all of it is a new experience.

I roll my hips, moving against him as he thrusts harder. My core tightens with each thrust, the promise of it being explosive shimmering to the edge.

When it all becomes too much, I lean back again, holding the pipe above me, needing something to anchor me as I shove down hard on him, needing that fullness only he can give me.

He growls as he captures my nipple with his mouth. The second his teeth scrape against the sensitive bud as he thrusts in one more time, I explode, screaming out the most powerful orgasm I've ever felt.

"Fuck," he groans, and it registers that I just pulled the pipe off the wall. It doesn't seem to matter because the second it breaks off, Drake slams his hand behind me, and I hear what must be the taps falling to the floor with a ping.

When the water stops, he pulls away, but only long enough to move us out of the shower and into the bathroom. He doesn't separate us, or make any move to, which only causes me to tighten around him, making him groan.

I'm sensitive, and each movement fires shocks of pleasure to my core and into my lower belly.

The feel of a towel wrapping around me has me confused. He didn't get to finish.

But I don't have to worry for long because the second we're in his room, he's dropping me on the bed.

I bounce, moaning at the loss of contact. I blindly reach out for him, to touch him, but he takes my hips and turns me.

Oh my.

We've done a lot of positions, but this is the first time he's ever taken me on all fours.

"Fuck, your arse is perfect," he growls, grabbing both cheeks and squeezing.

I moan, moving back into his hands. He lines himself up behind me and slowly, so painfully slow, enters me.

"Yes!"

"I'm not going to last long," he groans, pulling out before slamming back in.

He feels deeper, hitting a spot that's driving me wild. When he doesn't move, I slam back, taking matters into my own hands.

The hands on my arse tighten to the point it will most likely leave a bruise. But the second he enters me again, I'm lost, riding back against him with each punishing thrust of his cock.

"One more, baby," he moans, reaching for my clit, smearing our juices over the sensitive bud until I cry out.

"More," I beg.

"Fuck, you're killing me."

He slams into me over and over, and when he tells me he's going to come, another orgasm tears through me, leaving me boneless as I flop to the bed, breathing heavily.

Something smashes as he continues to thrust, not even stopping to see what it is.

When he grunts through his own powerful release, he stills inside me, his panting echoing around the room as he tries to gain control.

I hiss when he pulls out to leave the room, coming back a few seconds later and cleaning me up. I don't move a muscle, too exhausted and numb to even try.

"Come on," he says softly, slapping my ass. "Let's get you into bed."

"Leave me alone," I grumble.

He chuckles. "Come on. I'll let you sleep... for a bit."

I scoff because we both know as soon as he touches me again, he'll be hard and inside me. And I'll love every minute of it.

"Nope. You broke me."

He laughs and picks me up, cradling me in his arms as he carries me up the bed, pulling the blanket back before setting me down. I flop down, not bothering to get my knickers or a nightshirt.

My eyes droop, exhaustion winning the chat I promised we'd have tonight. But like every other time, Drake's a true gentleman and doesn't bring it up. He climbs into bed behind me, pulling me against his naked body.

"Goodnight, baby," he whispers, kissing below my ear.

I snuggle back and mutter a goodnight, too tired to speak whilst promising myself I'll talk to him tomorrow.

Yes, tomorrow.

Chapter Twenty-One

*A*s the days keep passing, my time here coming closer to an end, the more anguished I feel inside. My heart is slowly crumbling; by the time we leave, it'll be nothing but flakes of ash.

After the wedding rehearsal last night, in a stupid drunken moment, I decided to see if we could continue what we have after the wedding.

But now another day has passed and the courage to bring it up to Drake has gone. I'd never be able to handle his rejection, not when I'm so madly in love with him. I'd never recover.

Being a chicken is starting to be a pattern where I'm concerned.

We've tried talking a few times, even went so far as to plan a time and place, but either something comes up or we can't keep our hands off each other long enough to get a word in.

Saying goodbye to him is going to be the hardest thing I've ever had to do. And with the wedding tomorrow, it's making me feel physically sick.

I'll even miss his family, including crazy Ada. My time here seems to have gone too quickly. If you'd told me three weeks ago that I wouldn't want to leave, I'd have laughed in your face. But here I sit, wallowing in my own self-pity.

But then again, if you had told me three weeks ago that I'd be madly in love with a man I'd never see again, I probably would've sectioned you.

I just wish I had more time with him, more time to savour every little thing so I never forget my time with him. Not that I will. I'll never be able to forget him or a single moment of our time together.

"Hey, are you okay?" Alison whispers as we wait for the rest of the girls to arrive. We've set up a pamper party for the wedding party as a treat. Pam's idea and present to everyone for taking time away from their lives to be involved in the big day.

They'll be pampered with facials, manis and pedis, eyebrow waxing and tinting and even a massage. They're getting the full works, and I'm envious.

My mood the past two days has been dwindling slowly, and I know people are beginning to take notice. I barely said hello to my mum on the phone this morning before she was threatening to come down here to see what was wrong with me.

Sometimes being the only girl in the family can be a tad suffocating. All the men in my life have babied me from birth, even my twin who is three minutes younger than me. But my mum? I'll always be her baby girl.

When Lola came along, it was heaven—still is, especially now that we have Cece to watch over. Poor girl doesn't know what's coming with the big brutes in our family.

"Yeah," I lie. "Have you brought the bride's pyjamas for her to change into?"

She throws me a dirty look as she hands me the specially made bride-to-be pyjamas. We also had maid of honour, bridesmaid, and mother-in-law ones made up.

"Don't lie to me," she snaps, clearly having enough of hearing "I'm fine" as my answer every time she asks. "You've been moping for days. Did something happen?"

"Don't shout at me!"

She pushes my shoulder with force, sending me back a step. "No! Now tell me."

I push her back, ignoring her cry of outrage. "No. Nothing is wrong. Now leave me alone."

"You're going to tell me."

I roll my eyes. "Yeah, and how are you going to make me?"

She scoffs at my sassy attitude and grabs my hair, tugging it roughly before pinching my side. "Tell me what's wrong, you bitch."

My fingers find a chunk of her hair, tugging it down so we're both bent forward, moving in a circle as I try to pinch her back, not quite reaching. "I said no. It's none of your business, you whore."

I cry out when she pinches me again, this time grabbing the sensitive skin under my boob. "I'm not going to stop until you tell me, Pagan."

"You're a crazy bitch," I scream, pulling her hair tighter.

"Now this is what I'm talking about," I hear. I can't even lift my head to investigate before she pinches my boob and I forget all about our company.

"Tell me, Pagan. I'm your best friend. I want to know what has you looking like someone shit in your bed."

"Classy," I mutter. "Now get off me."

"No!" she screams loudly and twists my nipple.

I wail in pain, gasping for air. "Because I love him, okay? And we leave in two fucking days. Are you happy now?" I yell, glaring at her.

She releases my hair and, thankfully, my poor abused nipple and steps back. We're both breathing hard, catching our breath.

"You love who?" Pam asks sweetly.

Horrified, I turn to find Amelia, Ada, Pam, Gabriella, Angela, Hallie and Hannah standing in the doorway. Pam, Harmony, Hallie and Hannah look confused, but Ada and Gabriella seem to be wearing matching grins.

Scary.

"No one."

"Was that so hard to admit?" Alison mutters.

"You abused my nipples." I glare at her, rubbing my boob for good measure. "I'm not talking to you."

"She's not the only one," Ada pipes up, and I turn my glare her way. I didn't even think she was talking to me after Drake confiscated the whiskey stashed in her bag, but here she is, making her point known.

"I'm so confused," Pam tells us, looking exactly that.

"Oh God. She's fucking your son, Pam," Angela snaps.

"Hey!" I shriek, feeling my face heat.

"Watch your mouth, young lady," Ada admonishes, and Angela cautiously takes a step back.

"And you love him?" Pam asks.

She's smiling, staring off into space. My guess is she's planning our wedding, but once she realises we live miles away from each other, that happy glow will soon fade.

I sigh. "Let's get started." Another round of embarrassment hits me when I realise the beauticians just had a front row seat to mine and Alison's performance. They're all standing in the corner, frozen in shock as they watch on. I clear my throat, getting their boss's attention. "Do you want to start?"

She shakes her head before smiling. "Hi, everyone. I'm Lynn, and these are my employees, Katie, Georgia, Lacey, Megan, Zoe and Sky. Which one of you is the lucky bride?"

Amelia steps forward, holding her hand up as she gazes around the room in amazement. She should—Pam spared no expense tonight. We've had furniture removed to make way for the two massage beds, foot spas, and recliner beds for facials and to relax. We had some dim lights brought in, giving the room a soft glow, and music plays in the background as lavender essence burns through the room, the aroma relaxing.

"I'm the bride."

"Do you know what you're having done first?" she asks, handing Amelia a glass of champagne as the other girls pass out the rest.

"Where are the snacks?" I whisper to Alison.

"Emily is bringing them up with the cucumber water."

"She wouldn't let you in the kitchen, would she?" I chuckle.

Pouting, she shakes her head. "I don't get it. I only wanted a midnight snack. I thought it would be okay, but it's like she has some sort of superpowers because she knew I was there."

"You dropped milk all over her oven," I remind her.

She rolls her eyes. "Only because she scared the hell out of me. I should've remembered the second night I tried to make hot chocolate, but she did the same thing then."

I giggle, knowing how much she loves her hot drinks, whether it's coffee, tea, or hot chocolate.

"Pagan?"

I look over to Amelia. "I'm sorry, what did you say?"

"We'd like you and Alison to have the first massages. I don't mind what I have first, I'm just too excited. I'm getting married tomorrow!" she squeals, grinning ear to ear.

I look to Alison, whose shocked expression probably matches my own. I just wanted to go to my room, leave the girls to relax so I could wallow in self-pity by myself.

I'm about to excuse myself when Alison jumps up, clapping happily. "Really?"

Amelia turns to me. "I want to thank you for everything you've done. Ours hasn't been a typical wedding, I'm sure. You've worked so hard on it and ignored certain... incidents that would normally send people packing. You deserve to have a night to fully relax."

My eyes water hearing her words. But as much as I'd love to lie down and get a massage, I just need time to think, to process everything and find the courage to say goodbye to Drake when the time comes.

I'm about to decline and thank her for such a generous gift when Alison steps forward, hugging Amelia briefly. "Thank you so much. Pagan was only telling me yesterday how much she could use a massage."

I did say that.

"Good. Now go get into something more comfy. Pam had some dressing gowns brought in today for you."

"Are you sure? This is your night, after all."

Amelia smiles. "More than sure. Go get changed," she orders as Pam hands me a dressing gown, still dreamy-eyed.

Oh Lord.

~

"Pagan."

Something soft runs down my back, making me shiver and snuggle closer to the warm towel beneath me.

"Pagan, baby, wake up."

"Go away," I groggily tell Drake.

"You have to get up," he whispers softly, kissing the back of my neck.

"No! I'm having a massage."

I keep my eyes closed, ignoring his chuckle as he runs his fingers down my bare back.

"It's time for bed, baby."

"Go away, Drake, or so help me God, I'll set Ada on you."

"You wouldn't." The amusement in his voice says he doesn't believe me. But I'm so goddamn tired, I really would do anything at this point.

And it's all his fault.

He's kept me up all night, every night, getting to know every inch of my body and making me scream his name from every position known to man.

"I would. Now go away. You're not allowed in here. We're being pampered."

He chuckles, pressing another kiss to my lower back. "Mum came to fetch me when they couldn't wake you up."

I open one eye and, sure enough, no one else is in the room. "Um, where did everyone go?"

I sit up, pressing the sheet to my chest and rubbing my tired eyes, wishing I could just stay in here for the night.

"They went to bed. It's midnight."

I must have dozed off during my luxurious massage, because I don't remember much after feeling the pressure of Megan's hands on my back. "Why didn't they wake me?"

"They let you sleep because of how hard you've been working. When the ladies needed to go, they tried to wake you up then, but you wouldn't budge."

Yeah right. Like Ada or Alison would let me stay asleep. "Where're your grams and Alison?"

He chuckles, shaking his head. "Alison wouldn't do anything with everyone here, but she did tell me to get her if you didn't wake up. Grams wanted to cover you in seaweed or something they had, but Mum wouldn't let her. She threatened to remove all the alcohol from the wedding."

Saving grace for Pam and Alison being too professional to throw water over me in front of clients.

God! Even calling them 'clients' doesn't seem right anymore. They feel more like family to me and have been a delight to work for. I wish all my clients were as pleasant as the Donovans.

I bite my lip to stop the tears from forming. "It's not work that's tiring me out, you know." I glare at him for good measure.

His lips twitch. "Whatever do you mean?"

Rolling my eyes, I try to push him away, but I'm just too tired to move. I yawn, not even covering my mouth.

"Come on, sleepyhead. Let's get you to bed."

"I don't want to mo—" He sweeps me up into his arms, carrying me bridal style out of the room. "What are you doing?"

"Carrying you. You're too tired, baby."

God, he's such a gentleman. And the endearment melts my heart. I thought hearing someone call me 'baby' would make me want to gag, but when it comes from Drake, I feel precious.

We're silent as we make our way to his room. I don't even bother arguing over him not taking me to mine or tell him that his mother knows about us. It can wait until tomorrow.

Ah, tomorrow. I inwardly roll my eyes because I know it's not going to happen.

I'm only wearing knickers, so when he lays me down in the bed, he only has to remove the towel I had covering my chest. I watch as he pulls his T-shirt over his head. I'll never getting tired of his body, or how good it feels to run my fingers through his fine sheen of chest hair, or the ridges of his abs.

Drake unbuckling his belt gains my attention, and I go from staring at his amazing abs to the V dipping into his faded jeans. His fingers slowly undo the top button before he unzips, leaving the fly hanging open.

My thighs begin to quiver and a shock of wetness surges between my legs when I notice he's not wearing any underwear. The tip of his dick pokes out and I lick my lips, remembering how good he tastes.

A loud groan fills the room and I look up to meet his gaze. His eyes heat as he steps forward. "Oh, Pagan, you really shouldn't have looked at me like that," he whispers, dropping his trousers before me.

His large dick springs free, pointing directly at me as he stands there unashamedly naked as the day he was born.

He steps forwards again, pressing his knee to the bed before lying above me, his gaze never once leaving mine. I can't look away, not even when his lips meet mine, licking the seam and demanding entrance.

"I will never get enough of you," he whispers, kissing me slowly, passionately, stealing all coherent thoughts from my mind.

His dick pressing against my wet heat has me moaning and arching my back, but he pushes me down to keep me still.

I don't fight, not when I feel the tip of his dick enter me. His movements are slow, agonising, as he enters, never picking up speed or thrusting harder.

I don't know whether to scream in pleasure or frustration. After what feels like an eternity, frustration wins out because I need him more than I need my next breath.

"Please, Drake. More."

His hold tightens, not letting me move. "No. Tonight I'm going to fuck you slow and sweet, baby."

He moans when my walls clamp around him like a vice. Every time he fully fills me, he hits the spot that drives me wild, heightening my pleasure.

He nibbles my neck, moving lower towards my breasts as he goes. My hands move to his ass, my nails digging into his skin as I pant.

When he latches onto my nipple, I cry out as a tingle shoots straight to my clit. The tension is slowly building, torturous yet satisfying as I try to move with each thrust.

His mouth latches onto my other nipple, paying that one the same amount of attention. Sweat beads on my forehead and back as I struggle to prolong what he's doing to me. But each time he hits my cervix, my orgasm comes closer and closer. I know when I climax, I'll never be the same again.

"More," I plead, tears in my eyes as I grip the man I love with everything I have.

"Let go," he grits out, his breaths coming faster.

He pinches my nipple whilst sucking on the other and it's enough to make me explode, my core clenching tightly around him as I scream out my orgasm, calling his name.

"Pagan! Fuck! Pagan." He roars out his release, his cock swelling inside me before his whole body tenses and he buries his face in my chest.

I feel completely boneless as I lie there trying to catch my breath after the most incredible sex we've ever had together.

When I read 'made love' in a book, I always scoffed and wondered how stupid it sounded. But Drake Donovan just made love to me.

To *me*.

When the first tear falls from my eye, I know exactly what I'll be doing tomorrow.

I just hope what I'm about to do is the right decision.

Chapter Twenty-Two

With the big day finally here, everything is all go, go, go, and I'm thankful.

Keeping busy means I've had no time to think about what's going to happen in the future or about leaving Drake. It's hard to concentrate on what needs doing when all I want to do is curl up in a ball and cry.

When I woke up this morning, my heart was heavy. Time was of the essence, and I think Drake felt that too.

He made love to me like he knew it was our last time. He was silent as he thrust inside me, his gaze never wavering from mine. It was sweet, tender and slow, like he was in no rush for it to end.

Then again, I wasn't either.

It was hard to leave him in bed when I had to get ready.

My throat clogs with emotion and tears burn at the back of my eyes. I try to shake myself out of it. All I need is someone to question what's wrong with me. I don't know how I'll react if that does happen. But getting my head on straight is easier said than done. There's only so much pretending I can do.

"Hey, where do you want me?" Jessica asks. She has her earpiece in, something I'd normally be wearing, and is dressed in our normal black suit attire.

Glad she could make it on such short notice, I force a smile and hand her the clipboard. "They brought in the wrong placemats, so if you could go into the kitchen and see where the ones we ordered are, that would be perfect. I need to see where the white runner is for the aisle. It still hadn't arrived as of an hour ago."

"Pagan, we have a problem."

Worst words you can here in this job.

I turn to Lauren, one of our catering staff. "What's wrong?"

"Three of the waiters and waitresses haven't turned up. We're short-staffed."

I groan, wondering what else could go wrong today, but then think better of it.

"I'm going to check the placemats. I'll also get the champagne in the ice buckets and placed on tables. If you need anything else, call me," Jessica says, picking up on my high stress level. I'm usually calm and collected, but all I want to do is scream at the top of my lungs at how unfair the world can be. Why put Drake and I together if we were only going to end up apart?

Life can seriously suck sometimes.

I nod, watching her go before turning to Lauren. "I have backup staff. The number is on the clipboard in the kitchen. I need you to make sure everyone knows their roles and what tables they're working. You'll need to fill in the rest when they arrive."

She nods, seeming to relax. "Okay, thank you."

I sweep a hand over my hair, making sure my bun has stayed in place before turning back to the issue I was dealing with before I was interrupted.

"Cain, why aren't they working?"

He looks up from the table he's under, shrugging. "I don't know. I'm going to check in with the owner and see where the—" The lights on the artificial garden trees, which are shaped into hearts, finally light up.

I smile, and this time it's a real one. It would've been a travesty if they hadn't worked. "Yes! They're beautiful."

"Huh?" Cain looks at them confused before something dawns on him. "I didn't switch the main socket on."

My smile drops and I want to kick him in the shin. Why the hell Jessica hired him, I'll never know. He's supposed to be her tech support, but the only thing I've noticed he's good for is his good looks.

I'll have to make a mental note to talk to her about him when I'm back home. He's a liability, and a danger to others and himself if he ever messes up.

"Okay, can you go make sure you turned the outside ones on, please? They're running from the generator at the side of the house."

He nods, getting up and dusting his thighs off. "Sure thing."

Nervous, I follow him outside, making sure he heads in the right direction. He does and I sigh with relief.

I look around the garden, smiling widely at how beautiful everything turned out. We really did do an incredible job. I had our web designer come in and take some pictures for my website. As soon as she gets back, she'll upload them to our page. I can't wait to see the finished results; it could mean big things for Salvatore Events.

I sigh in relief when I see the white runner has finally arrived and been put down. It looks perfect between the rows of white fold-out chairs. Metal glass pedestal vases run down the inside of the aisle, all with bouquets of pink and white roses, finished with white bows. They look elegant and enchanting, the pink rose petals running down the side of the runner only complimenting their beauty more.

The wedding arch at the end of the aisle has the same arrangement of roses, tangled in vines and thin white chiffon. The table behind it has two caged doves, ready to be released when the couple finish their vows.

It really is a dream wedding. I can only hope mine will be as special one day.

My gaze shifts over to the doors leading into the ballroom. Tall tables covered in white thick chiffon are lit up from underneath, ready for when the sun goes down and the stars come out. On top of each is an artistic glass vase filled with an array of pink and white flowers and pebbled stones. They're also on the tables inside, brightening the room gloriously.

The only thing that didn't pan out was the twinkle lights and white

WISHING FOR A HAPPILY EVER AFTER

chiffon Pam wanted hanging from the ballroom ceiling. We would need scaffolding to attempt it, so we used the materials for the gazebos outside, making sure to decorate them the same as the wedding arch.

Everything looks incredible.

The only thing left is for the couple to walk down the aisle.

Strong arms wrap around me, a hard body pressing against my back. I breathe Drake in, a small smile on my lips at the same time sadness hits me.

"Hey. You look beautiful," he whispers, kissing my neck.

"In my uniform?" I ask before leaning my head to the side, moaning as his lips continue along my throat. "Shouldn't you be doing best man duties?"

"Jesse will understand," he chuckles, turning me to face him. He pulls me against him, smiling wide as he kisses the tip of my nose. "I miss you."

"You saw me this morning," I whisper, feeling a deep pang of guilt for what I'm going to do.

"I'll never get enough of you," he tells me adamantly, his gaze never wavering.

He leans down, kissing me deeply as his hand roams down my back, squeezing my arse. I moan, my traitorous body responding to his touch. The need to be closer almost consumes me, and a familiar feeling stirs in the pit of my stomach. Reluctantly I pull away, breathless. Now is not the time to be doing the naughty.

"We need to stop before we get too carried away."

He smirks down at me, his hands never leaving my backside. "I'm down with the getting carried away part."

I smack his arm lightly, grinning. I love this side to him, so flirtatious and playful. "Drake."

"What? You know you want me too." He grins.

I do. I want him more than I've ever wanted anything in my life. I'd happily give up everything to be with him. But he hasn't once asked me to stay. And the thought of him rejecting me and reminding me that this thing between us was to end when the three weeks were up would be too painful.

"Drake, Pagan, what a pleasant surprise," Aaron calls out in a sickly-sweet voice. I raise my eyebrows at Drake but he shrugs, seeming as confused by the happy tone in Aaron's voice as I am.

He's with a beautiful woman with bright red hair down to her shoulders, looking like a million dollars in a pale green dress that fits her like a glove, showing off her slim, fit silhouette and creamy pale skin. She's freakishly beautiful.

Far too pretty to be an escort.

Which begs the question, what the hell is she doing with someone like Aaron?

It's shocking, to say the least. The guy really doesn't need to send out any warning signals; him opening his arrogant mouth should be enough for anyone to steer clear. Hell, his whole persona screams player.

Drake's hand tenses in mine. My gaze drifts back to him to see his jaw tight, eyes hard.

"I want you to meet my date for the wedding." Aaron smiles as he reaches us, holding the woman's hand like she's some grand prize.

"Um," I mumble, unsure what to say. I really didn't care who he brought to the wedding, or if he turned up or not. Him thinking we would care is kind of awkward.

"Oh, Aaron, we know each other already." The elegant woman giggles, her whole face transforming into something ugly as she eyes Drake. My heart rate picks up as the animosity between the two increases. "Don't we, Drake."

I want to scratch her eyes out when she looks him up and down, licking her lips. When Drake still doesn't answer, I step forward, reaching out my hand. "Hi. I'm Pagan."

She looks at my hand, then grins, turning back to Drake. *Okay then. Whatever.* "Are you not going to say hello? We were once going to get married, so you could at least be polite."

My gaze snaps away from Drake's working jaw to... oh my God, it's Leanne, his ex-girlfriend. Aaron pulls her against him and my teeth grind together at the smug look on his face. He did this on purpose. I can practically see the wheels spinning as he stares at Drake and me with an evil gleam in his eye, smiling smugly.

"Hello, Leanne," Drake bites out. "I didn't know you were invited."

And my fears are confirmed. I squeeze Drake's hand supportively, and his fingers twitch around mine.

Her catlike smile is wicked when she finally gets a reaction from him, one I think she was expecting. "I wasn't. I found it disappointing when Bradley mentioned Jesse was getting hitched and I wasn't informed... *or* invited. But then I met Aaron here and what do you know? He needed a date for the wedding."

Aaron grins like he's won the lottery. "I really did. Such a shame for my plus one to go to waste."

"What are you really doing here, Leanne? And with this tool!"

Ouch, that hurt. It sounds like he still cares for her. Though the hostility in his voice still registers.

"I'm his date."

Aaron kisses her temple, seeming pleased with her answer before he smugly smiles at me. I narrow my eyes, pulling my hand away from Drake's. He doesn't seem to notice, and that stings.

"Well, it was lovely to meet you, but I have work to get done."

"You work here?" Leanne asks, acknowledging my presence for the first time.

"No, I'm the event organiser," I answer, feeling small when she looks revolted.

"I see."

"Cooey," Ada sings. I sag with relief when I see her strut outside in her wedding outfit, a simple cream dress that fits her small frame and a matching hat. She looks incredible and at least ten years younger, but then I see her feet and frown.

What the ever-loving hell.

"Ada," I groan, my eyes never leaving the offending items.

She ignores me, saddling up next to Aaron. "Hey, hot stuff. You ready to escort me to the wedding?"

Aaron clears his throat, choking. "Um, I have a date. Meet—"

"I know who the trollop is." She sniffs like she smells something rotten, shocking me at her blatant dislike for the woman—not that I can blame her.

"Ada!" Aaron snaps, looking surprised.

"What? She wasn't invited, and for good reason. When my grandson finds her here and learns you brought her, be prepared. She's not liked here... at all."

Aaron actually looks worried for a minute, biting his bottom lip. "But I—"

"Ada, I see you haven't changed," Leanne comments sweetly, but there's venom in her gaze.

Oh dear.

Ada narrows her eyes on Leanne. "Neither have you. Are you here to get your claws into my grandson? Because it's a waste of time, you know. He's got taste now. My lovely Pagan is good to him."

All eyes shoot to me and I take a step back.

"They're not going to last," she sneers. "We belong together."

"No, we don't," Drake snaps, stepping to my side like I can protect him, but I'm still a little hurt by his earlier actions.

"What?" Aaron yells, facing her with horror written across his face. "You said you liked me."

Leanne pats his cheek, batting her eyelashes. "I do. I really do." He relaxes, buying her lie like the fool he is.

Ada scoffs. "You're wanted upstairs, Aaron. And if I were you, I'd get rid of the trash before any of my family sees her."

"Well it was nice speaking to you all," Aaron rushes out. He places his arm around Leanne's waist before pulling her towards the house.

After he's gone, Ada turns to Drake. "Your brother is going to go apeshit when he sees them together. He hates her more than you do."

"Why?" I blurt out. I know the Donovans are close, but this doesn't seem like a big enough issue for Jesse to fall out with Aaron over. Not when he's done other unforgivable things.

Ada rolls her eyes, Drake answering. "Because she tried to seduce him. It was after we broke up. She wanted back in with the family once she realised what a mess she made. Her family cut her off completely after that stunt."

"Darn tootin'" Ada snaps.

"Okay. This is so bizarre. Do you want me to do something? Ask Shane to escort her out?"

"Yes," Drake sighs.

"No! I want to see what my grandson will do. Anyway, I came down to tell you the photographer wants some pictures of all the men together."

"I'll go up in a sec. I just want to talk to Pagan."

Ada nods, then goes to turn, but I call her name. "Why are you wearing glittery pumps?"

She lifts her foot, twisting it side to side with a smile on her face. "Exquisite, aren't they?"

"Um no, they aren't. Where are the shoes I bought you?"

"Those death traps?"

I roll my eyes at her dramatics. "Yes, those."

"I threw them in the bin."

She says it so matter-of-factly, I want to strangle her. "Please tell me you're lying."

"I'm not. Check the bins if you don't believe me."

"Ada!" I yell, throwing my hands up. "They cost three hundred quid."

"Thieving bastards." She walks off, muttering something under her breath.

"Where are you going? I'm not finished." She waves her hand, ignoring me as she continues on to the house. "I'm going to kill her. Would it hurt her to wear what we put out?"

Drake chuckles, pulling me against him. "Forget about Grams. Are you okay?"

I raise a brow. "Shouldn't I be asking you that?"

He smiles, kissing my nose, and I melt against him, forgetting all about earlier. "No. I only care about you."

My heart stills and those damn tears threaten once again. "I'm fine," I answer softly, too choked up to say much more on the subject. "How are you?"

He chuckles darkly, a shadow crossing his face. "I'm not going to lie —seeing her here is a surprise. I never wanted to see her again. She nearly broke Jesse and Amelia up with her games and nearly broke twenty years of friendship our parents shared. I don't like her, never will, and I'll never understand her motives. I'm just sorry for the way I reacted. I guess I was stunned."

I run my fingers along his jaw, my features softening. "I understand.

Hopefully she leaves before Amelia sees her. I can't have her being upset. It's her wedding day."

"I'll make sure she leaves. Although, I think once Mum sees her, I won't have to. I'm actually surprised Grams didn't try to do something just then. She really showed her maturity."

That makes me pause. I glance nervously to the house, thinking intently. "She wouldn't do anything today of all days, would she?"

He follows my gaze, shrugging. "Who knows, it's—"

"It's Ada, I know," I mutter, my mind still on the house and what she's up to. He smiles, pulling me against him once again. "You, mister, need to go upstairs and get the group photos taken. You're running behind already, and I need the photographer down here to set up."

"Yes, boss," he says seriously. "Always working."

"Always."

He smiles, kissing me one last time before staring down at me. "Tonight, I need to talk to you about something. We can go to the gardens. Is that okay?"

Knives stab into my chest. If I attempt to speak, I'll give everything away with the emotions bubbling inside me, so I nod instead, giving him a forced smile as I lean up and kiss him one last time.

Then I watch him walk away, knowing he's taking my heart with him.

Chapter Twenty-Three

The wedding ceremony was a fairy tale, beautiful in a magical way. Tears of happiness and sadness burst free as I watched the happy couple swear their vows to one another. I tried everything to hold back my emotions, but the minute I watched Jesse's eyes fill with tears when he saw his stunningly beautiful bride step into the aisle, I was a goner.

I've seen so many couples in my line of work get married. Most of them claim to love one another, but when I watched them exchange vows, they missed the spark that couples who are truly in love possess.

On rare occasions, there are couples just like Jesse and Amelia, who couldn't be more perfectly matched in every way that counts.

They shared their vows, promising to love one another, and I'm so caught up in the moment I can barely catch my breath. The way they stared into one another's eyes, I could feel they meant and breathed every single word they vowed. It's a blessed gift to witness such a special moment.

I swear I felt everything they felt for one another. They poured that love from their very souls in front of everyone who mattered.

There wasn't a dry eye in the house.

Jealousy crawled up my throat. I want what they have, crave it, and now more than ever, I wish I had it.

It wasn't going to happen for me though.

But I am human enough to be happy that Jesse and Amelia have it. They deserve to spend the rest of their lives happily married to their soulmate.

The day has been truly blissful, a huge success all around.

That is if you don't count the black eye Aaron now has, courtesy of Jesse.

The shouting began as soon as Drake stepped foot in the back door. I'd gone running, both of us heading to the attic where all the men were gathered, waiting to have their group photo taken.

What I walked into jolted me. Jesse had Aaron by the scruff of his collar, pinned against the wall. I'd never seen the man so mad. I had shakily stepped in to intervene, since none of the men seemed at all fazed the groom had punched his best man.

It seemed seeing Leanne didn't go over well with any of the Donovans though. Once Jesse demanded Aaron choose between their friendship and Leanne, it was absolute chaos. Aaron wisely chose his friendship, surprising everyone and me. He really did value his friendship with Jesse. Bros over hos and all that.

But the minute Jesse nodded and stepped back, the other males were yelling at him, threatening his manhood.

It didn't stop there though. The women had also found out about Leanne's appearance—no doubt from Ada—and somehow managed to corner Aaron on the stairs on his way down to escort Leanne out. They dragged him into a nearby room by his ear. Amelia got so mad, she landed the slap to end all slaps to his right cheek.

It was truly a beautiful moment. And if you look closely, you can still see her handprint on his face.

Aaron took it, apologising profusely until Amelia stopped screaming at him, finally calming down enough to hear him out.

That set the women off all over again. In the end, Ada took matters into her own hands and volunteered—rather giddily—to get rid of Leanne. So while the rest restrained Aaron, making sure he didn't intervene, she left the room with a Cheshire cat grin on her face.

I followed behind in case I needed to be peacemaker or call for Shane, but I shouldn't have bothered. Ada could certainly handle herself, not to mention a raging, crazy woman.

When Leanne refused to leave, putting up a fight and asking to speak to Aaron, Ada had calmly nodded and left the room.

That's when shit really hit the fan.

Ada walked out carrying a basket of eggs, like Little Red Riding Hood with her apples. Before Leanne could open her mouth to ask what she was doing, or even scream, Ada took aim and fired.

It was messy.

No one, not even Pam or Mary, the sanest of the group, stepped in to help her. They kept watching long after she was run out of the manor.

I have to admit, it was amusing as well as entertaining to watch her run whilst covered in egg yolk.

The other fun part? Alison recorded the whole thing as a wedding present to Amelia and Jesse.

She's a real giver.

"Hey, are you okay?" Alison asks, walking up to me.

And it begins again.

She's been asking me if I'm okay every twenty minutes or so, as if my answer is going to change. I know I've not been in the best of moods, but it's beginning to wear thin on my already shaky nerves. It's only a matter of time before I burst.

"Yeah." My voice is hoarse, and Alison links her arm through mine, squeezing me to her side.

"Are you sure about this? It's okay to change your mind."

I turn to her, tears brimming. "I-I can't," I choke out. "I love him so much." At the moment, everyone is sat eating their meals, so thankfully their attention isn't on me. I'm sure it will raise some questions if they see me bawling like a baby.

Her eyes soften as she runs a finger down my cheek. "You don't have to do this. We'll miss you if you change your mind, but I'll be there for you, always."

As tempting as that is, I have my reasons for what I'm doing. I love her for being there for me, but as much as she tells me she understands, I know she doesn't. She wants me to speak to Drake first before I make any rash decisions. Not doing so is selfish, I know, but I'm trying. Be that as it may, I'm still trying to protect my heart from something it will never recover from.

Even Jeff had something to say when I approached him late last night after sneaking out of bed, leaving Drake sleeping soundlessly. He begged and pleaded with me to talk to the Donovans, but after one look at my tear-streaked face, he gave up and agreed to have our car ready with our bags inside.

Which reminds me.

"They're going to start the speeches soon. We should go now before they notice something's wrong or that we're leaving."

As soon as the speeches are done and Drake's best man duties are fulfilled, he'll come find me; the heated look he's been sending me all day promises that. I knew when I decided to leave that this would be my only window without having to worry someone would see us. All I need is to face one of the Donovans.

Saying goodbye, even the best of goodbyes, is always hard, but saying goodbye to the Donovans and to Drake... I can't bear to think about it. They've come to mean a lot to me.

"Okay. I'll just let Jessica know that she's in charge and we're heading out now."

I nod, then grab her bicep. "Make sure she tells Drake about the note."

She doesn't look happy when I mention the note, but I'm not all that surprised. She said it was the coward's way of dealing with things, but it's the only way I can say goodbye without breaking down and embarrassing myself.

We fought for hours this morning when I told her my plans, her trying to talk me out of it whilst I tried to explain my reasons without sounding like a sad case.

"I'll meet you outside," she says, then walks away shaking her head.

I know she's upset with me. Fuck, I'm upset with myself. A part of me knows I'm making a tremendous mistake, but I've had my heart broken before. I've been betrayed. I can't go through that again, not when Drake hasn't told me how he feels. I won't put myself out there like that—not again, not ever. I'd rather leave here with the happy memories of our time together than memories of him telling me this was just a little bit of fun to him. I know it wasn't just about the sex; we connected on a deeper level. He feels *something* for me, but love? Men don't fall in love with someone in three weeks. Not with a woman like me. Not with my past luck.

So I'll treasure the memories I have. Everything else... well, what I don't know can't hurt me. And I'm willing to risk everything so I don't get burnt again. I'd never recover.

When I walk outside, Jeff greets me with a sad smile. "Pagan, are you sure you shouldn't talk to the Donovans before you leave? They're going to be very sad that you didn't stay to say goodbye."

I force a smile as a tear slips free. "Will you tell them I said I'm sorry I had to leave so suddenly? It's just too hard to say goodbye to them. They've been so good to me. I'm going to miss them all like crazy, including you and Emily."

"Oh, Pagan," he sighs, surprising me by pulling me in for a hug. I hug him back, more tears falling from my cheeks.

"Hey," Alison says softly as we pull apart. She takes one look at my face and growls—yes, *growls*—at me. "We're not going."

I blink, thinking I misheard her. Jeff squeezes my hand before wisely leaving us and walking over to the front doors. "No, we *are* going. We've been through this a million times already," I snap.

"You're already a bloody mess, for Christ's sake. Just tell him you love him, woman."

There are times when I want to slap my best friend. Now is one of those times, because as right as she is, she's also extremely wrong.

Before arriving, all I wanted was a break from my job so I could find a life. Now I've found someone I picture a life with and it scares me. It petrifies me to no end. But it's a vicious cycle. I can take a chance, tell him how deeply I love him, and can either have him tell me he loves me back or have him run away.

There's no denying the connection between us is sizzling, but I've read emotions wrong before, more than I care to count.

If I'm honest with myself, truly honest, I know I'm running away because I'm scared. I'm scared of what it would mean if he does love me back, but mostly I'm scared as hell because there's a fifty percent chance that he doesn't. If I try to tell Alison that, she'll never let me leave this property until I find out.

"I said no, Alison. Now please, just drop it," I choke out. More tears fall and her face softens as she reluctantly nods and moves to the car.

"Pot and kettle," Aaron sneers and I jump, turning around to face him.

I shield my eyes from the bright sun to see him glaring down at me. "Excuse me?"

"You. You're a hypocrite."

I eye the man who I once thought was my world and bite back a curse. "How?" I don't owe him anything, but I guess hearing what he has to say is another way of punishing myself for what I'm about to do. Leaving here without a goodbye isn't just rude, it's going to hurt those I've come to care about.

"You're about to leave him without saying goodbye. You're just going to leave him a shitty fucking note. I heard that one tell the other chick inside." He points to Alison, who's stepped out of the car, ready to intervene. "I followed you out here to see what was going on to hear more fucked-up bullshit."

"And?" My voice sounds stronger, even though I feel anything but. My insides are twisting up and I'm seconds away from vomiting all over the gravel driveway. His loathsome expression is scorching and I look away, uncomfortable.

"And?" he laughs humourlessly. "You've made my life a living hell for three weeks for doing exactly what you're doing to him." He laughs again, narrowing those beady eyes on me. "You think I didn't know it was you? I also know you had help. I just don't know who."

Well shit.

My eyes widen. He never let on that he knew who it was. Not once.

I shrug, pretending indifference, though the harsh words slice through my heart and I struggle to breathe. "It's different."

"How?" he bites back.

I'm stunned for a minute at the bitterness in his voice. He doesn't even care about the emotional turmoil going on inside of me, or that he's making everything feel much worse—making *me* feel shittier than I already do.

The angry expression on his face and the disappointment shining in eyes swirl the anger inside my chest. He has no right, no right at all. And who does he think he is, thinking he has the right to be mad at me?

"Because we were together, Aaron. You cheated on me and got another girl pregnant. You didn't even say sorry to me. You just left without a word, not even a goodbye."

"I didn't have a choice back then, Pagan. You have one now."

It's my turn to laugh, glaring at him. "No choice? There's always a choice, Aaron, but you chose to run away."

"Which is what you're doing!" he yells, throwing his hands up. "And I didn't get a choice. As soon as Loraine told my parents she was pregnant, we were shipped away to my grandparents' house. We were married a week later. We didn't even like each other. It was a drunken one-night stand, a stupid mistake. One I've been paying for ever since."

I stagger back, floored by the declaration and the hurt in his eyes. But it doesn't change anything. And it certainly doesn't matter to me anymore; that ship sailed a long time ago. He still made the choice to cheat on me and act indifferent about it. His message was cold, uncaring, and it cut me deeper than him actually cheating on me.

"I don't know why you're telling me any of this now," I whisper, wiping away my tears.

"Because I don't want you to make the same mistake I did, Pagan. You'll regret it for the rest of your life. Trust me, I know first-hand how the guilt can eat away at you. I'm not saying we'd still be together if I hadn't done what I did—I'm not stupid—but this... this isn't right. You should say goodbye."

The sincerity in his voice surprises me. "It doesn't matter anymore. I'm leaving. You don't deserve my reasons, Aaron, but it's for the best. For once in my life, I'm protecting myself. I've been made a fool of too many times. I won't let it happen again."

He shakes his head sadly, looking disappointed in me. "He loves you."

Narrowing my eyes, I take a step forward, poking him in the chest. How dare he be so cruel. He's only telling me so he can try to manipulate me into doing something stupid, something that will most likely destroy my soul. Because Drake doesn't love me.

"Screw you, Aaron. Screw you! You don't know anything!" I scream, banging my fists against his chest.

"You're a bitch if you do this. You're not the Pagan I remember," he sneers, looking appalled.

He doesn't know the first thing about me or what I've been through. He wasn't there.

With an angry cry, I knee him in the balls. He falls to the floor with a howl, his face turning red.

"Fuck! Really? The balls?" he wheezes.

"You deserve more than a knee to the balls. You may think you never had a choice, Aaron, but you did. You only had to come to my house and tell me what was happening. I wouldn't have liked it but I would've understood it, especially if what you're saying is true. I knew what your parents were like, how they threw a new girl at you every weekend. But you didn't believe in me. Not once. I deserved more than you gave me, and I deserve more from you now. Don't ever play with my emotions like that again. It's cruel."

I'm breathing heavy, my nails digging into the palm of my skin, cutting into me. Too many emotions are swirling around inside me, and it won't be long before the dam breaks and I'm inconsolable.

"I would never have been able to face you, Pagan. I did stupid things. We were young, but I did love you. I know I don't stand a chance now. I've seen the way you look at him. I just want you to be happy, Pagan, and he makes you happy. More than I ever did."

"He doesn't love me," I murmur, shaking my head.

"He does," he insists, leaning up on his knees. "Just tell him. What do you have to lose?"

Our gazes meet and lock. "Everything," I whisper before turning and walking away, my heart starting to crack as I struggle to take in a breath.

"Pagan," he calls but I ignore him, getting into the passenger seat without turning back.

"Drive! Please just drive," I plead, tears clogging my throat as I try to hold on a little longer. My throat burns and I rub over my heart with the palm of my hand, trying to ease the pain. It doesn't work and a tear escapes, my world crumbling around me.

"Okay, Pagan. Okay," Alison tells me softly, taking my hand in hers and squeezing. "Everything's going to be okay."

I turn to look at her profile, more tears falling. "It's never going to be okay again."

"You can't believe that."

I turn away from her, staring out the window as we drive through the manor's gates. I don't answer her and she doesn't press me, for which I'm thankful. I don't think I could handle hearing her beg me to go back anymore.

My phone starts ringing, Drake's name flashing across the screen, and my heart lurches. I suck in an unsteady breath, raw primal pain consuming my whole body as I continue to stare at the screen.

My chest feels hollow, like there's a big gaping hole where my heart used to be. I'll never be whole without him.

I crave his embrace, to feel the safety of his arms wrapped around me as he tells me anything and everything. I already long for one of his kisses and wish I had made our kiss this morning last longer, to savour the feel of his soft lips and his hands on my body.

But I'm gone.

He's gone.

And in five hours, we'll be miles apart from each other.

With a heavy heart, I switch the phone off, throwing it back into my bag where it will remain. There's no way I can turn it on to hear his voice or read his messages asking where I've gone. It would be too much, and I'm not ready to feel that kind of heartache.

I'm thankful for the silence, to try to calm my breathing as I struggle to come to terms with what I've just done.

Because the farther we travel from the manor, from Drake, I know wholeheartedly that I just made the biggest mistake of my life.

I curl up on my side, staring blankly out of the window as more tears fall free. I try to bite back a sob, but the farther we go, the more painful it is to keep inside.

Somewhere along the way, Alison pulls over, undoing my belt and pulling me into her arms.

The dam breaks and the most gut-wrenching sobs tear from my throat as I cling to my best friend, wishing I could make this pain go away.

"I'm here. I'm here. Let it out. It's all going to be okay."

"It hurts so much," I sob, clinging to her as my body shudders.

She rubs my back soothingly, kissing my temple. "Shh, it's okay. Everything's okay."

I shake my head against her. "I can't breathe. God, it hurts. Why does it hurt so much?" I cry.

"Because you love him, Pagan. I know it hurts now, I know it does, but it will be okay. It will." She says it so adamantly, like she's trying to convince herself more than me.

But she's wrong. This pain is scorching me from the inside so badly that I want to scream until my voice is hoarse.

I cling to her like she's my lifeline as she rubs my back, like she has all the time in the world and isn't parked on the hard shoulder of a motorway.

I don't know what I'd do if she wasn't here.

Her soothing voice does nothing to calm me though. Nothing can. Because by the time the last sob breaks free, I pull away from Alison, curling into a ball as I face the window once more. I feel dead inside, numb as I ignore her pleas to talk to her as she begins to drive.

Nothing will ever be the same. Not without him.

I really have messed everything up.

Chapter Twenty-Four

ONE WEEK LATER

Seconds turned into minutes, minutes turned into hours, and hours turned into days, but no matter how much time passed, the hollow, empty feeling inside my chest would not go. The loneliness of not seeing Drake every day is devastating and consuming. He's all I've been able to think about.

But that's the funny thing about time—it's always the same. It ticks with each second, with each minute, and with each hour. But so much can happen within a moment of time. It only takes a second for your heart to break. Minutes to make the biggest mistake of your life. Days to fall in love.

There is no time limit when it comes to the choices we make in life.

And in three weeks, I royally screwed mine up.

Dramatic? Maybe, but that's what you get when you're the girl who feels everything on a deeper level. Who loves unconditionally and forgives easily. I'm that girl. The one easily broken.

The second Alison and I arrived home, I used her phone to tell my parents I wouldn't be back until Tuesday. It gave me a few days to just be me—to mourn my loss, if you will. I felt bad for lying to them, but I needed space to feel a resemblance of normalcy.

It didn't work.

Even now my heart is heavy, and I've been walking around like a zombie since I got back.

I've avoided everyone at all costs. When I 'arrived home', I went to my parents' house, pretending to be happy, like there was nothing wrong. It took the very little energy I had left to pretend I wasn't falling apart from the inside.

After that, I just wanted to be by myself. I lied to them, telling them I had to work on another event and would be busy for a few days. That was five days ago.

They've knocked on my door a few times, and I swear I've heard either my mum or Alison try to use their spare keys to get in. Thankfully I thought ahead and bolted the door. I even ripped my home phone out so I didn't have to speak to anyone or hear their voice over the voicemail.

I just wanted to be alone for a while longer. It wasn't a lot to ask.

For the past two days, all I've done is sleep and watch TV. I couldn't even tell you what was playing. I was looking, but I wasn't really watching; everything's been a tearful blur.

Until today.

My eyes are red and puffy from crying non-stop. You'd think after seven days I would've pulled myself together, but if anything I feel even more lost now. I keep thinking 'what if' on so many things, that maybe things would be different. I wouldn't be hurting, wondering if the man I love loved me back or not. Every scenario of what I could've done differently runs through my mind. But it doesn't matter what I change, because the results are always the same.

I fucked up.

Big time.

The banging that woke me from my afternoon nap continues, thumping through my sore head. "Pagan, open the door!" Dean yells, banging some more—you know, in case I didn't hear the first ten times.

Groaning, I hold a pillow over my head to block him out. I can't deal with my brother right now. I feel like shit, and I have the headache to end all headaches from crying non-stop. Listening to Dean will just make it worse, and the second he sees me, he'll know something's up and demand answers... or someone to punch.

"Open the door, sweetheart," my dad shouts.

I lift my head from under the pillow, wondering if I'm hearing things. *I'm not.*

"Come on, Pagan, open up." My mother's voice is calmer, yet full of concern.

"If you don't open the door, I'm kicking the fucking thing down," Dean threatens, banging again.

"Dean, calm down. You'll scare her," Lola chides.

Oh God.

They're all here.

"Come on, Pagan, open up. They know everything," Alison calls out.

I groan into my pillow, wanting to strangle my best friend. I don't even know why we're friends anymore. "Go away."

There's no point in pretending I'm not in. Alison's been delivering containers of food every day to make sure I'm eating, though they're still in the kitchen where I left them. I didn't want to have her overreacting, calling the police, ambulance, and fire station, telling them I'm dead.

She'd do it too.

"Open the fucking door, Pagan, and let us in. We're worried fucking sick," Dean shouts.

"I don't think she'll answer with you going all macho like this," Lola snaps. "Pagan, open the door for me. We want to check that you're okay."

I'm actually tempted to open the door to her. I just don't have the energy right now. Hearing her sweet, soothing voice makes me feel guilty for ignoring her, but I just want to be left alone.

I hear muttering, then a few curses before silence falls outside my door.

Well, that didn't take long. I thought they'd be out there all day.

Rolling over and facing my bathroom door, more tears slip free. I hate feeling weak and pathetic, but right now, that's who I am. And it's infuriating.

A rapping gains my attention, and for a minute I think my brother is picking my lock, but then rustling follows, sounding a lot closer. I turn to the noise, a scream bubbling in my throat when I see a large form in a hoody climbing through my window.

Before a gasp of air can escape, I see my twin brother's handsome face and hiss, "What are you doing?" My voice sounds foreign, raspy. I wince, wishing I didn't sound as bad as I look.

They're never going to leave now.

"What am *I* doing? What are *you* doing? You look like shit." His gaze sweeps over me, looking for any signs of injury. "We've been worried sick. And what is that godawful smell?"

Discreetly as I can, I smell myself, wincing when I do. I really should've taken a shower last night.

"I'm fine, as you can see. And I don't smell anything," I pout, glaring at him.

He tsks, shaking his head. "What's wrong, Pagan? Do you need me to go sort him out?"

My eyes water. "No! I just want to be left alone." I sound like a whiny teenager.

"So you can rot?" he snaps.

"Ugh, can you just climb back out of the window?" I growl, lifting the blanket over my head, trying to ignore him.

He walks towards the end of the bed and I relax, glad he got the picture and is leaving—

"Hey, what the hell are you doing?" I scream.

He rips the blanket the rest of the way off with a smug grin. "You're getting out of bed and showering. Then you can talk to Mum about what's going on. I don't need to hear about my sister's sex life."

"I want to be left alone!" I shout, thumping my fists on the mattress.

"Tough shit. I'm not letting my sister lock herself away. It's not you. It never has been. Even at your worst, you always manage to find the positive in life. You've never given in, and you never wallow. *And* you never blow off family, ever. I won't let it happen now. Not to you."

"Get out! I want to be left alone, just for a few more days. Please."

"No! Now get up."

I get up, but only because I want my blanket. He smiles like he's won, but then I grab the blanket off the floor. He sees and growls, grabbing the other side and pulling. I stumble and grit my teeth, pulling it away.

"Go away, Sid. I want to go to fucking sleep. I'm tired."

"At three in the afternoon?" he retorts, pulling sharply.

Giving up, I slap his hands away. Distracted, he tries to grab mine but I move quickly, pulling his hair. "Let me go to sleep."

"Get off my hair, Pagan." His voice is high-pitched; if I wasn't in a mood, I'd be teasing him right now.

"Not until you give in and go away."

"Never!" he screams, but I keep pulling. One thing he can't stand is having his hair pulled.

He's such a girl.

It's the easiest thing to grab a hold of since he's always kept it long, saying it goes with his bad boy image. But that's just an image. He's the softest lad I know.

The banging on my door starts up again, their shouting echoing around the room.

I pull harder, but before I can dodge him, he's pulling my hair back, both of us bent over like teenagers.

"Get off my hair before I have to remove you myself, Pagan."

"Like you ever could," I growl.

He kicks my feet out from under me and I scream, landing with a thump on my back.

Wood splintering rings in my ears and I groan. Footsteps come running into the bedroom as Sid pins me down, sitting on my stomach to make sure I'm nowhere near his nether region.

He knows me too well.

"What on earth?" my mum gasps, taking us in and snapping, "How old are you?"

We both groan, turning to look at her.

"He started it."

"She started it."

We glare at each other. "You started it," we say simultaneously.

"It's like we've time-travelled back twelve years," my dad groans, stepping forward. "Get off your sister, Sid."

"What is that fucking smell?" Dean grunts, looking around the room with his nose in the air.

I moan, wishing I had my blanket to hide under.

Sid jumps off me, looking at Dean as he points down at me. "That."

"It is not," I snap, sitting up.

Mum steps forward, bending down towards me. She reaches out for me but then pauses, her face scrunching. "Um, Pagan, sweetheart, I think it is. You need to jump in the shower."

"I want to know who to fucking kill first. She isn't going anywhere until I get a name and address," Dean growls.

"I told you it's not like that," Alison tells him.

I glare at my best friend. She tries to not meet my eyes, but after a few seconds she turns my way, shrinking behind my brother.

"I hate you!" I snap. "We're no longer best friends."

"I'm sorry, but you left me no choice. I'm worried about you, and I had every right to be. You have food growing fur in the kitchen, and this bedroom? It stinks."

Way to point out the glaringly obvious, bitch.

"Did you really need to point that out? In front of everyone?"

"Clearly," she snaps, pouting.

"Whatever. Can you all go now? I want to be left alone for the night. You can see I'm fine."

"You're not fine," Lola whispers. Hearing her voice brings more tears to my eyes, and when I look up, I'm met with her watery, sad smile. "You haven't smiled once since we walked in. You always smile."

"Yeah, well...." I shrug, not knowing what to say as guilt consumes me.

"Okay, boys, you go get us some takeout. Her kitchen isn't fit for me to cook in. Alison, you get the bin bags and gut the whole kitchen. Lola, you strip her sheets," Mum orders, then looks at the sheets again. "And bin them."

Everyone moves all at once.

"Wait... what... but...," I stammer.

"No, no talking. You, my girl, are getting in the shower. Come on."

With no choice, I let my mum help me to my feet, feeling a little weak. I haven't eaten in two days, which probably wasn't the wisest choice, a wave of dizziness hitting me.

"What am I going to do with you?" she murmurs sadly.

I stare at the troubled look in her eyes and burst into tears. I hate feeling so hurt, like such a failure.

"Let it out," she whispers, pulling me in to her. I hold on for dear life, breathing in her fresh, earthy scent.

"I was such a coward, Mum. I just left without even explaining or telling him how I felt." She rubs my back, cooing soothingly in my ear as I let it all out. I didn't believe I even had any more tears to shed.

"You're not a coward. Don't ever say that again. You fell in love and got scared. What girl who's been through the heartache you have wouldn't do that? You have such a big heart, my darling girl."

I cling to her harder, needing to be held. She does, wrapping her arms tighter around me, kissing my temple.

"I really messed things up with him. Now it's too late to do anything about it or see if he feels the same. And even if he did, he wouldn't now, not after what I did. I feel so stupid."

She sighs. "You haven't messed anything up. Have you tried calling him?"

Pulling away, I look up at her as I wipe my tears and shake my head. "I'm too scared to even turn my phone back on. I wouldn't even know what to say to him. What do you say to someone you spent three amazing weeks with and then left without a word to?"

She runs her fingers through my hair, tilting her head. "Why don't you start with sorry, and why you ran away?"

I laugh at that. "It won't be that easy. He's been hurt before, worse than me. His fiancée cheated on him with his best friend. But before he found out about them, he found out she was pregnant. He thought it was his. And according to his nan, he was hurt by the betrayal." I pause, taking a deep breath. "I don't even know why we're talking about this. It's not like he has feelings for me. I'm just some stupid event organiser he had a three-week fling with."

Narrowing her eyes, she steps forward. "Stop! Stop talking about yourself like you don't mean anything, Pagan Lily Salvatore. I won't have it. You aren't someone to have a fling with. You're more than that, and any man, even the slimiest, can see that. And from what Alison told me, he was infatuated by you. So you, my daughter, are going to get in that shower, wipe those tears and come out as the Pagan we all know and love. Then we'll talk about what you should do next. Now go!"

My eyes widen at the heat in her voice. She's shouted at us plenty of times, but never like this.

"But—"

"No buts, missy. You'll do as you're told. When you get out, we'll put a plan of action together. You're going to eat first though. You've lost too much weight."

"But—"

"What did I say?" she says in that mum voice of hers, giving me a pointed stare.

"I know, but—"

"But what?" she asks, sighing.

"But I love you," I blurt out, because anything else can wait. More tears spring to my eyes as I pull her in for a hug. I'm grateful for my brother climbing through the window because I really did need my mum. I just didn't know how badly until she was here in front of me.

A thought occurs to me.

"Mum?"

She pulls away, sighing again. "What now?"

I give her a weary smile, concern worrying my bottom lip. "Um, who's going to fix my door?"

She rolls her eyes. "If you had answered the door, then you wouldn't be worrying over it. We should make you live without one for the worry you put us through."

"But?"

"But we're not going to. I'll have Dean get a new one when he gets back. Now go shower. You really do stink, darling."

I roll my eyes at my mother, then head to the bathroom.

My only concern now is what plan she's going to cook up. There's no way I can go back to the Donovans, and a phone call seems insulting somehow. I can't possibly see how we can fix this.

But there's no denying that the thought of talking to him again, maybe even seeing him, has lightened my mood a little.

Mums really can fix everything.

Chapter Twenty-Five

TWO WEEKS LATER

*W*hen my mum told me her plan, I happily went along with it. More so to get her off my back, knowing she wasn't going to drop it until I gave in.

It was supposed to be simple.

All I had to do was call Drake, explain, say I'm sorry and that I'm madly in love with him.

So I promised her I'd do it tomorrow.

And we know how well *they* turn out for me.

I got my phone out of my bag, all geared up to call him. But the minute I pressed my finger over the button to switch it on...

I dropped my phone back into my bag like it was on fire.

And then promised myself *tomorrow*.

Days went by, and before I knew it, a week did. Then another.

I've resigned myself to doing nothing. It's pointless and too late to do anything.

I'm hopeless when it comes to love.

Even my dreams are screaming at me, reminding me of what a failure I've become. A little girl, one I've dreamt about for a while now, haunts me. She comes to me each night, crying and breaking my heart all over again. I've never met her, but my feelings for her, even when I wake up, are fervid. It's scary how much I care for her.

Everyone's been by every day to check in on me. I've worked from home most days, but others, I've left Alison and Catherine to deal with it.

I tried escaping to the cabin my family uses for the rangers, but with my brother and my pestering mum, I only lasted an hour before one of them showed up.

The one day I went, I walked to the meadow—a place special to Dean and Lola.

And in a meadow full of wild flowers, I picked up a lonesome dandelion. It reminded me much of myself, surrounded by a lot of people but feeling utterly alone.

I picked it up, closed my eyes and blew, wishing for a happily ever after.

The past few days though, I've managed to spend my time alone, sitting in the back of Lola's book/coffee shop. The place totally rocks and is very chic. She has the bright sofas with different-coloured pillows cleaned every two weeks so they stay fresh and new and oh-so-comfy. They're my favourite place to sit, and for the past two days I've hogged the entire sofa, not letting anyone sit beside me or on the sofa opposite.

If asking for them to move didn't get them to go away, me glaring at them surely did.

Which is what I just finished doing to a couple who thought it was okay to disturb me whilst reading a favourite book of mine. No one should be disturbed whilst reading about sexy military men.

"Pagan, you really need to stop glaring at my customers. Even Lorelei is scared to come over and serve you. She's also getting a lot of complaints."

"I'm okay with getting up and getting my own drinks." I smile. "And I'm not glaring, per se. I'm just encouraging them." I shrug.

"Encouraging them to take their business elsewhere?"

Now I feel bad.

I look over to the door, and sure enough, the couple are grabbing their coats and leaving, clearly pissed. It's pouring down rain, the skies dark. When I look back at Lola, guilt tugs at me.

"I'm sorry. I'm being a bitch. But in all fairness, I did ask you to have a 'reserved' post put on the table."

"And I told you no," she reminds me, her lips twitching.

"It would be so cool though. We could be like *Friends*, have our own table for the gang." I beam, loving the idea.

"You kicked your brothers out when they tried to keep you company." She takes a seat on the arm of the sofa.

I scoff, waving it off. "I was reading about Sawyer."

She rolls her eyes. "If I think about the sign, will you back off my customers?"

"If you put the sign on the table, you wouldn't need to worry about your customers," I argue sweetly.

She sighs, shaking her head. "I'll think about it. But please, just for today, let people at least sit opposite you. The storm is bad outside. They need somewhere to go."

Since I love my sister-in-law, I'll agree just this once. It's a small sacrifice in the grand scheme of things because I know she'll give in where my sign is concerned... eventually.

The door jingles and she gives me a pointed look before turning to greet the customer. Only my name is shouted as soon as they step inside.

"Pagan! Pagan!"

Alison, soaking wet, rushes in, heading straight for me with a panicked look on her face.

"Oh my God, what's wrong?" I ask, dropping my book on my seat as I shoot up, meeting her halfway.

"It's—oh, my God, Pagan. Your flat," she gasps, pointing behind her.

My pulse starts beating wildly. "What? What about my flat?"

Oh God, it better not be on fire.

Please no.

I have things that are unreplaceable in there.

"Flat," she gasps, still pointing.

But I know Alison. If my flat were on fire, she'd already be dragging

229

me across the road with buckets of water, not standing here leaving me in suspense.

I glance at Lola, who looks as confused as I am. "Breathe, Alison. Tell me what exactly has you freaked out."

She breathes in, calming herself before looking me dead in the eye. "There are people taking your stuff, Pagan. I told them you weren't moving or anything, but they told me to take it up with the boss. You aren't moving, are you?"

"You're moving?" Lola asks, hurt evident in her voice.

My eyes widen as I look between them. "No!" Then I run without thought until I get to the door, turning back when I realise they aren't following. "Are you coming?"

Lola steps forward but Alison stops her, shaking her head. "It's best if you deal with this. Go on."

Shrugging it off, I open the door and race across the street in the pouring rain. I see removal men walking down the side alley with boxes and my anger surfaces.

"Hey! Hey, what are you doing with my things?" I yell at the nearest man, stepping in front of him.

He stares down at me, clearly not worried in the slightest that he's taking my things against my will. "I'm just doing my job, miss. If you go upstairs, our boss can assist you."

"Boss?"

"Yes, miss."

"Stop calling me miss. I'm not a fucking teacher. Now go put my things back," I snap, pointing towards my flat.

He shakes his head. "Our orders are to pack everything into the truck. If you're worried we haven't packed anything, don't. We got everything but the furniture."

Worried he hasn't packed everything?

Has he lost his goddamn mind?

I growl and step forwards to take the box away from him. "My things aren't going anywhere with you."

He sighs like I'm annoying him. "Look, I don't get paid by the hour, so if you could just let me do my job, that would be great."

I notice three more men walking back into my flat. "Where are they going?"

"To get the rest of the stuff. There're only a few boxes left, miss."

I stomp on his foot, ignoring his hiss of pain and cursing as I march to the side entrance to my flat. There's an entrance at the back of my office, which is the one I mostly use since I don't like the alley, especially when it's dark.

I take the stairs two at a time, then come to a full-blown stop when I reach the front door, my eyes fixated on the man sitting on my mini purple sofa, making the thing look even tinier.

"What?" Tears spring to my eyes and I pinch myself, making sure this isn't some dream. "Ouch," I gasp, and more tears fill my eyes.

It's real.

Very real.

Drake Donovan is really sitting in my front room, leg crossed over his other knee as he eyes me with a devilish smirk.

"All done."

What the...?

I spin around, coming face-to-face with Ada. "What?"

She grins. "You can't get rid of me that easily. I'm taking the boys out for something to eat before we head on. See if you in a few."

"Take your time, Grams," Drake orders, his voice raspy.

"Sure will. Got me some eye candy."

Slowly, I turn back to the man of my dreams, my mouth opening and closing.

"Is this real?" I whisper.

His lips twitch as he stands, walking towards me. "You tell me. You're the one who left me in the middle of a wedding—luckily not our own—and didn't explain why or even say goodbye. So you tell me, Pagan Salvatore. *Is* this real?"

The heat in his tired eyes and the way his arms clench at his sides tell me it's not about the situation, but about *us*. Vulnerability flashes in his eyes, but it's gone within a second.

A tear slips free and he steps forward, wiping it away with his thumb before it can fall down my cheek.

"How?"

He smiles sadly, tucking my wet hair behind my ear. "It's not the how you should be asking but the why. Why would I come all the way here, steal your things, and wait for you to come home?"

"Why?" I croak out, blinking back more tears that threaten to fall. I can barely see through them. I want to reach out and touch him, make sure this is real, that *he* is real.

He's more beautiful than I remember. His hair is a lot shaggier, and he looks like he hasn't shaved in a few days, but he's still ruggedly handsome in the best kind of way.

Mine.

"Because six weeks ago, a woman walked in on me naked and molested me."

Tears of laughter bubble free. "I didn't molest you."

My face heats at the reminder of our first encounter.

He smirks, stepping closer so our chests are touching, and looks down at me. "You did. But it wasn't just that. It wasn't that you assaulted me with a door, got itching powder on me, slapped me in the face or threw me in a pool. You walked into my life and gave it meaning, a purpose. I wake up every morning picturing your pretty face, go to sleep each night thinking about what you're doing. You gave a man with no hope for a future a better one. You, Pagan Salvatore, gave me life. You became my life and without you, I don't have any meaning, any hope or a purpose. Because my purpose in life is to love you. I love you, Pagan. I love you so much that the minute Aaron told me you left, I felt my heart break, truly break, for the first time in my life."

Gobsmacked, I can only stare, tears trailing down my cheeks as I stumble forward, clutching his biceps.

His words....

"You love me?" I croak.

He loves me.

This can't be real. It can't. I feel like I'm floating underwater right now.

"With everything I am," he tells me fiercely.

"But I left," I choke out, gripping him tighter.

He laughs, and God, I've missed the sound so much it brings a fresh wave of tears. "Pagan, I tell you I love you and that's all you can focus on? You should know me better. I was never going to let you go."

"But... it's been three weeks."

He smiles, running his hand through my hair again before cupping my cheek. I lean into his touch, savouring it and hoping I never have to give it up again.

I've missed him so much.

And seeing him reminds me of the pain I've felt without having him in my life, in my arms.

"I had some plans I needed to take care of first."

"What plans?" I'm still whispering, though I don't know why. It could be because I'm scared if I talk too loud, then everything around me will come crashing down. I'm not ready for whatever this is to end.

"Well, I'm now owner of a medical practice and have three other doctors coming to work for me. I also bought a house."

"You're leaving?" My chest hurts and I sag forward, breathing deeply as I try not to collapse.

He shakes his head, wiping my tears once again. "Yeah."

My heart drops and a sob breaks free as I try to pull away, but he tugs me against him. It feels good to be in his arms, but I know he'll be gone again soon.

"Why did you come, then? Tell me you love me?" I cry, wishing he didn't have such a tight hold on me. I'd punch him right now. Maybe even knee him the nuts.

I hate that I love him so much.

"I'm getting to that part." He glances away for a second, seeming to think about his next words.

I stop struggling so I can narrow my eyes at him. "Get on with it, then."

He chuckles at my sass, kissing the tip of my nose. I sigh, melting against him even though another part demands I run away again and hide.

"My practice is in town—" He starts to say something else, but he doesn't get a chance when I push him away.

"What?" I screech, looking at him with wide eyes. "In *this* town? Here? Where I live?"

He laughs, moving to pull me back against him. I go because, well, the love of my life just told me he'll be working in my town. Here. Where I can see him every day and...

"Why have you taken all my stuff?" I ask warily.

He laughs harder at my expression. "Because until the house sale goes through, I've rented it off the owners. We're free to move in."

"Move in?" I ask, confused.

"Yes, move in."

"With my stuff?"

He nods, grinning. "You're moving in with me."

"Am I now?" I ask, biting back a smile because the idea of living with him excites me. "And when were you planning on telling me?"

"Right after I told you I loved you. But you wound me, baby. I came all this way—"

I launch myself at him, wrapping my legs around his waist and kissing him, pouring all my love into it.

We moan, clinging to each other as he steps backwards, sitting on the couch. I straddle him, not wanting to break the kiss for a second.

But I do.

To tell him the one thing I wish I had told him all along.

"I love you, Drake. I love you so goddamn much. I'm sorr—"

"I love you too, Pagan. And I understand why you left. I wasn't happy, but I understood. And it worked out in the end. Alison filled me in two weeks ago on why you weren't returning my calls."

"Alison," I growl.

She's no longer on best friend status.

For real this time.

He chuckles, pecking my lips before pulling back. "Don't be mad. She helped me understand better."

"How did you do all of this in two weeks though?" He looks sheepish as he turns away, not meeting my gaze. "What?" I ask, wishing I didn't when he answers.

"Grams. It seems she planned this all along."

"Elaborate," I order, wondering how she could've foreseen this coming in the three weeks I was living with the Donovans.

He holds his hands up, his eyes twinkling. "Easy." He grins. "It seems she knew you before you knew her."

That's all I'm going to get, really?

"Are you trying to annoy me?"

He shakes his head. "No, but you won't believe me anyway."

"Try me."

"Okay," he says, giving me a warning look. "She met you at a charity fundraiser last Christmas. It was a masquerade ball."

My eyes widen because that ball was here, on my father's property. We were raising money for a children's hospital.

I try to think back, wondering if I met her, but I don't recall ever bumping into anyone who remotely resembled Ada.

"I don't remember seeing her there," I tell him, still wary about the whole thing.

"She said she spoke to you for about an hour about the kind of work you do and what you liked to do in your free time. And she helped you spike your brother's drink."

Now I remember.

"Oh my God, that was Ada? I didn't even know. She was talking to me for ages, following me around everywhere I went and asking questions, not just about the event but my personal life. I don't understand though. What does this mean?"

I'm trying not to freak out, but how can I not?

She knew me this whole time and never said a thing.

Then I remember.

Drake opens his mouth to answer but I interrupt, wriggling on his lap and making him groan. "Oh my God. She made a comment one day down at the pool. She said, 'It's why I picked you.' I never understood until it now. Well, I kind of do. I think. It still doesn't really make sense."

He shakes his head, not seeming surprised. "She planned for us to get together. She was going to set us up, but we set ourselves up. She didn't need to lift a finger."

I shake my head.

Devious woman.

"But how did she know I would leave?"

"She didn't see that coming, so expect a telling off when you see her next. But she planned everything. It wasn't until Alison called two weeks ago that we made a different plan."

I smile, no longer mad at my best friend. How could I be when he's here, beneath me? "What were the plans?"

"The first plan was to force you to love me back," he chuckles.

"You never would've needed to force me. I thought you didn't love me, and the thought of you rejecting me scared me."

"Pagan, I fell in love with you the second you fell to your knees and touched my cock."

My face heats as I giggle. "Typical man."

He laughs, shrugging. "I didn't realise what I felt for you until the moment we first kissed. I knew then that I'd never be able to live without you."

"But you said you wanted three weeks with me, then agreed to walk away when it was over."

He looks disappointed. "No, baby. *You* agreed to those terms. I just stood there and listened to you ramble on. I never agreed to anything. I knew I'd never let you go. I let you do what you needed to do to protect yourself."

Shocked is an understatement. It also makes me love him more.

"And now you're here? Really here? For good?"

"I'm not going anywhere. Grams had everything sorted but the house. She purchased the building for the clinic, even had investors lined up with other doctors ready to start work. She thought we'd want to invest in our own home, so she left that to me. With Alison's help, we found the perfect home fifteen minutes from here."

"Fifteen minutes?"

He smiles knowingly. "Yeah, there's a house just on the outskirts of the bridge leading onto your parents' property."

I gasp, nearly falling backwards. "You bought Old Weller McDonald's home? The big white one with pillars?"

"Jesus, is that his name?"

"Yes. He would never sell that property."

Even as a girl, I pictured myself living in that home. It has decking at the front, with pillars at the top of the stairs leading to the front door that look amazing in the winter with decorations and lights on. The garden is massive, big enough to play five-a-side football and the kitchen... the kitchen is beautiful.

But he would never sell.

I should know. I tried asking on more than one occasion.

"He has. He's signed the papers and everything. It wasn't easy, but the second I told him who I was buying it for, he agreed. He told me you were the only person he'd ever consider selling it to. He's moved to a retiring home where he can get around easier, said the stairs were doing his back in. He's been there for a few months, just never had the heart to put the house on the market."

My eyes water as I take his face in my hands. "This is really happening?"

I'm in awe, completely lost to the emotions swirling around inside me. Nothing feels real. Nothing but Drake beneath me.

"Yeah, baby. It took me three weeks but I'm finally here. With you. Where I belong."

"A lot can happen in three weeks." I nod, my double meaning subtle.

"Yeah, it can," he replies softly.

"I love you," I breathe against his lips. "So much."

"Show me," he says huskily, his eyes darkening.

I know that look.

It's the one he gives me every time our clothes are about to come off.

I smile, running my finger down his chest before moving in and kissing below his ear. "Gladly," I whisper, earning a deep growl from him.

I'm ready to tease, but the minute he sees the gleam in my eyes, his hands are at my waist and he's lifting me over his shoulder.

I squeal, laughing when he takes me to my room.

My *old* room.

Because now we'll have *our* room, and I'll get to spend every night making love to my man.

He pulls me down his body as we stand at the end of my bed. I sway towards him, not wanting to be apart for even a second.

"I'm going to love you for always, Pagan."

"And I'll love you forever, Drake."

Epilogue

TEN YEARS LATER

*H*earing my husband walk through the door, I smile wide and turn to greet him.

"Hey, baby. Sorry I'm late. I had a few emergencies at the practice. Is everyone here?"

Every month we have a get-together with the whole family, alternating between London and here.

I wrap my arms around his neck and kiss him. He's been working a lot more lately, ever since he lost one of his doctors. We miss him dearly when he's gone but understand his practice means a lot to him.

It's very rare I get to have a minute to devour my husband without being interrupted, so I take pleasure in our moment of peace, kissing him like there's no tomorrow.

He pulls away, a smirk on his gorgeous lips as he looks down at me, his eyes soft. "What was that for? Not that I'm complaining."

I shrug, pressing against him. "I just missed you."

His eyes sadden. "I've missed you guys too. I've finally got interviews lined up, so the late days shouldn't continue for much longer."

I nod. "Okay."

"Are we alone?" He smirks, looking around the kitchen for one of our monkeys.

I inwardly roll my eyes. "They're in the garden with everyone else."

"They won't miss us for five minutes," he tells me, running his hands down to my ass, squeezing me. I grin and press harder against him. "Maybe we could—"

"Aunt Pagan, I think you should come outside," Cece says, biting her bottom lip. At fourteen, she's grown into a beautiful woman, very much like her mum with her head always stuck in a book. And her putting one down to come get me can only mean one thing.

My twin boys have done something—again.

"What did they do?" Drake and I say simultaneously. At six years old, they're little terrors.

She grins, looking at both of us before shrugging. "They changed Granddad's password, spent a fortune with Uncle Sid's bank card and are in the middle of tricking Daddy into eating one of their cupcakes." She scrunches her face adorably. "He really should learn."

I glance at Drake, both of us wearing 'oh fuck' expressions before we race for the back door.

We both make it outside in time to see Dean open his mouth to take a bite.

"No!" I scream, while Drake just starts laughing.

Dean pauses but doesn't heed my warning. He takes a bite before choking and then gagging when worms start falling out.

Disgusting.

And now I know why they were so quiet when I was baking them.

I gag, looking away as he spits the bite on the floor.

My twins, Calvin and Reece, are mini Adas. Before she sadly passed away last year, she taught the monkeys everything she knew. Literally. They're terrors in their own right, but once they were old enough to get technical, and learn more stuff, they became destructible.

"Boys!" Dean yells, throwing the cupcake across the garden. "Why would you do that? It had sprinkles on it."

Lola laughs, shaking her head at her husband. I don't blame her. He really should've learned after they made him drink laxative—a stash Ada left with them, amongst other things—to not take anything from them, especially if they're willingly giving it to you.

"Calvin and Reece Donovan, get your behinds here right now," I snap, using my best firm mum voice.

"But Mum," they whine.

"Nope, I'm not having any of it. I've told you not to play jokes on people."

"No you didn't," Calvin says.

"You said to not play pranks on the girls," Reece finishes, saying 'girls' like he swallowed something sour.

"What?" the men in my family shout at once, looking like they want to throttle me.

I step back, shrugging sheepishly. "It didn't seem fair. Plus, they cut their sister's hair while she was asleep."

"Baby," Drake murmurs, stepping up behind me.

"I can't believe you'd do this to your own twin," Sid snaps. "And you owe me three hundred pounds. I don't even know what they've subscribed to or spent it on either. I just know my bank is missing freaking money and that it was them."

I turn to my boys, scowling. "What did you do?"

They look at each other before nodding and turning back to me. "We bought you a Mother's Day present."

My heart melts at my sweet boys, and I have to stop myself from smiling. "And what did you get me?"

"With my money?" Sid growls.

"It's a surprise," Reece says, the most confident of the two, so I turn to Calvin and stare him down. "Don't do it, Cal."

"I won't buy you any more Smarties if you don't tell me. Like ever. Not even after school." I keep my face firm, but all I want to do is laugh at the sweat dripping off his forehead and the anxious look he keeps sending his brother.

"She's bluffing. She wouldn't do that to us. Remember, she thinks we're cute," Reece says, holding his brother's arm.

"And I'll remove your telly," Drake butts in, probably annoyed he has to give money back—again.

They really are too clever for their own good.

"But—"

"No buts. Tell us now. You have three seconds," I warn them. "One, two—"

"We bought you the new Xbox," Calvin blurts out.

Reece groans, throwing his hands up. "Way to go, loser."

An Xbox, really?

Drake chuckles behind me, but I don't find it amusing. The boys asked for one for Christmas. We said no after they downloaded a virus onto Brooke's computer. Then they asked again for their birthday, and once again we said no. They sank my dad's boat in the lake after we told them not to go on it. Thank God they were wearing life jackets. I was going out of my mind, along with everyone else.

"You two are grounded for two weeks. No park after school, and no treats for a week. And you'll be sending the Xbox back whenever it arrives."

"But it's already paid for," Calvin argues, and I give him a look that shuts him up. "Okay, whatever."

"I'm sorry, Sid."

His lips twitch, looking to the boys. "Is it the Xbox five?"

They nod, grinning madly. "Yeah, it has these 3D features and you can—"

"That's cool," Sid interrupts before looking at me. "When it gets here, let me know. I've been wanting one for a while."

"Can we go on it?" two extremely excited boys ask in unison.

Sid pretends to think about it for a second. "Um, no."

"But—"

"Just give up, boys," Drake chuckles.

I look around the garden, noting Adaline isn't with everyone or with Cece, who she usually shadows.

"Where's your sister?" I ask my boys, who look so much like their father. They're going to be heartbreakers when they're older. Either that or they're going to be imprisoned for disrupting the peace. But Adaline, she's all me: blonde hair and ocean-coloured eyes.

Reece scrunches his face up but mumbles, "She's in her stupid den."

"Yeah, she wouldn't let us in," Calvin grumbles, crossing his arms over his chest.

I roll my eyes and tell everyone I'll be back in a minute so I can go look for her.

Adaline, who we named after Ada, is seven. When Drake asked me to marry him after not even a year of living together, we started trying for a baby. But sadly, it didn't happen. We tried everything the doctors told us to, but the disappointment each month was gut-wrenching. We decided to wait a year so we could adopt, but then a miracle happened. The minute we stopped trying, I fell pregnant with my darling daughter. The day we found out was the happiest of our lives. She's our baby miracle.

She's also the best behaved, an angel to have around with two bois-terous boys wreaking havoc.

Looking up at her tree house, I don't see her. "Adaline?" I call, shielding my eyes.

She doesn't answer and I begin to panic, hoping she hasn't run off. The girl follows butterflies without watching where she's going. She could be anywhere.

"Mummy, Mummy!" her sweet, soothing voice calls out for me and I relax.

I see her running from the back of the garden where all the over-grown bushes and trees are. We're saving up to let the boys have their fort there. They would've had it by now if it weren't for all the damages they cause to other people's property and our own.

"Hey, sweetheart. Where have you been?" Her hair, hands, and clothes are covered in dirt, yet she still looks adorably beautiful. "And what is that you've got?"

"Isn't she beautiful?"

"Oh my, is that a kitten?" I ask when she gets closer.

She nods, running a hand over the dirt-caked animal. "Yes. I found her in a bush, stuck in one of the holes the boys dug." Her eyes narrow when she mentions her brothers, no doubt willing to give them an earful over them digging holes.

"Oh no. Let's have a look." I take the kitten from her and check her over. Apart from being a little underweight, she doesn't seem to be hurt.

It's hard to tell if she's grey or white with the amount of dirt on her, but she does have the bluest eyes I've ever seen. She's beautiful.

"Can we keep her?"

Oh no!

"Um, I don't think that's a good idea. She could belong to someone else."

"They don't deserve her. I'll look after her and protect her. Not like them," she pouts, still stroking the kitten.

I really should talk to Drake about this, but the look on my daughter's face has me giving in. She never asks for anything, never complains, and always goes with the flow where the boys are concerned.

"Okay, but—"

She squeals loudly, startling me and the kitten, then jumps at me, wrapping her arms around my neck. "Thank you, thank you! I love you. I promise to take good care of her. I can't wait to show Nanny and Cece."

"Baby, you're getting dirt all over Mummy," Drake chuckles. I rise from my kneeling position and paste on my best smile. He shakes his head. "I heard. I guess we have our first pet."

"We really should've gotten one before we had the boys," I remind him, something we were talking about before I fell pregnant.

He shakes his head and walks over to his daughter, picking her up. "How are you, love bug?"

"I'm really good," she beams. She's a daddy's girl through and through. "I've got a new kitten. She's going to be so loved."

"I bet she will. Now why don't you go wash up, then ask Aunt Gabriella to get a towel for the kitten to keep her warm."

Adaline looks from her father to the kitten and back again, nodding solemnly. "I will. I promise. I love you, Daddy."

"I love you too, bug."

She kisses his cheek before wiggling to get down, carefully taking the kitten from my hands.

"Be careful," I warn. She nods and rushes off, then turns back.

"Thank you, Mummy. I love you so much. You're the best mummy in the whole wide world."

"I love you too." I kiss her dirty forehead, chuckling as I watch her run back to the house, her excitement infectious.

"You spoil her," Drake says, wrapping his arms around me from behind.

I scoff. "You do too, mister."

He laughs, kissing my neck. "It's the best thing to do in this world—spoil my girls."

I melt against him, placing my hands over his covering my stomach. "You do. You've given us everything, more than we could ever imagine," I whisper, emotion clogging my throat.

"You're wrong," he tells me huskily.

"About?"

"It's you who gave me everything. I love you. I love you more every day and will continue to until the day I die."

Tears spring to my eyes and I grip him tighter. "Drake."

"It's true, baby. You've given me more than I could ever hope for. You make me happy, so fucking happy. We have three—okay, we have one amazing kid. The jury's still out on the other two, but we've got them. Every day I count my blessings, and I'll always, *always* be indebted to you. You've completed my life like no other woman ever could. I love you."

A tear falls and I turn, wrapping my arms around his neck. "We were born to be together, Drake. You don't owe me anything. You never have and never will. You love me more than any girl could wish to be loved, and I love you more than I could ever love anyone. It's us. It's our happily ever after."

"Happily ever after," he whispers against my lips.

I press them against his, needing to taste him.

Forever will never be long enough, but I can live with happily ever after with him.

For as long as we both shall live.

The End

Made in the USA
Monee, IL
05 January 2021